1984

How to Gain
(and Maintain)
the Competitive Advantage
in Business

How to Gain (and Maintain) the Competitive Advantage in Business

WILLIAM E. ROTHSCHILD

McGraw-Hill Book Company

New York • St. Louis • San Francisco • Auckland
Bogotá • Hamburg • Johannesburg • London • Madrid
Mexico • Montreal • New Delhi • Panama • Paris
São Paulo • Singapore • Sydney • Tokyo • Toronto

Library of Congress Cataloging in Publication Data

Rothschild, William E.
    How to gain (and maintain) the competitive advantage in business.

    Includes index.
    1. Competition.   2. Corporate planning.   I. Title.
HD41.R67   1984   658.4'012   83-16260
ISBN 0-07-054031-4

    34567890 DOC/DOC 8987654

0-07-054031-4

The editors for this book were William Sabin and Christine Ulwick,
the designer was Jules Perlmutter, and the production
supervisor was Teresa F. Leaden. It was set in Meridien
by Achorn Graphic Services, Inc.
Printed and bound by R. R. Donnelley & Sons Company.

To my own *personal* competitive advantage,
my wife Alma

Contents

Preface

During the past twenty years, I have been involved in all phases of strategic planning and have helped corporate and operating managers improve strategies and strategic insights. This work has included teaching, consulting, writing, and doing. I have witnessed a significant improvement in most phases of the strategic-thinking discipline with the exception of competitive assessments and the use of these assessments to determine the "competitive advantage."

This book is aimed at correcting this deficiency and helping executives improve their competitive position by consciously identifying, anticipating, and analyzing current and potential competitors. I focus on both "competition" and "competitors" and provide techniques to enable managers at all levels to know how they compare in the present and will compare in the future. Each chapter is organized to enable the reader to apply the principles as he or she progresses and to use the insights to improve strategy and implementation.

This book is not based on theory. It is based on experience and application. The techniques and concepts have been tested and have proved to be useful in improving strategies, developing options, and determining timing and execution. Each technique provides an insight valuable for understanding the next one, and therefore it is recommended that all the techniques be used in a planned, systematic way but in a thoughtful, not mechanistic mode. The competitive advantage is a result of thinking, evaluation, and hard work, and this book can be a significant help to you.

William E. Rothschild

1 Winning and Competition

This book is about winning and being competitive—winning because you know how you stand against the competition and have been able to identify, create, and defend a competitive advantage. Winners are those who never forget that they are in a continuing competitive game and that it is important to understand and monitor current competitors and also new or potential competitors. Competitive understanding and monitoring are key elements to strategic thinking, since they help you to see the relationship between customers and resources. They force the answering of questions like:

- What is the customer buying?
- How can these needs be filled?
- Who does the best job?
- How does my company compare?
- Can I change the positioning and be the clear winner?

The major concepts of competitive evaluation include the need to compare and identify relative position and the need to identify changes which can influence these positions.

America Was the Clear Winner

During the post–World War II period, American companies were the world leaders in all the key industries. The Big Four automobile companies dominated their own U.S. market and controlled a number of European automobile companies. Except for a few specialists like Rolls Royce and Mercedes-Benz, they led in all measures, and the competition was among themselves. The Japanese were not even in the race, and their unsuccessful probe into the United States in the 1950s made them the laughingstock of the industry. Within a decade this situation changed. Today, it is the Japanese and Europeans who are the winners, and the Big Four have been cut to the "Big Two and a Half." The same situation prevails in steel, textiles, factory equipment, electrical goods, and consumer durables. The American companies have lost share in exports on a world scale and even in their home markets. The threat and challenge has come from companies that had unknown names and that in some cases were so small that they were ignored.

This message is not new, and it is not my intent to embarrass, criticize, or berate the executives of American companies or even to applaud the executives of Japanese or European companies that are challenging them. The purpose of this book is to demonstrate the need for competitive thinking and to recommend ways for those who are winning and those who are being challenged to continue to win or fight off the challenge. Competitive thinking is vital to success, and we must recognize its value, make a commitment to it, and find the proper aids. Competitive thinking and its supporting intelligence and analysis must pervade the entire organization from top to bottom, and it cannot be delegated to "specialists" or to some function like planning, finance, or marketing. It is a continuing job and not merely something that "happens in the spring or fall." Losers are those who either ignore or underestimate the competition.

The Failure to Think Competitively

Most of you will agree with the opening commentary, and as you reflect on your own company or institution, you will most likely also agree that such *critical* thinking and activity are not done well and possibly are not done at all. Why? Why aren't they done, and why are they delegated to the lower not the higher levels of the organization? I would like to review a few of the reasons that account for this situation and then suggest how they can be changed. This will provide an outline of the content of the book.

Success Breeds Complacency

The discussion about the success of American companies in the postwar period illustrates the primary reason that chief executives and their staffs ignore or downplay competitive thinking. Winners have proved they can beat the competition. So why should they worry about competitors? This superiority attitude causes them to forget that the reasons for their past success may change in the future. They begin to believe they are invincible, and they may give away what contributed to their success. This may be productivity, innovation, efficient marketing, or any of a number of things. They forget that their strength is relative and that they can deteriorate or the competition can improve. Complacency is the result, and this can become the fatal flaw. In addition, winners have a lot to lose if there is a change, and so they may consciously or unconsciously rationalize that the new product or substitute will not become a factor. This is what has been repeated in the new technology races, and this is why even large, successful companies like IBM have missed opportunities or been forced to follow others in word processing, personal computers, computer-aided design (CAD) and computer-aided manufacturing (CAM), and so on.

The message is clear: Competitive analysis is critical to the winners as well as the challengers.

Ignoring the Customer's
Changing Needs and Wants

The second reason that competitive analysis may be underestimated relates to the last point that I just made but is worth elaboration. Substitution, surprises, and defeats are caused by ignoring or underestimating the concerns, problems, and needs of customers. You cannot separate competitive analysis from customer analysis. They are related, and complete analysis is the only way to anticipate changes. New competitors with unknown products or services must spend considerable time understanding and satisfying customers. They win by demonstrating uniqueness, additional value, and lower costs against the existing offering. When an industry is matured, this concern usually declines and the attitude that "customers will buy what we give them not what they may want" begins to grow. So the second reason for failure to think competitively is that the company forgets that it is relative advantage not merely internal strength that counts.

Collecting Information
Is Not Intelligence

Competitive analysis suffers because of the confusion between information and intelligence. Many companies have competitive fact gathering and analysis but not intelligence. They go through a ritual of collecting information, putting it in files, and writing reports, but they do not ask what the information means and whether it requires a change in strategy. Companies often know a great deal about their competitors. Salespeople meet representatives of other companies daily in the marketplace. They talk to customers, they know the pricing approaches being used and the features being emphasized, they see the advertising, and, of more strategic value, they know the customers' reactions and how the customers compare their company with the competition. The engineering staff will most likely know the competitor's design and development approach. They may even be aware of the new products coming along—possibly through the talks or publications of the competitor's manufacturing, finance, and human-resource personnel.

The problem is not a lack of information. There is plenty of information and data, but it is not systematically retrieved and used for strategy development. I will discuss how this can be done in a later chapter.

Legality

Tied to the last reason is the concern on the part of many corporate officers, especially attorneys, that the only way to get competitive information is to revert to espionage or other illegal, unethical means. I will describe all the major sources of information and their assets and liabilities. This will include public, government, investment, and internal sources. There is no need for using unethical or illegal approaches; in fact, it is foolish.

Not Understanding the Full Value

Finally, companies fail to use competitive analysis because they do not understand its full value. Competitive analysis has many uses. It can be a valuable aid in providing a new or different vision of the business, identifying the changing or consistent success factors, assessing your relative position in the market, anticipating changes and consequences, generating alternative strategies, and assessing the potential success of a proposed change in strategy. In other words, competitive analysis has a number of rewards, and if these benefits are understood, then more commitment and involvement of higher levels may result. Let's look more closely at a few of these unrecognized benefits.

A Different View

Even though companies all use the same type of information and possibly the same system, they have different perceptions of the world. They may see new or different opportunities or threats on the horizon. For example, Volkswagen, Toyota, and Datsun all saw the automobile market differently from the American Big Three. They bet on the small car while the U.S. giants were dedicated to the large, high-horsepowered automobile. They recognized that small cars were not equivalent to economy cars. They load them with "extras"—stereos, reclining seats, rear-window defrosters and wipers, and so on—and they included them as standard equipment.

The Japanese had a different vision of the television business. They recognized the potential of adding accessories to the television receiver instead of emphasizing the receiver itself. Thus, they have created new markets for videotape and videogames, and they recently added stereo television through the use of videodisc and videotape. Today the Japanese are number one in this market and the reputed technology leaders.

Thus by studying competitors, you may find that they have identified new growth opportunities. The same may be true of threats. General Motors had a different perception than Ford and Chrysler. They began making smaller cars earlier because they perceived a major threat to large, gasoline-inefficient cars. The same is true of Goodyear, which invested extensively in radial tires while other companies did not.

Success Factors

The critical requirements to win are strongly influenced by the competitors and what motivates them. If you participate in an industry where competitors invest heavily in research and development, possibly 5 to 6 percent of sales, then it may be a necessity for you to invest at this rate. There are industries that are capital-intensive because of the way companies compete. Automobile companies have traditionally had model changes every two or three years. This has significantly increased the cost of participating. The cost of the recent retooling required to build small, fuel-efficient autos has been enormous. Some industries require a constant increase in capacity because of competition and demand. If you compete against companies that have strong relations with their governments and are supported by them, this may become a critical success factor. Thus, competitive assessment will permit you to examine these factors and your relative strengths and limitations. Further, it may change these success factors to your advantage. For instance, you may be able to make the business more cash-intensive by offering products on a lease rather than direct-sale basis. Or you may be able to create a new type of distribution that can give you the competitive advantage.

Relativity Assessment

Another benefit of sound competitive assessment is the recognition of relativity. You must compare your product, salesforce, and cost position with the competition's. This enables you to get a perspective on the differential advantage or disadvantage. However, it also forces you to probe how well the product or service you provide meets the customers' expectations and needs. This is covered in our discussion of functional substitution.

Changes and Consequences
The fourth benefit is the ability to anticipate change and its implications for potential rewards, costs, and risks. Which competitors are likely to become more aggressive or increase concentration by acquisition or mergers? Are there any partnerships or joint ventures in the making? What about exits or divestitures? Thinking about these types of moves can enable you to calculate changes in the financial commitment required or can even provide an early warning of when to get out.

Generating Alternatives
Just as competitors may have different perceptions of the market needs and thus stimulate different opportunities and threats, they may also have different strategies. In every industry there are a number of successful companies that have different strategies. For instance, Maytag has followed a selective, high-reliability and high-quality major-appliance strategy while Whirlpool and General Electric have concentrated on a full-line, high-volume, distribution-driven strategy. All three have prospered and survived the fate of Frigidaire, Westinghouse, and several others. Later, I will demonstrate how you can systematically evaluate these differences and determine the viability of using these analyses to modify your own strategy.

Contingency and Review
Finally, competitive intelligence is a help in determining the potential effectiveness of your current or new strategies. You can see how and if changes need to be made, and as I just said, you can see the options available. This option listing can also be very helpful if you need to implement a quick change. Contingency planning is difficult, but a lot of problems arise because companies believe there is only one viable strategy and have not thought through the options.

Approaches to Be Discussed

You can see that competitive thinking, analysis, and intelligence are the bases of developing and implementing strategies and are integral parts of strategic planning and thinking. They contribute to all phases, and they are not extra exercises or just nice activities if you have the money and the time. I would now like to summarize the approaches that will be covered in this book.

Mapping the Battlefield

The first step is to determine your battlefield, which simply means understanding the customers and their needs and wants. Competitors and competitive products and services must satisfy customer needs in order to be successful. Thus, the first assessment will probe into what the customer is really buying and how well the current offerings are satisfying the customer's wants and needs. This will enable the analyst to identify ways that products and services can be improved to gain the competitive advantage. Further, it will enhance your understanding of how new products or technologies may be able to capitalize on a deficiency or unserved want and thus enable you to become the winner in the future. This reminds me of the statement made a number of years ago by the managers of Black & Decker. They pointed out that consumers and industrial users of their products were interested in making holes with some speed and precision and could not care less whether it was done with a drill or by some other means. This struck me at the time as funny and almost irrelevant. But upon reflection, I saw that it was profound and the essence of good business thinking. When you define your product by the function that it serves for the user, you then are in the position of understanding what competition is all about. You immediately think about all of the ways that you can make a hole and the relative advantages and disadvantages of each. But even more important, you begin thinking about changes in the way that hole can be made via new technologies. Now you think about lasers, sonics, and small explosives and ask whether they could be a threat or, if you are an optimist, how they may present opportunities. This will be the subject of our first approach, and it will be illustrated and discussed in more detail.

Winners and Losers

The second approach will focus on the current and potential competitors in your served and related unserved markets. We will ask you to separate those that have been successful from those that have been unsuccessful; *the winners versus the losers*. This will force you to define the criteria of success and then to identify the reasons for past success or failure. For instance, you may decide that winners are those with the highest return on investment over the past decade. If you were to apply this to the automobile industry, you would have General Motors on one side and Chrysler on the other. The issue is, why? Why have some succeeded while others have not? Is it because of superior products or unique production and the ability to make less costly but quality products? Or is it explained by distribution strengths and a longer-term image and reputation? Or is it because of some strategic decisions made by the predecessors? Or is it merely being in the right place at the right time? Or is it some combination of these characteristics? This is called a factor analysis, and it tries to account for differences in performance. However, it won't stop there; it will require a look ahead and an assessment as to whether these same critical factors will be valuable in the future. What will be the impact of environmental and governmental changes? Suppose the cost and availability of fuel was significantly different. Would this change the winners and losers in automobiles? Suppose there was a different set of government regulations in the United States that supported U.S. industries instead of putting them in an unattractive position. Suppose there was a sudden reduction in the cost of money or a decline in the inflation rate. What would this do to the competitive scene?

The list can be extended, but the point is clear: Today's winners may be tomorrow's losers because of some external factor or because of the loss of some resource, skill, or ability. This will be discussed later.

Total Industry Review

The third analysis we will recommend will be focused on the entire economic situation, that is, on understanding all the actors and where the industry makes its money. We will look at those that supply the industry and those that are the intermediaries between your industry and the user. Intermediaries will include wholesale distributors, retailers, original equipment manufacturers (OEMs), and system assemblers. In this review, we will examine the objectives, goals, and strategies of suppliers and intermediaries and also what may motivate them to become full-fledged competitors. It will be my contention that both forward integration (when a supplier becomes a direct competitor, for example) and backward integration (when a customer becomes a supplier, for example) can be anticipated. Further, they might be prevented if the company is aware and ready. There are numerous illustrations in all industries. Recently we saw this take place in the watch and calculator markets when the semiconductor manufacturers moved forward and became major competitors, if not the victors, in both of these situations. It took place years ago in the automotive market when General Motors and Ford made backward moves and drove many of their suppliers out of business. The timing and motivation will be discussed in depth and illustrated.

Demographics

Competitor demographics will be the topic of our fourth approach. Most of us are familiar with consumer or user demographics, which divides users by some characteristics such as age, sex, income group, profession, and so on. This permits segmentation and the development of strategies to deal with this segmentation. The same logic pertains to competition. By grouping competitors into different types, you can gain insights into the type of industry in which you now participate or plan to participate.

There are two characteristics that are useful for segmentation of competitors. One deals with the degree of specialization or diversity, and the other emphasizes the degree of globality of the competition. I have found that through such segmentation you can understand the degree of aggressiveness and the nature of likely rewards and risks within an industry. For instance, industries dominated by domestic specialists will be different than those dominated by multinational, multi-industry competitors. This will influence the planning horizon, the reaction to threats, the type of measures, and the type of management. As these factors change, there will be changes in the rewards, risks, and costs of participation. For instance, the television industry was significantly different two decades ago, when it was controlled by U.S. specialists, like RCA, Zenith, Magnavox, and Admiral, than it is today, when the major companies have become the multinational giants, like Philips, Matsushita, and Sanyo. These changes have intensified the need for innovation and product development and may modify the role of the television receiver from a self-standing component to part of a home information, communications, and entertainment center.

In-Depth Evaluations

The last approach we will describe is the in-depth review of the current and potential key competitors. This will probe into the competitor's total portfolio, investment and strategic driver for each segment of the portfolio, and finally all the major programs that together will enable implementation. A comprehensive checklist will be provided, which can also be used to compare each competitor against the others and also against you. For instance, questions will include:

- What are the product-development strategies?
- What is the type of distribution?
- What are the promotional strategies?
- What is the pricing approach?
- What is the service-support strategy?
- What is the production strategy?
- What is the financial strategy?
- What is the human-resource strategy?

By probing each of these and comparing one against the other, you can determine whether your strategy is similar or different as well as whether the supporting strategies are internally consistent and will be capable of meeting the objectives and goals. If there are inconsistencies, these may be the elements to attack in achieving your results.

Competition and Competitors Covered

Thus the book will cover all aspects of the competitive scene and permit the development and review of strategies. In addition, there will be a chapter on sources and resources to use in doing this type of analysis. This will be divided into sources from investment, public, trade, and governmental organizations and groups. Often the data you seek is already available within your organization, and I will describe how you can go about obtaining this information in the most effective and cost-efficient manner. For instance, we will discuss how you can find out what competitors tell the world about their future direction, and what others say about competitors, and how they believe competitors will change in the future.

Unfortunately, the best intelligence is of little value if it is not communicated and documented in a way that can become ingrained in the corporation and used by the corporation to develop strategic responses. This will be the topic of our last chapter, and I will provide several illustrations of documentation and communication.

Not a Financial Analysis

As you have read this material, it may have occurred to you that I have not spent time discussing the traditional financial analyses that are often equated with competitor analysis. This is not an unconscious omission on my part. I believe that these analyses are useful and are part of the assessment but that they are overplayed and misrepresented. They are useful in validating your assumptions and estimating the viability of competitors to implement their plans. This is their major contribution.

Layout of Each Chapter

In each chapter I will first discuss and illustrate the concepts and approaches. Most of these will be based on my own use of the techniques, and I will try to explain both their assets and liabilities. My objective is to enable you to gain from my experiences and those of others. But this will be of limited value unless you think about the techniques and try to apply and adapt them to your own needs. Therefore, at the close of each chapter I will provide application sections. They will summarize all of the key questions that should be asked in order to do the type of job that I believe is necessary. I would recommend that these questions be answered as you progress and not left until the end. The reason is that each new section will build on the ones that went before and will yield better results if you have completed the work as you progressed. These sections can be reproduced and used, and they should help you apply the concepts and determine their utility.

2 Mapping the Battlefield

Where to begin? To start your own strategic thinking and planning, you must ask yourself what business you are in now and what business you want to be in in the future. In the competitive arena, you must ask the same questions. The answers will determine how you define the battlefield in which you are to participate. Many planners and businesspeople believe that the answers to these questions are their own personal domain and that they can make them as broad or narrow as they wish. In fact, ten years ago I would have been in this camp and would have insisted that any company would be able to determine the answers for itself. The problem is that the events of the past decade have proved to me and others that the answers must be decided by a careful review of the entire competitive screen and of others' behavior in the market.

The Need for Mapping

The first place to start, as is true with all good strategic thinking, is outside, specifically with the customer and his or her needs and wants. The key issues are what the customer is buying and what there is available to satisfy these desires or needs. Knowing these things helps you to anticipate changes, especially in the form of new substitute products and services. The inability of companies to understand other ways that customers can be satisfied and the fact that their changing needs and wants may make yesterday's also-rans tomorrow's superstars has proved to be the major flaw in the strategies and management of all companies.

If this is true, then the place to start is with a map of the entire competitive battlefield, including all the ways that customers can obtain what they want in a given *functional area* as well as the solutions available to solve their problems. This is like the general of the army looking at the entire war map and then gradually moving to the specific terrain or site where the enemy will be met. Like the general, we will need broad overview maps and specific battlefield maps. In the army, the four-star general will be concerned with different levels of detail and specification than the colonel, the captain, and the unit commander; in the business world, the chief executive officer (CEO) of a large corporation will have different maps than the head of one of the business units. In this chapter, I will illustrate a number of these types of maps, beginning with the broad, total functional-need map and moving to the more specific market-segment maps. Thus, one of the maps will be highly conceptual and cover large markets and industries while the others will be more traditional market-segment charts. I will even provide the map for the small businessperson who is competing on a local scale. *The message I will emphasize is that it is important to have a map that will enable you to avoid winning just the battle and losing the entire war.*

What Is a Competitive Arena Map?

A competitive arena map is a visualization of a broad functional need and all the ways to satisfy this need. You can have a map for transportation, communications, energy, financial services, food, or, in fact, any human or organizational need. On the map will be complete specifications of the products and services as well as the components and parts that are used to satisfy the need. Let's take an example of a map that would be useful to a company in the transportation business as well as those who supply components and parts to this industry.

Refer to Exhibit 2-1, Transportation Battlefield. This map visualizes the major parts, components, products, and services related to transportation. They are further categorized by land, sea, air, and space. Some of the parts, like electrical parts and fuels, cut across all the categories, while others, like tires, are in only one or two categories. The same is true in the components grouping; some components, like controls, cut across all the categories, while others, like structures, are in only one or two categories. Moving up the map, we see the specific products that serve these categories. Automobiles, buses, trucks, and motorcycles are in the land-product category; boats, ships, and barges are in the sea-product category; and so on. You can extend each of the categories and become more specific. For instance, you can divide boats into motorboats and sailboats, and you can further divide these by sizes. The map should be as detailed as required to understand the competitive scene and no more. Finally, related services have been included; some services cut across categories, while others are pertinent to a specific category, for instance, parking services for cars, marinas for boats, and airports for air transportation.

What Do You Have?

You now have a visual aid that portrays how an individual can satisfy his or her needs for transportation or the parts, components, and services related to it. It is like having a map of the total battlefield for the transportation dollar. No one individual wants and needs all of the items, and not all areas are attractive and profitable. The use of colors, codes, and sizes may be helpful to display these characteristics.

This map is a tool to plot the current and future competition. For instance, suppose you want to plot General Motors Corporation (GMC) on this map (Exhibit 2-2). You would circle or box automobiles, buses, trucks,

	Land	Sea	Air	Space
Services	Tourist and Travel Parking Rental and Leasing Financial and Insurance Distribution and Retail	Tourist and Travel Marinas Rental and Leasing Financial and Insurance Distribution and Retail	Tourist and Travel Airports Rental and Leasing Financial and Insurance Distribution and Retail	
Products	Automobiles Buses Trucks Railroad Cars Motorcycles	Boats Ships Barges	Business Jets Aircraft Helicopters	Satellites Missiles Guns Rockets
Components	Controls Drives Motors Diesels Structures	Controls Guidance Diesels Steam Turbines Structures	Controls Guidance Jet Engines Motors Airframes	Controls Guidance Power— Supply Structures
Parts	Electrical Tires Fuels	Electrical Fuels	Electrical Tires Fuels	Electrical Fuels

Exhibit 2-1. Transportation battlefield—ways the transportation needs can be satisfied.

and locomotives in the land products, all of the land components, and several of the land parts. GMC also provides diesels for sea transportation, jet engines for aircraft, and a variety of controls and systems for space. Interestingly, they do a lot of business in the leasing, renting, financing, and distribution of their own and complementary products. The question this may raise is whether GMC will be content to remain in these markets or will consider moving into other transportation products and services. The key is to think about changes and how a specific company's portfolio might change. For instance, if you plotted Chrysler's portfolio in 1979, you would include automobiles, satellites, boat engines, and financing along with the land products and components. In order to survive, Chrysler has sold its defense and financing businesses, thereby concentrating on automobiles and key components. The issue is whether they will continue to focus on their current fields or again move into other related fields.

The map will also force you to recognize that the transportation arena is not restricted to only the Big Three and their multinational counterparts, such as Toyota, Nissan, and Volkswagen. There are many companies in the services and components segments that are not viewed as transportation companies. For example, RCA is a participant in rentals and leasing (Hertz), financing (CIT), satellites, and controls. General Electric partici-

	Land	Sea	Air	Space
Services	Tourist and Travel Parking Rental and Leasing Financial and Insurance Distribution and Retail	Tourist and Travel Marinas Rental and Leasing Financial and Insurance Distribution and Retail	Tourist and Travel Airports Rental and Leasing Financial and Insurance Distribution and Retail	
Products	Automobiles Buses Trucks Locomotives Railroad Cars Motorcycles	Boats Ships Barges	Business Jets Aircraft Helicopters	Satellites Missiles Guns Rockets
Components	Controls Drives Motors Diesels Structures	Controls Guidance Diesels Steam Turbines Structures	Controls Guidance Jet Engines Motors Airframes	Controls Guidance Power– Supply Structures
Parts	Electrical Tires Fuels	Electrical Fuels	Electrical Tires Fuels	Electrical Fuels

General Motors Corporation

Exhibit 2-2. Transportation battlefield—General Motors Corporation.

pates in controls, locomotives, jet engines, satellites, and missiles as well as auto rentals and finance and insurance services. This raises the question of whether these companies might move into other products and services, thus changing the competitiveness of the industry.

As you plot each of the key and relevant participants, you should look for changes in direction and focus. You may discover that some have identified a new growth opportunity and that it appears to be their own domain. An example is the locomotive, which has been a GMC game for some time, and none of the major transportation companies have followed. On the other hand you may discover that several of the key players are headed for the same target, which, therefore, may become costly and require extensive resources. All of the automobile companies are focused on the automobile market, and it will continue to be highly competitive. The leasing and renting field is also highly competitive now that transportation-based companies are heading into it.

Thus, the map can graphically show change, impending conflict, new competition, and even unserved opportunities.

Communications and Information

Several years ago I was introduced to the work of the Center for Information Research Policy at Harvard University. This center was the pioneer in the mapping approach and has done excellent work in depicting the emerging conflict in the information and communications arena. It was their work that caused me to develop other maps to be used in my own competitive and industrial analysis work. Exhibit 2-3 contains a copy of their current information-business map.

They have grouped content-related businesses on the right side of the map and conduit-related businesses on the left, with those overlapping in the middle. The product and service distinction is used for the vertical axis. Thus, you can see traditional information and communications items such as paper, dictation equipment, books, and newspapers commingled with computers, broadcast equipment, and satellites. Immediately it illustrates that substitution is taking place and that a newspaper must recognize that it competes against teletext, computers, and broadcast stations as well as other newspapers. It also explains why A T & T and IBM are taking steps that will result in intensive head-on competition among the giants. If you plot companies like McGraw-Hill, Dun & Bradstreet, Citicorp, CBS, RCA, and GTE as well as foreign multinationals like Hitachi, Sony, Toshiba, and Siemens, the size and complexity of the confrontation will become apparent. Companies are moving from all directions of the map and appear to be heading toward the products and services in the middle ground. Almost all of these offer either computer, communications, or information services that will compete against each other. Some of these are defending their

The Information Business

Axes: Services ↑ / Products ↓ (vertical); Conduit → Content (horizontal)

Services (Conduit → Content):

U.S. Mail
Parcel Services
Courier Services
Other Delivery Services

Telephone
Telegraph
Mailgram
IRCs

SCCs
VANs
Multipoint Distribution Services
Cable Operators

Broadcast Networks
Cable Networks
Broadcast Stations

Satellite Services
FM Subcarriers

Paging Services
Industry Networks
Defense Telecom Systems
Security Services

Time-Sharing

News Services
Financial Services
Advertising Services
Professional Services

Data Bases
Teletext

On-Line Directories

Service Bureaus
Software Services

Printing Companys'
Libraries

Retailers
Newsstands

Loose-Leaf Services
Directories

Products (Conduit → Content):

Computers

PABXs
Telephone Switching Equipment

Modems
Concentrators
Multiplexers

Radios
Television Sets
Telephones
Terminals
Printers
Facsimile
ATMs
POS Equipment
Antennas
Fiber Optics
Calculators
Word Processors
Phonographs, VTRs, Video Discs
Microfilm
Microfiche
Business Forms

Text Editing Equipment
Communicating Word Processors
Mass Storage

Printing and Graphics Equipment
Copiers
Cash Registers
Instruments
Typewriters
Dictation Equipment
File Cabinets
Paper

Software Packages
Newspapers
Newsletters
Magazines
Shoppers
Audio Records and Tapes
Video Programs
Books

Legend:

ATM—Automated Teller Machines
IRC—International Record Carrier
PABX—Private Automatic Branch Exchange
POS—Point-of-Sale

SCC—Specialized Common Carrier
VAN—Value Added Network
VTR—Video Tape Recorder

Exhibit 2-3. The information business. (From John F. McLaughlin and Anne E. Birinyi, *Mapping the Information Business,* Harvard Business School, Cambridge, Mass.)

17

traditional turf while others are diversifying. The conflict will require creativity and commitment for the long haul, with the need to have sufficient resources to sustain losses. Another interesting aspect of the work of the Center for Information Research Policy is that they have demonstrated how legislation and regulation will play a role in this complex battlefield.

Many of you may be thinking that the map has value for the billion-dollar company but not for the small businessperson. Suppose you are the proprietor of a small television store. On the map, you find the words "television sets." But they are surrounded by other familiar products like radios, terminals, printers, facsimiles, and personal computers. If you put on your thinking cap, you might recognize that these other products are related to your own and that the television set is a communications and information product not just an entertainment vehicle. Further, you could add to what you offer, thus increasing sales. From a competitive point of view, you could plot other retailers, like Radio Shack, Sears Roebuck, and even the telephone companies. This may cause you to change your perspective and recognize that it is vital for you to expand just to survive.

Whether your business is big or small, the map helps you to see change and also to see the relationship between products and services.

Other Battlefields

Let's take another battlefield, namely leisure and entertainment. This arena may be segmented by seasons, since leisure and entertainment will vary by season. In winter, football, skiing, ice-skating, ice hockey, and snowmobiling are very popular. In summer, there are swimming, boating, sailing, waterskiing, tennis, golf, baseball, and softball. Thus, you could list all of the related products and services. However, many of these sports are now played year-round because of the creation of indoor facilities. Further, there are some activities that are not seasonal, such as vacationing and bowling as well as theater, video, audio, cultural, and community activities. This may be the midpoint of our map. As before, we should use the map to plot all of the current and potential competitors as well as changes in strategy and direction. AMF, for instance, spent the decade of the 1960s and part of the 1970s creating a conglomeration of leisure activities and products. They even used "We make your weekends" as their motto. Their portfolio included bowling, tennis, and golf equipment, powerboats and sailboats, basketballs, baseballs, motorcycles for pleasure not just transportation, and so on. In the early 1980s, they have begun to dismantle this portfolio and focus on industrial, not leisure-time, products.

Another use of the leisure and entertainment map is to depict how social and demographic changes can alter the size, growth, and relative attractiveness of the various activities. Age is a major cause of change. In the

1960s, youth was the idol and the major growth category. As the population ages, there will be a move to some sports that can be played as you grow older. This would include golf and tennis. The change in sex roles and the recognition that women as well as men can participate in what were considered to be primarily masculine activities have changed the leisure and entertainment industry. Body building for women is increasing in popularity. Colleges have been forced by law to allocate funds and facilities to women's sports as well as men's. This illustrates that there is a changing need and that as you proceed through your assessment, you may have to add products and services to your map.

This map would also be of interest to small local retailers. They could use it to determine trends and also changing competition. It may become apparent that there is a need to have a full line or possibly that there is an opportunity to emphasize one or two sports in depth instead of using a broad approach.

Energy is another key sector, one in which the competitive scene is changing. In this case, you could use the horizontal axis to depict types of fuel. The same logic should be used. List all products and services and then the major competitors that presently participate and possibly those that may find it attractive in the future.

The Need for More Specification

Macromapping gives the broad picture of the total arena and shows how companies are changing position. This is useful at the corporate level to determine new opportunities or threats, but it is not that valuable to those at the product and market level. At the product and market level you need more detail and specification. This will include more coupling with the various customer segments and an expanded listing of products and services. It is similar to moving from the national map to a city map or some step in between, such as a state or a region.

Let's take an example. Suppose you are interested in increasing your participation in the auto leasing and rental business. This segment appears to be one of high growth and profitability. A traditional market-product matrix might be of use to gain more insight into what is happening on the competitive battlefield. In order to do an effective job in preparing the matrix, you must determine how you wish to group customers and what you think are the most effective means of segmenting the product and service. In Exhibit 2-4, I have listed a number of ways you can segment the product and the market. For instance, you can segment the product by material, size, manufacturing process, model, cost, price point, base product, complexity, quality, or function. The auto leasing and rental business can be segmented by price point: high, medium, or low price, that is, luxury, utility, or economy cars. Or it could be separated into product, accessory, and service. Suppose you decide to use the price point. In Exhibit 2-5, we use three categories, economy, utility, and luxury, to represent price points. This provides the vertical axis of the matrix.

In Exhibit 2-4 I have also listed the various approaches to segment the market or, to put it another way, to group customers. Suppose you decide to use the characteristic of the size and frequency of purchase. And further, assume that the breakpoints are one to two purchases every five years, two to ten every two years, ten to twenty every year, and twenty or more every year, as illustrated in Exhibit 2-6. This correlates with the difference in frequency of purchase between individuals and organizations of various sizes.

This map provides more detail of the auto leasing and rental business and provides a means of portraying the competition. You will find that some companies lease and rent across the board while others are focused. Hertz and Avis lease and rent primarily in the utility and economy product segments to individuals. Others may focus on the large accounts, like

PRODUCT SEGMENTATION	WAYS OF SEGMENTING OR AGGREGATING CUSTOMER GROUPS	
By Material	LOCATION	—Worldwide
By Size		—Regions
By Manufacturing Process		—Urban Centers
By Model		—Population
By Cost	PURCHASING	—Size and Frequency of Purchase
By Price Point	BEHAVIOR	—Decision Makers (National or
By Base Product versus		Local)
Accessory		—Economic Focus
By Complexity		—Channels of Purchase
By Quality		—Lease versus Buy
By Function	PRODUCE USE	—End User
		—Applications
		—Experience with Product or
		Technology
		—Service Requirements
		—Quality and Reliability Needs
	CUSTOMER	—Size or Diversity
	CHARACTERISTICS	—Investment Strategy
		—Degree of Integration
		—Financial Condition

Exhibit 2-4. Product segmentation.

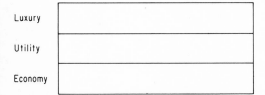

Exhibit 2-5. The vertical axis of a segmentation matrix depicting a price segmentation.

banks and insurance companies, and provide operating leases to corporations. A few leasing specialists are in the luxury category. Many of these lease cars are made by Mercedes-Benz, Rolls Royce, Cadillac, or Lincoln.

Large automobile companies like GMC and Ford might decide to increase their emphasis on leasing and renting because they want to maintain an even load of work at their plants and also because they might find leasing more profitable than direct selling. If they were to make this move, they would most likely aim first at the large accounts and then at the smaller ones. Since the luxury segment is not their traditional strength, they might ignore or only dabble in this area.

The market-product matrix can help you identify changes of emphasis and direction and uncover new opportunities.

Another Example—
Video Products

The television market has changed during the past decade to such an extent that the traditional segmentation no longer pertains. Just five years ago it would have been appropriate to segment by screen size—large, medium, and small. The addition of accessories, namely videodisc,

	1 or 2 (5 years)	2 to 10 (2 years)	10 to 20 (1 year)	20 or more (1 year)
Luxury				
Utility				
Economy				

Exhibit 2-6. A product matrix using price and quantity and frequency of purchase characteristics to scope the market and competition.

Television Receivers	
Accessories	
Program Materials or Software	

Exhibit 2-7. Segmenting the television market.

videotape, cameras, and even personal computers, would indicate that a more insightful means of segmenting would be by television receiver, accessories, and programming materials, or software. This is depicted on the vertical axis of Exhibit 2-7.

The market segmentation has also changed. Again, five years ago, it would have been most logical to segment according to the income or purchasing power of consumers. Consumers were the primary users of television sets, and their incomes correlated with the prices of the televisions they purchased. Since the television has become part of an entertainment and information system, customers now include commercial, industrial, and educational institutions. Thus, the market segmentation might be more appropriately focused on this grouping (note Exhibit 2-8).

The matrix can show the changes that have taken place and are continuing to take place. The traditional television receiver leaders, RCA and Zenith, have moved downward to include accessories, including computers. Sony has moved downward to include accessories and across to include commercial, industrial, and educational users. Some companies, like Tandy (Radio Shack), have moved upward to include television and across to include commercial and industrial users. In the future, you would anticipate the entry of IBM and A T & T, since receivers will be in the systems they offer. This is depicted in Exhibit 2-9.

	Individual Users	Commercial or Industrial	Educational
Television Receivers			
Accessories			
Program Materials or Software			

Exhibit 2-8. The television product offering and types of customer groups.

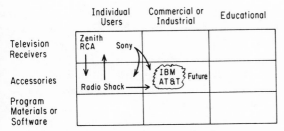

Exhibit 2-9. The changing television competitive scene.

Review and Application

Now it will be helpful if you take some time and apply the concepts to your own business or one with which you have some familiarity.

Step 1—The Macromap

1. Define your business in terms of what need, want, or pleasure you provide—energy, food, shelter, education, financing, or any other.
2. Draw a macromap of the arena you serve. This should include all the products and services that fit the arena. Normally, you draw the map to show the move from the simple to the more complex: parts and components are on the bottom, followed by products, systems, and services. This is illustrated in Exhibit 2-10. The horizontal axis can be used in any way that helps you understand various types of customers: land, sea, and air for transportation; content to conduit for communications and information; and so on.
3. Plot the current providers of the products and services, indicating current and anticipated offerings. Begin with those providing the same

Services	
Systems	
Products	
Components	
Parts	

Exhibit 2-10. Using the vertical axis to depict the move from parts to systems and services.

type of products or services. It may be useful to note size or growth of the products or services to determine whether some competitors are focused on the high-growth or biggest segments and whether they are selective or indiscriminate. If you note the regulated from the non-regulated companies, this may also be insightful. Some companies may be burdened by regulation and may be diversifying to prevent this in the future. When you have plotted the direct competitors, it might be helpful to plot the indirect. Observe whether the indirect competitors are moving to become more direct and whether they are bigger, more rapidly growing, or more or less regulated. Finally, think about those just entering the market, and plot any of these that may become your direct competitors.

Probing Deeper

Studying the map and the competitors' interactions, ask yourself the strategic questions:

1. Which segments of the market are under attack, and what will this mean to sales, rate of growth, cost of participation, and increase in risks within the industry as a whole?
2. Which segments are declining in popularity? Why is popularity or degree of competitiveness declining? Would you find this segment attractive, and do you have strengths that will permit penetration?
3. Do any of the products or services have distinctive advantages or disadvantages inherently? Would the leader in this area have uniquenesses that can by parlayed into your area of strength?
4. Does the map enable you to deduce some broad strategies in the industry that may help you to integrate and direct your own?

Step 2—The Segmentation Matrices

Having completed your map and gained information about the "war" and the major battles, you should move to the local or regional confrontation. The segment matrix is the tool for this activity.

1. Select the products and services you will analyze and determine how they can best be described. This might be by size, horsepower, price, complexity, completeness, ease of operation, quality, and/or standards. The descriptors of the product or service should reflect economic differences and be comprehensive enough to include a complete spectrum.

Exhibit 2-11. Your product or market matrix.

2. Select the best way of describing the market or customer group. This might be by type of institution, age, sex, regional participation, knowledge and skill, affluence, nationality, and so on.
3. Draw the matrix, as illustrated in Exhibit 2-11, using the descriptors you have selected.
4. For each cell in the matrix, record:

 • Size and growth of the segment
 • Profitability or margin
 • Uniqueness or characteristic
 • The key competitors and the share of each

Probing Deeper

1. Are you participating in the largest or the smallest segment, in a rapidly growing segment or a slower one? These questions address the relative attractiveness of the mix.
2. How does your mix compare with others?
3. What is the ease of moving from one segment to another? Which competitors are on the move, and does this enhance their position?
4. Which are the strongest? Are there broad or only selective leaders? Are there advantages to being broad or narrow?
5. Are changes in the wind? Will the leaders change?

3 The Winners and Losers

Identifying Winners and Losers

If you were a professional sports coach, whether it was in baseball, football, basketball, or soccer, you would easily be able to identify the historical winners and understand what made the difference between those who won and those who lost. In some cases, you would know that the difference was a result of pure talent. In others, it might be the coaching or just being in the right place, like being in the easiest division of the league. Winning can also be the result of a misfortune of the competition, such as having their best player hurt before a crucial game. Sometimes the winners have all of the above advantages, and they create a dynasty that is hard to beat. The New York Yankees of the 1960s are a good example. They had a combination of talent and good management, and they were in the easier of the major leagues.

In business the same logic should hold. It is important to determine which companies have won and lost and to understand the reasons why. Why has IBM been the traditional winner in computers, A T & T in telecommunications, GMC in automobiles, and GE in electrical equipment? Every businessman or -woman must know who the winners are in their industry and why they have won. If they do, then they will know what the criteria of success are and how they stack up. But there is one problem in business that does not exist in sports, namely deciding on what it means to be the winner, on what criteria should be used to measure success.

Determining Criteria

There are some who would argue that the answer is simple—winners are those that make the most money and losers are those that make the least. This seems to be the major criterion in the United States, and each year the major business magazines provide the standings of all the major players in each industry. The listings of *Business Week, Fortune,* and *Forbes* are useful references. In fact, the Fortune 500 is normally used to list the top 500 U.S. companies. But profits can be evaluated in several ways, and each method will yield a different listing of winners. If you use return on sales, you will get one listing; return on investment, another; and return on capital and equity and cash flow, another. So even if profits is the end of the game and is the means used to decide which firms have won and lost, you still must decide on which ratio or measure to use.

Using the *Forbes* listing of the heavy-construction field, you would find that Parsons, Parker Drilling, Fluor, and Halliburton would be considered the winners if you used return on equity as the primary measure, while Dravo, U.S. Filter, Pernini, and Dynalectron would be the losers. On a return of total capital, Parker would drop into the mid-range of the listing and Turner Construction would take its place. On the loser listing, Dravo would be replaced by Sedco and the other three would maintain position. A return-on-sales criterion would change the listing, with Sedco moving from a low, even loser, category to the top of the listing. Santa Fe International would look attractive as well. This demonstrates the need to specify the criteria and be careful in the selection.

But profit is not the only measure. In the March 22, 1982, issue of *Business Week,* there was an article on the oil industry, which used another measure to differentiate the winners from the losers. It used annual percentage change in U.S. oil production (1982 to 1985) as a means of identifying the winners and losers in the U.S. oil shakeout. The article identifies only three winners, Standard Oil of California, Union Oil, and Shell Oil, and two in a neutral position, Arco and Standard Oil of Indiana, with seven others on the negative side. These included Texaco, Exxon, and Gulf. I am not familiar enough with the oil industry to know whether this is the right measure to use, but it illustrates my point that you can use various measures and each will yield different perceptions and insights.

Matrices

In Exhibit 3-1, I have used a matrix showing the return on total capital and the return on sales in the heavy-construction industry, and you can easily spot those construction contractors that exceeded the industry averages in both criteria as well as those that were laggers. Clearly Halliburton, Parker Drilling, Parsons, and Fluor are on the winning side, while Pernini and Dynalectron are on the losing side.

I have used other matrices to plot companies according to return on sales (ROS) and return on investment (ROI) and to plot them according to growth of sales and growth of earnings. Illustrations of how such matrices can be constructed are found in Exhibits 3-2 and 3-3.

You will note that the intersection of the two variables will vary depending on what you consider to be the average. You might use your own performance as the key average, or you might use the industry average. Thus, the winners are those whose performance exceeds yours or exceeds the industry average.

Different Objectives
and Motivations

As I will emphasize in a later chapter, there are many different kinds of competitors and they each have their own priorities when they set their objectives and goals. Profits are important to the large U.S. firms but are less important to the smaller specialists that might be more concerned with cash flow, which is vital to their continuing survival. To the large multinational or state-owned firms, there may be several other criteria. These may include the creation of jobs and keeping unemployment at a low level or the assurance of a favorable trade and monetary balance. The key may be to provide prestige and build a spirit of success for the nation. These companies may use a matrix which plots employment on one axis and trade balance on another. Those with a favorable position would be the winners, and those that are negative on both would be the losers.

Need for Comparable Data

Regardless of the criteria used, you must recognize that it may be difficult to get comparable data. In the profitability area, each firm or country may have different rules to account for cost, investment, and profits. These practices may distort inventories, costs, taxes, and accrual accounts. The objective in some companies is to keep profits low so that they do not have to pay taxes or can avoid the criticism of being too profitable. This is the

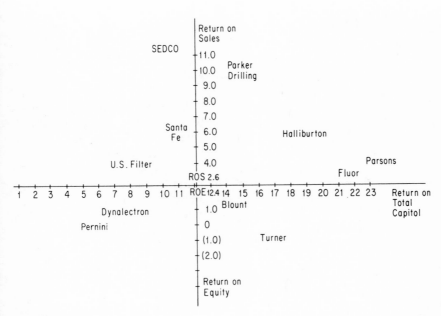

Exhibit 3-1.

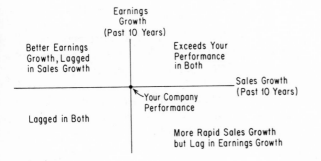

Exhibit 3-2.

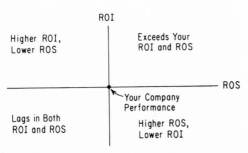

Exhibit 3-3.

case in Europe and to some degree in the United States. Therefore, it is important to choose the criteria carefully and then to make sure that the measures and results are comparable. I prefer to use multiple criteria and to see which companies fall in which positions. Some might be winners regardless of the measure. For instance, IBM would be the best regardless of which criterion is used. They have exceeded their competition in ROI, ROS, and sales and earnings growth. They have created jobs and improved the prestige and image of all host countries. They have created the standard of excellence—at least in the past. The same is true of a number of the multinationals. Certainly, the Japanese electronics companies have been winners, though in this case you would have to adjust earnings to reflect their way of accounting.

Why Success or Failure?

Once you have the criteria and the measures and you have completed your analysis, you will have a listing of the key companies on the success and failure sides of the ledger. Your firm might be on one side or another or might not be on the list at.all. This may be because you are in the middle or do not currently participate.

Now you need to try and explain what makes the difference between the two extreme groups. The differences may provide you with a listing of success factors that can be used in a later step to decide on how you stand via the competition and also to decide whether changes in the world or type of competition will change these factors. There are four fundamental aspects to analyze to determine why some win and some do not. These are: the vision, direction, and strategy of the firms; their assumptions about the future; the resources they possess; and just plain luck or lack of good luck. I would like to demonstrate how these have contributed to the industries with which I have had some experience.

Vision, Direction, and Strategy

There are numerous examples of companies that were gifted with having forward-thinking and visionary leaders who had the courage to make some tough decisions and then to implement a consistent strategy. In each of these cases, the vision was right for the time but not forever. In the automobile business, we are all aware of the vision of Alfred Sloane, who made General Motors into the giant we know today. His vision and strategy focused on providing the public with stylistic, quality automobiles, with numerous changes made annually at all price points. He established divisions in each price and status segment that could run their own show and yet capitalize on the volume advantages of mass production. He encouraged competition among the divisions and decentralized decision making. His strategy still exists today, and his company is still the giant of the industry even though it is under attack by others with different strategies and visions. He took on the industry leader, Ford, whose leader had a different strategy. Henry Ford based his game plan on the vision that the public wanted a means of transportion at low cost. This could be best achieved through standardization and few designs and changes. His was a cost-driven vision while Sloane's was a marketing-driven one. Ford centralized while GM decentralized. The point is that there was a winner and loser and the difference could be traced to a different vision and strategy.

In retail, the contrasts between the vision and strategy of Sears and Montgomery Ward were easy to see. Sears had a vision that after World War II America would move to the suburbs and use the car as its mode of transportation. Thus, their strategy was to build stores in the suburbs and not in the center of the cities. Ward's vision, on the other hand, assumed that the world would plunge into a recession, possibly a repeat of the Depression. Thus, they held on to their cash and concentrated on center-city stores. Sears was the better forecaster. Their strategy was the winning one, and Ward does not exist as a separate company today.

In the consumer electronics arena, the story today is not as clear as to who is the winner and who the loser. For over a decade RCA was a winner in the communications arena. General Sarnoff built a completely integrated system. He was able to get the United States and several Western Hemisphere countries to use the RCA system for color television. Simultaneously RCA used its NBC broadcasting network to lead in color broadcasting. He moved into records and other related equipment as well as programming. This made RCA the profit winner for a period of time, and the situation only changed when the company stopped following the original strategy. Today we have other examples of a consistent and winning strategy. Sony has been able to combine innovation and quality to become the reputed quality leader in the consumer electronics arena. Whether this is a lasting thrust, only time will tell.

Different Assumptions

The reason that there are numerous illustrations of companies that have different strategies is that the leaders of these companies make different assumptions about the future and then set out to make them self-fulfilling prophecies.

Thus, it is important to deduce the assumptions that are being made. Let's examine a few areas in today's world and see how the assumptions will vary and therefore influence the strategies.

Market Assumptions

In the communications and information arena, companies appear to have very different sets of assumptions about how and at what rate the market will develop. Wang Laboratories is betting on the word processor as the center of the office of the future, while IBM is betting on the mainframe computer, distributed processing, and the recently added personal computer as the main core of the office. Xerox would like to believe that it will be the copiers and its communication network. Some companies are assuming that the office will develop gradually and that you do not have to be a leader. Others see it growing rapidly and believe you must lead in some aspect of it. The same is true of the factory of the future and the home of the future. In the factory field, companies disagree on the key to the future. Some believe it will be the machine tool, others robotics, and still others the computer-aided design and manufacturing systems. Of course, as in the office field, there are some that are waiting to see what happens and planning to then move in. Others believe that success will be the reward of those that create the modules and then put it together.

In energy there are also a number of assumptions that will differentiate the ultimate winners. Some are assuming that conservation is only a fad and that it will disappear once oil or gas become plentiful and their cost stabilizes. Others, however, are making different assumptions and are focusing on providing products and services to meet the conservation and efficiency needs. There is disagreement about which form of energy will evolve and be the most popular. There are companies that believe it will be multiple types, and so they are acquiring a number of forms and resources, while others believe that it will be one type, and they are putting all their eggs in one basket.

There are also assumptions about the industry as a whole. Will the industry decline and how rapidly? If it does decline, who will survive? Is it better to diversify or even to get out of the prime business? General assumptions about the industry will clearly determine the future of many companies in the maturing commodity industries, such as steel, aluminum, autos, and transportation. U.S. Steel took a chance and acquired Marathon Oil; National Steel acquired a savings and loan association; while Bethlehem Steel has decided to continue to concentrate on the core industry.

Technology Assumptions

Companies and nations are making significantly different assumptions about the future technologies. Some are rushing to displace the traditional for the new, while others are merely making the existing technology more competitive or even ignoring the entire question. Will electronic controls substitute for the electromechanical controls? Will very large integrated circuits (VLSI) displace all of the traditional integrated circuits? What are the new applications for electronics, and what will be the displacement rate? These are the questions that are the keys to almost all companies in the industry. The Japanese companies are betting on the larger integrated circuits and have used electronics almost exclusively in their controls. American companies have been slower to displace and are betting on being able to buy the circuits rather than having their own internal production capabilities. Some believe that if you do not make the circuits, you will fail, while others believe that the making of them will reduce flexibility and increase the risks and costs of participating.

These differences in assumptions are also apparent in metallurgical and biological industries. What is the future potential of the biotechnologies? Do you have to participate now to win, or can you wait to have it developed and then buy in?

Supply Assumptions

Another area that may make the difference between success and mediocrity is the area of supply. Assumptions are made about money, people, and natural resources. I mentioned earlier that Ward's management thought that there would be a recession or even a depression after the war, but it turned out to be a period of rapid growth, and they were not prepared to take advantage of that growth. The same situation is occurring today. There are a number of companies that are not very aggressive, because they believe that the economy will not grow. Many are assuming a continuation of high interest rates and cost of money. There are others that believe that inflation will remain at a high level and so are reluctant to use their own funds. Thus, they are increasing debt. This can dramatically change the strategy of a company. If the world does not turn out to be so pessimistic, these companies may miss the growth and thus be another Ward. Of course, there are others that have the opposite opinion, and they are betting on growth. If correct, they may be tomorrow's Sears. You must think about your own situation and identify those companies that have the optimistic and pessimistic perceptions of tomorrow.

Assumptions about the workforce and the strategy to deal with it are also crucial and may separate the top and the bottom. Some believe that the American workforce is inherently unproductive, and so they are moving their plants to the lower-cost parts of the world. There are also those that believe there will be a shortage of trained electronics engineers, and they are establishing elaborate and expensive training programs or investing in automated equipment that will reduce the need for this type of professional. Assumptions about relative wage rates and salary structures can lead to different location and manufacturing strategies.

On the natural-resource end of the spectrum, there can be a variety of opinions and actions. Some believe that there will be a continuing abundance of resources and that they will be available when and if needed, while some have the opposite belief and are setting up long-term contracts to assure supply and cost control. Finally there are those that are backward-integrating. This is what has happened in the energy field over the past decade. DuPont's expressed motivation in the acquisition of Conoco was to assure a supply of petroleum-based materials at a reasonable price. The same kind of thing may happen with copper, coal, tungsten, bauxite, and other natural resources.

Macroenvironmental Assumptions
The most crucial questions about the future may be not in the microenvironment but rather in the macroenvironment. In some countries, like Spain, it may be the question of the stability of the government or whether the country will move to the left. Unfortunately this may be the issue in most nations of the world, even the United States. In 1983, there are those who believe that the Reagan program will be a failure and the country will return to the liberalized policies of the past. This is not a trivial assumption, because it may determine how business measures itself in profits or the creation of jobs. One question that I mentioned early in this chapter is: What are the assumptions that are being made about the societal configuration of the future? If you are in consumer products, this question may separate the winners and losers. Will the trend toward working wives and feminism continue? Will individuals continue to marry later, and what will be the number of children in a typical family? If a company decides that the current trend toward working wives, smaller families, and smaller homes will continue, it may decide to focus on smaller appliances and the more expensive, higher-priced merchandise. If, however, the assumption is that this trend is merely another fad and that there will be a return to the more traditional family, then the decision may be the opposite. Some may hedge their bets, and this may not be the best thing to do, since those caught in the middle are often destined to be mediocre and are often the long-term losers.

The key point is that assumptions influence strategy, which in turn will result in a company being on either the high or low end of the listings. But this is not the only factor that has an impact on the results, and so I will now discuss how different resources may be the determinant.

Resources

We all know that people are not the same. Some individuals are smart, others handsome; some have a pleasing personality, and others are good salespeople. The same is true of enterprises. Some companies are gifted with innovative people, strong images, and good salespeople. There are companies that know how to make superior products cheaply. Some companies are rich, and others are located in desirable countries. Of course, there are also companies that can innovate but cannot sell and ones that produce well but are dull in their offerings. Others could be strong but are located in countries that have troubles. These differences can be crucial to success or failure. It is important to analyze the companies that you have identified and to compare their resources. Let's look at some resource areas in which companies differ.

Marketing Skills

We normally think of marketing only in relation to the salesforce. But this is too limited. Part of the difference between winners and losers may be found in the ability to work with customers to determine what they need and then to satisfy them. You may need to know what customers want even before they know themselves. For many decades IBM has proved that it is willing to work with customers to determine needs and then to help satisfy them. The same has been true of General Electric in the electrical generation and distribution markets. The materials companies also have had this talent, and they have often developed unique materials to satisfy their users' needs. This may become so vital that it becomes a critical success factor. Other marketing talents may be related to advertising, which can be used to build the feeling of differences even if they are not real. This is the talent of packaged-goods companies, especially Procter & Gamble. They combine real distinctiveness with perceived distinctiveness. Thus they are able to demand a premium price for commodities like toilet paper, napkins, tissues, and soaps.

Design and Product Differences

The difference may be in the ability to design and produce new products and services creatively. This may be done by a small group of professionals or even the owner. Such talent may not be replicable, and so it may disappear with the exit of the key people. The talent may be restricted to one or a few disciplines and thus not be applicable to other sciences or technologies. Success may have been achieved by the application of someone else's ideas or even their patents. In such cases, it may not have been the initial entry into the market that mattered but rather being able to provide the service or product at a lower cost. The history books are full of stories of inventors who died poor while those who followed them became rich. Of course in the eyes of some, the winner may be the poor inventor rather than the rich follower; it depends on the criteria, as I discussed before.

Sustaining Power

The differing resource may be sustaining power. It can take years, even decades, to develop a market and create a new industry. Thus the leader may be the one that can sustain its funds and its aggressiveness. Unique patents are often the key to success, and these may be so protected that the competition cannot move or follow. At other times, quick following may be the key to success. Take a few minutes to think about your industry and to determine if its resource differences are in the type of people, the funding, the uniqueness of a patent, or the ability to follow.

Production

There are numerous examples in which winning was a result of the ability to deliver the product in a unique, quality, and economical way. This clearly is the distinction in the fast-food industry. McDonald's has been a winner because it combined a fast, consistent-quality product on an economical scale. The skill of producing products that have few defects and that do not require extensive service networks can be the deciding factor, or it might be the productivity of the workforce or even of the total system. Controlling materials and inventory or striking the proper balance to serve the customer may be the fine line between the winner and the loser. The list is long and the examples are numerous of companies that combined the proper levels of productivity, quality, and service. It was not one or the other that made the difference but rather the combination and the mixture of several of these factors.

Financial Differences

There is a saying that "Being rich is not everything, but it beats being poor." I indicated before that having enough money to stay in the game for a long time may be the key to winning, sometimes even more important than having the best or even the second best product or service. Money can be important. I believe that one of the main reasons IBM was so successful in the early days of computers and was able to beat many larger companies, including GE, RCA, and Westinghouse, all of which were larger when the computer industry began, was that it was able to use its cash flow to create a barrier. Other companies lacked the willingness to use cash or were unable to raise enough to participate. IBM had excellent cash flow from its old keypunch business and used the money to enable its customers to rent or lease computers rather than buy them. Thus, leasing became a key factor to success in the computer business, but it became too expensive for other companies. In fact, most of the other companies were interested in selling and even being paid in advance. Thus having cash was a key to IBM's success.

There are other financially based criteria. Having a strong credit rating may enable a company to obtain funds at attractive rates at a time when others cannot even get funds. This has proved to be the case in the past decade. Access to low-cost loans was vital to the success of the American companies in the 1950s and 1960s and has been the key to the success of the Japanese and European companies in the past ten years. Are there any companies in your industry whose progress has been dependent on this factor?

Managerial and Workforce Talents
We all recognize the genius of Sloane, Land, Edison, and others who created enterprises that prospered, and indicated how they personally contributed to their development. But the competitive advantage and the reason for winning may be that a company can attract and retain key people or that it has been smart enough to develop people at all levels. Thus, the company may be able to make better analyses and faster and more precise decisions and plans. I once gave a talk in New York in which I described what it took to be a strategic winner. The talk focused on things like developing options, being committed, and consistently rewarding people to achieve the desired results. Following my talk, the president of a major electronics company described his company and indicated that I had left out one of the most important ingredients, namely people. As I thought about his remarks, I decided he was right. I had not been complete. Certainly companies need something to work with, and it is helpful if they have a strong marketing, product, and production system, but quite often the only thing that appears to separate the winners from the losers are the people. Talent is important, and it should not be overlooked.

Luck

We have looked at vision, direction, and strategy; assumptions about the future; and resources. They may explain the differences between winners and losers. But there is a fourth aspect that should also be looked at. It may be tied to the others, or it may just stand out by itself.

It is important that a company be lucky, and luck cannot be underestimated. Luck includes being in the right place at the right time. The key words are time and place. I mentioned that some people are too early and don't have the staying power to wait for the "right time." There were people who developed lamps before Edison, but they are not even known today. The companies with the energy-efficient cars, motors, appliances, and generators have prospered because of the energy crisis and concern about availability and cost. Those who have the software to match the computer or the ability to respond rapidly to a given fad or unique once-in-a-lifetime need are the winners for the short term if not necessarily the long term. Often success has nothing to do with great planning or forecasting but rather is purely a function of timing.

Location can also be a matter of luck. American companies certainly have an advantage over other companies because their country is large, affluent, and rich in resources and human energy and has a climate suitable for almost anything they want to do. Many Americans look at the Russians' inability to provide wheat for their own use and believe that it is because the U.S. farmer is smarter or more skilled. This may be partially true, but it is also a fact that the Russian climate is not as supportive to agriculture.

The Saudis and the Kuwaitis are not smarter than anyone else; they're just lucky to have all that oil in their country. The South Africans are fortunate to have coal, gold, and diamonds as well as other strategic minerals. Your competitors may be in a country that is very supportive of industry and that provides financing and protection. Some believe that this is the reason some Japanese companies have done so well. I don't share this generalization. However, it helps these companies to be in a country that has priorities favorable to business and a willingness to support their implementation. Some U.S. companies are located in a state that has low taxes and a uniquely skilled workforce. This may be part of the resources you just noted, but it may not be, since it is available to all companies in that state and not just the ones you are evaluating.

Changes in Success Factors

Success factors can change, and a winner can lose position and even fall into the loser category. There appear to be several causes.

Complacency and Fear

Clearly the winner becomes the model and the target of all the competition. Unfortunately, many winners become complacent and fear that they will be affected negatively if they change. Clearly A & P stopped innovating and leading. They refused to follow their customers to the suburbs and did not offer a combination of brandname and store-label products. Their stores became outmoded, and their prices became uncompetitive. This was caused by complacency and/or fear of losing what they had. The American automobile companies became complacent and assumed that the imports were too weak and fragmented to become a serious threat. In addition, they feared that the smaller car would erode their overall profitability. This is a classic situation. New products often take share from the older line that is more profitable.

Substitution

Winners have the most to lose from the introduction of a new and different way of providing the same function or an improved version of it.

Most people have never even heard of the American Locomotive and Baldwin Lima Hamilton companies, since they do not exist today. These were the winners in the steam-locomotive markets. The advent and success of the diesel locomotive not only threatened these companies but actually led to their demise. The same is true of many companies that were displaced by substitute products. Addressograph Multigraph and AB Dick were the leaders in office products. Xerography substituted for the wet copiers and thus changed their standing. Curtis-Wright was one of the early leaders in propeller-driven aircraft. They were successfully displaced by the jet engine and by Boeing and to some extent McDonnell Douglas. The list can be repeated in every sector of the economy, whether it is food, lodging, transportation, or metals or even one of the emerging industries such as chemicals and electronics. Sometimes it happens in specific niches rather than in total industries. It will be interesting to see who the ultimate winners are in minicomputers, biotechnology, and engineering materials.

Environment

In the previous chapter I stressed the need to start with the customer and his or her needs and wants. Missing changes in these needs and wants can be devastating to the leaders. Again, examples abound. The most recent is in the automobile industry, an example I have used before. Missing the change from concern for style and power and little concern for energy efficiency to the current concern for quality, reliability, and high mileage put the American leaders in the position of having to aggressively move to catch up with their new foreign opponents. Clothing manufacturers who missed the desire for lightweight garments that are easy to wash and clean were negatively impacted. The trend toward designer jeans caused a number of position changes in the industry and opened the way for the entry of previously unknown brands. The need for improved productivity in industry and commerce has led to the entry of several new forces in industrial machinery and automation and the decline of a number of previously well-known companies. Many of these companies have been merged into other corporations. In farm equipment, several companies missed new opportunities and were forced to consolidate or even liquidate.

Governmental regulations and laws can be a major reason that companies fall from the top and new ones take their place. These regulations can vary from country to country. Certainly the restrictions placed on American companies selling nuclear power plants abroad enabled French companies and may enable Japanese companies to move up rapidly and possibly displace the leaders. The restrictions on the use of asbestos and the subsequent suits to claim damages to users and workers resulted in the recent bankruptcy of Johns-Manville, the reputed industry leader. Often these regulations impact the means of production and force the addition of new antipollution and environmental-protection devices on manufacturing facilities. These devices may result in a decline in productivity or the allocation of funds from productive to nonproductive projects. Thus, the cost positioning may change, and this may result in a decline in relative position. This has caused a number of American companies to lose their competitive edge to companies located in nations with less stringent regulations or no regulations at all.

The rise of worker demands and militancy may influence the success factors, and the environment may change the attitude and willingness of professional and managerial workers to work in a given industry. For instance, the anti-Vietnam movement in the 1970s resulted in a decline in defense-related expenditures as well as a decline in the number of engineers and scientists seeking employment in these industries. Therefore, success depended on the ability to retain the people you had and get a higher share of the smaller number of applicants. Companies that are most capable of dealing with their workforce, attracting and retaining key people, and maintaining peace and stability may become the winners, provided they can achieve equality in other factors.

The facts are that changes in the customer, industry, government, society, and so on can result in changes in the factors of success, and this can result in changes in the relative position of the major firms.

Innovative Followers

Quite often the threat to position comes from those who are smarter in adapting and even following the leaders. In other words, it is not just substitution or new products that can cause displacement, it is also the competitor that adds or innovates on what currently exists. This ties to the timing concept discussed earlier. Again, some of the best examples come from the Japanese. Most successful Japanese companies were originally not innovators but rather followers. They took U.S. and European technologies and applied them creatively to create new needs and wants. Sony, Canon, Panasonic, Nissan, and Toyota all added value to the offering and were able to penetrate at the expense of their often larger competitors. Most would agree that IBM did the same in computers, Pratt & Whitney in jet engines, McDonald's in fast food, Hyatt in hotels, and Merrill Lynch in financial services. The industries and markets already existed. Others already had position and had been innovators, but these companies were able to move aggressively and create new success factors that the leaders either missed, ignored, or followed too slowly.

Thus quality and reliability were added to autos because of the innovative followers; systems service, and leasing were added to computers; clean, attractive, limited menus were added to fast food; elegance at moderate prices to hotels; and full services at moderate fees were added to the financial service markets.

Review and Application

Let's review the logic and sequence I am suggesting for winner and loser analysis.

Step 1—Criteria Determination

Determine what best differentiates the winners and losers.

- Is it total profits? Return on sales? Return on equity or total capital or investment?
- Is it sales and profit growth?
- Is it cash flow?
- Is it market share?
- Is it the creation of new markets?
- Is it the provision of employment?
- Is it the development of future reserves?

Think about your own situation and pick the criteria that best meet your needs and will mean the difference between success and failure.

Step 2—Matrices to Visualize

Once you have decided on the criteria, you can use them to evaluate the performance of *all* the key participants. If you use more than one criterion, it may be useful to use a series of matrices to plot them. These matrices might show a combination of ROI and ROS or other profitability measures or they may show growth in sales, employment, or other factors. Remember our caution about the need to have comparable data, since you may be over- or underestimating the performance of competitors. There is also the need to determine what will be the intersection of the axis. Some may decide on average performance, thus highlighting those that exceeded, equaled, or were below the average. Others may use their own companies' performance, thus highlighting those that exceeded, equaled, or did not do as well as themselves.

Step 3—Determining the Differences

What are those characteristics of the winners that distinguished them from the losers?

1. Is there a unique vision, direction, or strategy?
2. Were there different explicit assumptions about the market, technology, and/or supply?
3. Were there unique resources in any of these areas?

- Marketing
- Manufacturing
- Engineering
- Finance
- Management

4. Were there other unusual factors?

- Good timing
- Strong location
- Inept or conservative competition
- Government aid
- Proximity to unusual natural resources

Use these questions to determine the differences between winners and losers. List the success factors.

Step 4—Changes in Success Factors

Success factors can change, resulting in a change of winners and losers. These changes may be a result of overconfidence, complacency, or fear of change on the part of the leaders. They can be the result of substitution, innovative followers, or the impact of environmental changes.

Determine how these change agents can impact the success factors and how they can change the relative position of all the competition, as well as yourself.

Output

- Identification of winners and losers
- Clarification of present success factors
- Noting of key events, trends, or changes that can alter the future success factors

4 Allier Could Become Adverrarier

In the last chapter I described how to use a winner and loser evaluation to highlight the critical success factors. But this gives only a partial view of potential winners and the changing success factors. To be complete, we must evaluate the total industry structure and analyze how movement of various participants can change the factors and the players.

Industry Analysis

An industry analysis includes a total view of the entire industry, beginning with the current participants in your area of interest. This is equivalent to the winner and loser analysis just completed. For instance, suppose you were the producer of lawn mowers. You would list all producers of lawn mowers, both power mowers and hand mowers, whether they were domestic or international. This is depicted in Exhibit 4-1 as the first phase of the industry structure.

Next you would identify the major suppliers of the parts, components, subassemblies, and materials used in the production of lawn mowers. This is illustrated in Exhibit 4-2. This should include the major suppliers of the motors, blades, controls, cases for housing, and wheels, and even those

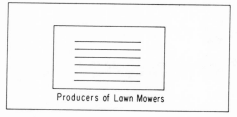

Exhibit 4-1. Phase 1 of the industry structure.

that produce the steel and aluminum. In other words, all of those that supply the lawn mower producers and that could decide to forward integrate and become competitors.

Next you should identify all those that serve as "intermediaries" between the producers and the end users of the product. These should include wholesalers, OEM, jobbers, agents, and retailers. The number of steps between the producer and the user will vary from industry to industry. In some cases, the producers sell to others that put the product in a larger system—as when a printer manufacturer sells to a computer manufacturer, which in turn sells a computer system. In our lawn mower situation, this is not the case. Lawn mowers are systems in themselves. Ordinarily, the producer sells to wholesale distributors, which in turn sell to retailers that service the user. At other times, they might sell to agents or to jobbers that serve retailers or sell directly to users. Each step increases the time the product takes to get to the user, and it might increase the markup as well.

When you complete the list, as shown in Exhibit 4-3, you should identify the winners and losers in each category.

One other group to identify in an industry is the companies that provide

```
Parts
____

Components          ┌──────────┐
____                │          │
                    │          │
Subassemblies       │          │
____                └──────────┘

Materials
____

    Suppliers _____ Producers
```

Exhibit 4-2. Phase 2 of the industry structure—the suppliers.

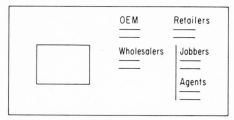

Exhibit 4-3. Phase 3 of the industry structure—the intermediaries.

similar products to the user or that sell to the same intermediaries. For instance, in our lawn mower example you could list those companies that provide other garden equipment, such as rakes, shovels, wheelbarrows, even lawn-care products such as seeds and fertilizers. It would also be helpful to list companies that provide motor-driven products, such as snow blowers, tractors, and trenchers. This is illustrated in Exhibit 4-4.

If you have followed this approach, you now have complete visualization of all those that supply and serve the intermediaries and even end users. In total this is an industry view.

The Use

This type of visualization can be very helpful in seeing the total industry and identifying the leaders, followers, and losers in each category. Some companies may participate in each category, in other words be totally integrated, while others may specialize in their specific category. The competitive issue is whether this situation will change.

- Will suppliers decide to move forward and become direct competitors? For example, a steel company may decide to make mowers instead of just selling steel.
- Will intermediaries decide to move backward and produce their own

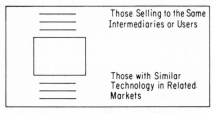

Exhibit 4-4. Phase 4 of the industry structure—others serving the industry.

lawn mowers or acquire a company that produces them? This happened when Sears acquired its own supplier of lawn mowers.

• Will those on the side—selling related products—decide to add lawn mowers to their line? Scotts Lawn Products did this.

• Will those selling other motor-driven products decide to sell lawn mowers? Toro did this.

All of these changes have happened, and many companies have been surprised or ill-prepared. The objective of this chapter is not to make you fear everyone but rather to increase your preparedness. As the Boy Scouts slogan says, "Be prepared."

The type of moves I am describing are pretty obvious, and I am not going to belabor them. I would like to discuss why they occur and what their significance is. Further, I would like to emphasize how often these changes can be anticipated, and how they can be neutralized or used to your advantage.

Why Do Participants Change?

There are four key reasons for backward, forward, and horizontal integration: (1) insecurity, (2) economics, (3) ability to do the job better and be innovative, and (4) change in grand strategy because of the need for diversified growth.

Insecurity

Often there are one or two critical components or materials that are so vital to a product that without them you would be out of business. For instance, a compressor is a key component to a refrigerator or an air conditioner. Without it, you cannot make them at all. A power source is a key to any transportation vehicle. Diesel engines are the key to trucks and locomotives; internal-combustion engines, to autos, lawn mowers, snowmobiles, and tractors; and jet engines, to the commercial aircraft.

We seemed surprised to find in the mid-1970s that petroleum was a vital fuel to propel most vehicles as well as to provide heat for industrial, commercial, and private buildings. Copper is critical to the wire and cable and electrical distribution and transmission businesses. There are a number of highly strategic materials that, though they are not used in quantities, are important catalytic agents for making steel and aluminum. The list is enormous. One or two key components or materials, if not available in enough quantities or in a timely manner or at competitive costs, can shut down or make a manufacturer noncompetitive. This is the reason that a number of users of these vital materials decide to backward integrate and make their own. Let's list a few illustrations.

Fifty years ago, General Motors initially purchased all necessary components from small suppliers and specialists. As time progressed, it recognized that it would be more secure if it made its own. So it acquired a number of these companies, primarily for its own use. The word "primarily" is important here. Many do not recognize an integrated producer that makes the product for its own use as a competitor, but since GMC also sells components to others in the industry, it is a true competitor.

Black & Decker is a major tool producer. Many of its tools are motor-powered. B & D started to make its own motors in the mid-1960s. Recently Whirlpool integrated into component motors and controls for its appliances.

Coal is a major fuel for electrical generation. Electric utilities have acquired a number of mines to supply their own coal. Chemical companies have backward integrated, and so too have mining companies and others. Quite often, this was done to assure a timely supply at a competitive price. This move puts companies in a stronger bargaining position with vendors, since they know the cost and the operating economics, even if they do not become completely self-sufficient.

Supplier Insecurity

Suppliers also have insecurities, and as a result, they take actions to become assemblers, wholesalers, and even retailers. Their insecurity is a result of the concern that intermediaries may become so powerful with the user that they can control the price and the terms of availability. At times suppliers take action because the distribution they receive is too weak and they lose clout in the marketplace.

Whirlpool is a major supplier to Sears and sells them all of their home-laundry products (washers and dryers). Whirlpool has its own dealer network and sells the Whirlpool brand as well as Sears. In recent years, the Whirlpool brand has been heavily promoted to assure that Sears does not control Whirlpool's future.

Originally, Howard Johnson's was primarily a supplier to its exclusive franchised dealers. It supplied them a unique structure, national brand advertising, site selection, architectural support, recipes, ice cream, foodstuffs, and condiments. The same was true of McDonald's. As these chains became successful, they recognized that it was difficult to control the quality and service of their franchises. Quality and service are key success factors in fast food, and if they are not consistent, they can negate other factors, such as recipes, motif, and national advertising. Both chains have acquired a number of their franchises and currently operate them.

Insecurity in the Auto Industry

They say that history often repeats itself. Traditionally, automobile manufacturers have relied on individual franchised dealers to market products, parts, and services locally. These franchises have been very attractive, and the automobile manufacturers were in a position of power and could make and obtain many concessions. One of the major concessions was exclusivity. A Ford dealer could sell only Fords and a Chevrolet dealer only Chevies. In fact, they were often restricted from handling other brands of the same producer—Chevrolet dealers could not sell Buicks; Ford dealers could not sell Lincolns.

In the mid-1970s the large U.S. auto companies were unable to meet the "sudden" demand for small economy cars, and many franchises added other brands to their offering. Buick dealers added Honda. Oldsmobile added BMW. The control of the Big Three was weakened, and ultimately I believe you may see mass merchants, such as Sears, K-Mart, and J. C. Penney, begin to sell autos, since most of them already sell parts and tires and provide service. Will auto companies move forward and begin to sell cars at retail? GMC could decide to acquire the independent dealers and become a retailer as well as a manufacturer. If it does, it will be a repetition of what has happened in other consumer products, such as Howard Johnson's, McDonald's, and International Silver.

Horizontal Moves for Security

Before we discuss other reasons for integration, it is worth looking at horizontal integration moves. In any hardware, food, or department store there are products from a number of vendors. Even in the same department of a store, you will find this situation. Suppose you supply pots and pans. You may not consider the producers of dishes, utensils, and rubber products as potential competitors, but they could be. These companies may be concerned that they will lose counter or shelf space to companies that have a larger offering or that can make special deals with the store owners and operators because of their more complete line and thereby sell a mix of products by the carload. In order to counteract this move, producers of dishes, utensils, and rubber products may decide to increase their offering and become "providers" of pots and pans. Note the word "provider." They may have someone else make the products and offer them for resale. Here are some examples:

- Maytag added dishwashers and ranges to its offering.
- Rubbermaid moved into all kitchen products as well as auto-accessory products.
- Midas increased its products to include a fuller line of auto parts.
- Toro added snow blowers to lawn mowers.

Economic Reasons

In the early stages of the product life cycle, most companies remain flexible and do not integrate backward or forward. There are a number of reasons.

The product will be changing, and it makes no sense to lock in too early. The cost of integration can be high, and the funds may not be available. A move may distract from the primary line. During the mature stage, the situation changes. With forward, backward, or horizontal thrusts, the economic rewards can be significant. You can use the same engineering designs and the same marketing and administrative skills. By making the products themselves or by becoming closer to the user, companies can change the volume produced and possibly reduce inventories and cut down on payables. Further, they can build facilities that can increase economy of scale, and they can even sell to competitors. Greater utilization of capacity often results in higher profits.

Examples
During the late 1960s metal-can manufacturers offered food canners and canners and bottlers of soft drinks and beer the opportunity to have canning facilities built in or close to their facilities. Many accepted and discovered the profitability of can production. Within the next ten years, the large bottlers and canners initiated their own can production. This increased their value added and decreased the market available to Continental Can, American Can, National Can, and Crown Cork & Seal, since the companies became internal suppliers rather than external purchasers.

Initially, Motorola was an innovator in automobile radios and a supplier to all auto companies. As the industry matured, General Motors began producing its own radios, and Ford acquired Philco—decreasing the size of Motorola's market and creating new competitors.

In the 1920s, electrical-products companies purchased motors, controls, wire and cable, and compressors from small specialists. As the volume increased and the components became standardized, the large companies such as General Electric and Westinghouse acquired or initiated their own manufacturing. Similarly they began to acquire or start up their own wholesale supply companies—giving birth to GESCO (General Electric Supply Company) and WESCO (Westinghouse Supply Company). These moves illustrate both forward and backward integration.

Retailers, such as Sears, J. C. Penney, A & P, and Safeway, recognized the economic value of controlling their suppliers. A & P acquired and operated their own food processors and canning facilities, offering Ann Page private-label products at lower prices. Sears did the same with its Craftsman and Kenmore brands, though they combined ownership and joint partnerships.

But, of course, movement is not restricted to just moving backward. It can also be forward. If a manufacturer controls the key components, it may find it beneficial to add other components or activities and move forward. Texas Instruments thought that its position in integrated circuits put it in a strong economic position to be the supplier of consumer products such as watches and calculators. It offered complete products instead of merely selling parts to calculator assemblers such as Bowmar. Its move was devastating to Bowmar but also not as successful as it anticipated, and it lost position in calculators and discontinued watches.

Aluminum and steel companies thought that since they produced the vital metal, they could be in the consumer-products business. Many of them sold garden tools, others baseball bats and tennis rackets. Others offered tractors, lawn mowers, and lawn furniture. Their understanding and ability to successfully participate were not adequate, and they, like Texas Instruments, gave up after an unsuccessful move.

Thus, not all forward integration moves are successful, but it still behooves companies to anticipate these thrusts and take steps to prevent or minimize their impact. Even an aborted or unsuccessful entry can change the profits and the economics of doing business.

Ability and Innovation

Even though the suppliers or intermediaries are not threatened or do not see a considerable economic advantage, they may be in a position to add to the construction, function, or utility of the product or component. This is a direct result of the knowledge they have as users or as direct sellers to users. They may spot limitations in the material or quality and reliability of the component. It may be possible that by combining the functions or materials currently used with new ones, they can make the product more durable or more functional. Likewise the intermediary might have an awareness of a user need that is not filled by a current offering or that can be satisfied in a better way.

It is difficult to separate the precise motivations of the companies already illustrated. The auto companies, aluminum companies, and Sears could all have made their moves because they saw ways to do the job better as well as because they saw ways to gain advantages of economy and control. However, as technologies mature, moves in order to innovate might increasingly occur. The semiconductor and integrated-circuit manufacturers might find that by compounding materials, they can increase yields, improve reliability, and possibly get more memory on a chip. The airframe companies could decide that it makes more sense to integrate the jet propulsion system into the frame and thus build their own. Many computer manufacturers are including firmware into their computers rather than using software additions.

Strategic Changes

Finally, a supplier or intermediary might change primarily because it has a new management and overall strategy. Instead of being content in a small niche, it might wish to expand, and the best bet is to build on its unique strengths or position. It may have unique design capability that would give it a competitive advantage, or it may have unique manufacturing, marketing, or financial clout.

Examples

The DuPont and Conoco merger made headlines in July and August 1981. The bidding among DuPont, Mobil, and Schenley was the topic of the news stories, but the change in DuPont's strategy was more dynamic. DuPont had stayed in its "specialty materials" niche for more than a century. It was the leading innovator in the field and had invented materials that created new markets and industries. It invented nylon, rayon, orlon, corfam, and other materials, and most were successful. Under Irving Shapiro, DuPont had continued this thrust and had announced its move into generic engineering, including several acquisitions. Mr. Shapiro retired; Edward Jefferson replaced him; the Conoco deal came up; and suddenly the entire strategy appeared to have changed to include significant backward integration moves. DuPont asserts that increased control of its supply and costs were the major considerations.

The Westinghouse acquisition of Teleprompter made history in the cable field. Westinghouse was one of the leaders in broadcasting, and Teleprompter was number one or number two (depending on whose figures you use) in cable. Westinghouse had a small cable system but was primarily focused on broadcast and leisure businesses. With the election of R. Kirby as its chairman, Westinghouse changed focus. It sold or closed down most of its leisure ventures, such as car rental. It has refocused and may become the leader in cable, which is a horizontal move, building on strengths in programming and broadcasting.

Timing

The issue of timing should be understood so that you can be prepared and possibly even prevent unfavorable changes. Surprise is unnecessary, since the changes I have described are often predictable. Surprise leads to costly errors and reactions.

Several times I have mentioned that placement on the life cycle is a key indicator. Normally, there is little movement at the embryonic and rapid-growth phases because of the need to be flexible, the lack of adequate capital, and the low level of learning. During the maturity stage, there are many changes. It is at this stage that the need to add value, the need to control supply or distribution, and the ability to finance are increased. Further, this is the period of concentration. The marginal suppliers or distributors have fallen out, leaving only the strong. The stronger the supplier or intermediary, the more the possibility of losing control—thus, increased insecurity. Normally concentration is directly related to the life cycle, and as the industry declines, there may be only one supplier or distributor. Thus, the need for movement may be increased, but this needs to be counterbalanced with the slowing growth rate.

Another key predictor is who controls the situation and can be the driver of change. If the supply industry has one or two dominant companies that are very aggressive and/or unpredictable, then it may be critical for the companies they supply to develop other sources or even to develop their own capability. They must also watch intermediaries and current full-fledged competitors.

A third indicator might be changes in management or problems that others are experiencing. The new management team's early vision and direction should be watched.

Why Are the
Changes Significant?

Now that we have discussed why changes in an industry occur, let's examine why the changes are significant. Much of this should be obvious. A change in status of one of the other organizations in your industry can have an impact on you in a number of ways.

1. It can deprive you of a significant portion of the market, and most likely it will be the growth area. This happened to the giant metal-can companies I described earlier. The fastest-growing segments were the beverage and soft-drink segments, and these were the companies which backward integrated. The loss of access to the shoppers at Sears, K-Mart, and J. C. Penney can have a sizable impact on the sales of many consumer-products companies.

2. If a company becomes its own supplier or intermediary, it can first satisfy its own needs and then sell its excess to others. To make matters worse, it can afford to charge less, because it has already covered fixed costs for its own needs and because the added volume will cost practically nothing. If it chooses to sell at manufacturing cost instead of considering total cost, it can do so and probably still make a profit. This is why many companies offer private-label products along with national brands. Added volume increases capacity utilization and ultimately increases profits.

3. If the new competitor decides to be innovative, you might be even more at a disadvantage. The improved product or service might make your own obsolete and force you to follow or accept a lower status

position. The use of electronic controls to replace electromechanical controls is a case in point. Texas Instruments appears to have tried unsuccessfully in this market, but if it had succeeded, it might have taken the next step and ultimately offered its own brand of household appliances.

4. Finally, the new competitor might change the entire competitive climate and ground rules. One example is the pricing action described above. This can reduce profitability for all and can make all competitors more defensive and reactionary. It can also force others to integrate backward or forward, again from necessity. The level of cash and capital required can be seriously raised. Instead of a genteel, complacent environment, the market may become a cutthroat, dog-eat-dog world.

What to Do!

The implications are serious and worthy of top management concern and action. There are a number of options available to reduce the impact of or even prevent the moves I discussed.

Prevention must be aimed at the reason for the change in status. If the supplier, retailer, or distributor can gain more control, increase profits, and add user value, then it will be impossible to deter the company, and you might as well be prepared for the inevitable. Suppose, however, that it will gain only one of these rewards, that is, that only one cause is the basis of the change.

If the reason is insecurity, then you should do everything to assure it that this is unwarranted. For instance, you might be able to guarantee the intermediary a certain price for a long-term period or you might build a warehouse or even a plant closer to it to assure it that you can provide a timely delivery. You might be able to assure it that you do not intend to forward integrate—thus, you won't be the aggressor. With the supplier, you might also be able to contract for a long-term period, providing fair terms.

If economic reasons are behind the move, then you make it economically unsound for the other company to move. This might be by being willing to provide some margin above what it could earn by selling. In other words, strike a deal that will enable everyone to win and is not so greedy that it forces the other to become a competitor. Negotiations should enable all parties to gain something they want. For instance, you might trade security for some cost or price benefit. Another way to prevent moves is to take some initiative on your own. You might be able to backward or forward integrate yourself to the degree that would permit you to know what the economic levels are, that is, the costs and profits. This might neutralize the other company, since it might wish to prevent you and others like you from completely integrating. I prefer a positive rather than a negative neutralizer.

If the reason for change is innovation, then the best move is to innovate first. Always be in the position of working on the next generation. This can be timed in such a way that when the supplier or intermediary believes they can leapfrog, you can introduce the improved version and send it back to the drawing board. The slogan of Panasonic, "a little bit ahead of our time," is the one that is appropriate to remember. This is how IBM and Xerox prevented new competitors from moving in. The key is to always be prepared and only introduce the change when the timing is correct—not too soon and not too late.

One of the universal preventions is to always keep your profits at a reasonable level. If you stack up huge profits, you will invite new entry. If the "umbrella" price is too high, you will encourage a number of entries. If you bargain so well that only you can win, then you will find that others will become aggressors not allies.

Reducing impact can be achieved by avoiding surprise, thinking through contingencies, and not panicking. For example, if a supplier decides to make its own assembled product, then you might wish to start to make a portion of your own supplies. This cuts off the volume the supplier has from you and puts it on notice. If you cannot move that fast, then you may wish to invite a new supplier to participate. Of course, one rule is to always have multiple sources. Another powerful neutralizer is to switch to another type of product or material—using plastics to replace steel or aluminum, for example. You might be able to venture jointly on such developments.

Another move might be to refocus your business on other products or services that use different materials or components. You are then less dependent, and you might even avoid a confrontation with your new foe. There have been situations where companies completely moved out of the business and gave it to the new entry over a period of time. This might include sale of your assets.

Review and Application

Step 1—The Total System

The first step is to gain insight into the total economic system, including those that sell equivalent products and services, those on your flanks (i.e., selling other products to the same customers), those on the supply side, those between you and the user, and, finally, the user.

One approach is to draw a map of the entire battlefield. The mapping technique I described in Chapter 2 can be used to identify potential moves.

Another approach is to merely list the participants in different categories, starting with your direct competitors. Use Exhibit 4-5 to do this. Next, list all those that supply the industry in which you participate:

Parts

Components

Subassemblies

Materials

The third list is of those that sell your industry's products. There may be several steps in this process.

Wholesalers   Retailers   Users

                OEM   Jobbers

             Assemblers   Agents


```
┌──────────┐
│          │
│          │
└──────────┘
```

Exhibit 4-5. Application Phase 1—the direct competition.

Fourth, list all those that sell other products to the same intermediaries or users.

CLOSELY RELATED PRODUCTS

NOT CLOSELY RELATED

Whether you use the mapping or the listing technique, you will be able to clearly visualize the total industry and where competitors may come from.

**Step 2—Spot the Leaders
in Each Part of the System**

It will also be helpful if you can identify the relative power or leadership role each of the companies in each category may have. This may be depicted by the market share each has or the total dollars it generates in sales or earnings. Make sure you plot the past as well as the present to determine which companies might be gaining ground and might displace the leader. Again, this could be a result of gaining share, or it could be a result of merger and acquisition.

Step 3—Leader Analysis

Starting with the leaders in each category, think through why it might be to their advantage to integrate backward, forward, or horizontally. Are they insecure? If so, what could be making them insecure? Would it be economically advantageous for them to change? If so, why is this true? How about their knowledge of user needs and wants? Have they recommended changes that have been ignored, or have they taken steps to increase their ability to satisfy user needs? Have there been or will there be major changes that can result in a new strategy, direction, and vision? Does this new thrust impact your area and expertise?

As you think about these potential causes for modification, you should rank them according to their strength. If all or most of them are strong, then you should be prepared for change.

Step 4—Surfacing
Specific Strengths

In Chapter 3, I discussed how comparison of winners and losers can enable you to determine the success factors. These might include specific abilities to innovate the product, which are typical of many new growth industries; unique talents in selling, promoting, and marketing the product, which are typical of packaged-goods and consumer-products industries; or the know-how of making, moving, or storing the product, which is important in the area of cash-intensive commodities. The ability to finance or manage can be the critical difference. By assessing the leaders from the also-rans, you can deduce the difference.

Now that you have the list of critical factors and have identified how they might change in the future, you can use them to evaluate the potential of your suppliers and dealers as well as those on the periphery. The issue is whether they can pull it off. Do they have what it takes to succeed? If not, what can they do to get it?

If you find they have a need to change, high reward for change, and the ability to do so and be successful, then watch out.

Step 5—Prevention
or Risk Minimization

The best way to prevent the forward, backward, or horizontal moves of suppliers, customers, distributors, or others providing complementary products is to attack the cause.

- If the cause is insecurity, how can you make them more secure?
- If the cause is economics, how can you make a move less economical for them?
- If the cause is innovation, how can you beat them to the punch?
- If the cause is strategic change, how can you make a move that would be harmful to you less attractive than other diversified moves?

Output

- Understanding of which suppliers, customers, and intermediaries are likely to move position and become competitors
- Listing of how to prevent change in status of these allies and how to minimize impact if it occurs
- Development of strategy changes appropriate for prevention and risk minimization

5 Competitor Demographics

In Chapter 2, we evaluated the users of the product or service and asked what they are really buying—leisure, security, warmth, nourishment, or status. How are these needs and wants filled now? How does the approach you sell compare with others? What is likely to change needs and wants, and will that have a positive or negative impact on your offering? In short, our focus was on "functional substitution."

In Chapter 3, we emphasized the need to understand who the winners and losers have been and why. The definition of success will vary from culture to culture and nation to nation. Thus, we discussed how to define success or failure. The comparison of companies in these two categories yields a listing of success factors. The caution was to be sure that you recognize that success factors can change and that what it took to be successful in the past may not be the same in the future.

In the last chapter, we used the output of both chapters to anticipate a change in status of suppliers, intermediaries, and those on the periphery. In the next few chapters, I will focus on the type of competitors you now meet and might meet in the future and then show you how to do an in-depth analysis of these competitors. The message will be the same—namely, think about change—but the viewpoint will yield different insights.

Competitor Demographics

There have been hundreds of books, articles, and courses dealing with customer demographics. These urge evaluations of how changes in the age, location, affluence, sex, and education of the customer can influence how the market develops and what it takes to be a winner. Strangely there are few publications on how competitor demographics can influence the industry and the success factors. Yet, if competitors are young, it can influence their behavior. If they are all located in one part of the world or are very affluent or highly educated, the success factors can vary.

I have evaluated competition from a number of characteristics and have focused on two key variables that seem to explain most of the competitive differentials. One key variable is the degree of specialization. An industry dominated by specialists behaves differently from one controlled by large, diversified or conglomerate companies. Another key variable is geographic focus. Industries led by domestic companies grounded in a single geographic location are different than those controlled by global, multinational firms. These two variables often explain the rewards, risks, and costs of participating better than other factors. In addition, they influence the type of analysis needed and the complexity of doing competitive analysis. Multi-industry and multinational companies are the most complex and single-industry domestics are the simplest.

In this chapter, I wish to take these competitor demographics and demonstrate how they can be used to understand and even anticipate competitive behavior. First, I will take each variable and demonstrate how it will change the strategy and programs. Then, I will interrelate the variables to demonstrate what the various combinations might mean to you and your industry.

Specialist Versus Generalist

Some industries are dominated by specialists, while others have generalists as their leaders. This can influence the type of management, the degree of commitment, the type of objectives and goals, and the reaction to attack. Let's examine a few industries and see who the leaders are and whether they are specialists or generalists.

Automobiles

I start with the automobile industry because it is so familiar to most Americans and businesspeople worldwide. The U.S. leaders have moved from being specialists to quasi specialists and back to specialists. All began as "auto" companies and then in the 1950s and 1960s diversified and have now moved back to the auto category. Even while they were diversifying, there wasn't any question that they were still wed to the auto, and their CEOs have always been from this business. General Motors diversified earlier than its competitors. It created an appliance business, Frigidaire, which became known as a quality and innovative brand. In fact, at one time Americans called a refrigerator a "frigidaire," since Frigidaire was synonymous with refrigeration. General Motors was also the innovator in locomotives—leading the way with diesel electrics—and for decades it has had the dominant share. GMC's Allison Division was also a leader in jet engines. Thus, at the beginning of the 1970s, General Motors was successful in its limited and selective diversification. By the close of the decade, GMC moved backward into its dominant business. It finally exited the appliance business after years of losses and declining share and image. Its locomotive position still seems strong, but it is reputed to be losing its position to others. Its jet engine was highly niche-oriented. In short, GMC is now a specialist again.

Ford also followed the diversification route with the acquisition of Philco. This put it into the consumer-electronics, appliance, and defense-systems businesses. Again, within a decade this move was negated, and by the end of the 1970s, Ford had exited the primary Philco businesses.

Chrysler was more profitable in its defense and credit businesses than its auto business, yet it sold off these divisions in order to concentrate on autos. It had already sold its Air Temp air conditioning and its appliance businesses. Within a decade the American Motors Corporation sold its Kelvinator appliance business. Thus, the U.S. auto industry is now dominated by specialists.

On the world scene the situation is a little different, since a number of the automobile companies have diversified or are trying to do so. Volkswagen had been the classic specialist and niche player. For years it was synonymous with the small car via its funny looking Beetle. In the late 1970s, it diversified and acquired Adler Triumph in an apparent attempt to become a factor in office automation. At the time of writing this book, this venture appears to be in trouble, and it may become a repeat of the GMC, Ford, Chrysler, and AMC aborted diversification moves. In Japan, there are a few diversified companies. Mitsubishi is a diversified multinational giant that appears to be making a move to improve its auto business. Subaru is owned by Fuji, which is also diversified.

In the United States, specialists are the key in the auto industry, while in other parts of the world, there are several diversified companies.

Office Equipment

IBM is clearly a specialist in my terminology and has focused its product offerings on computers, typewriters, copiers, and some office-related services. Xerox has tried to add to its line in the office by including computers and communications networking to build on its copier dominance. It too was a specialist, though its recent move into financial services could change its status. There have been some other quasi-diversified companies, such as Kodak in copiers and Honeywell and Burroughs in computers. Sperry is clearly a diversified company, having farm equipment and military systems along with Univac computers, with which they have been marginally successful. During the 1950s and 1960s, a number of fairly diversified companies made strong moves into computers. These included General Electric, RCA, Siemens, and Philips, but they did not make the grade and retreated either in part or in toto. Thus, until recently the clear winners were the specialists who focused and committed themselves to expanding the market. However, this may be changing with the entry of the Japanese. Clearly Hitachi, Toshiba, Fujuitsu, and Nippon Electric are diversified, and they are taking on the entrenched competition. Whether this attack will succeed is still uncertain, but if history is repeated, it may not.

Forest Products

The traditional winners in forest products have been Union Camp, Weyerhaeuser, and International Paper, all clearly specialists. There have been attempts by other packaging companies (Continental Can and American Can) to penetrate, but these have been less than successful, and both American Can and Continental Can have announced their interest in divesting themselves of their forest-products business. Other companies like Champion International and Georgia-Pacific moved in and out of other industries and have now refocused back on their core business.

Consumer Electronics

In the 1930s, General Electric and Westinghouse, both quasi-diversified companies, were the leaders in radio and even created the television business. In Japan it was Toshiba, in Europe AEG and Siemens that led in radio. Thus you could say this was an industry led by the diversified companies. There were some specialists as well, including RCA, Borch, Telefunken, and Motorola. Fifty years later a significant number of specialists or quasi-specialists have become the leaders in consumer electronics. On the specialized side we have Sony, Sharp, Pioneer, and McIntosh; on the quasi-specialized side we could include Matsushita and Sanyo, which both combine major appliances and audio-video equipment. The diversified companies, such as Westinghouse, have left the consumer electronics and the major appliance arenas. RCA, which diversified, has lost position and is now in the process of divesting itself of its other businesses to refocus on consumer electronics.

So What?

I could cover industry after industry and do a similar type of analysis. In some cases, you would find that the clear winners are now and have always been the specialists. In other cases, you would see that the winners have always been the diversified companies. In still other cases, leadership has varied over time and has moved from specialists to generalists to specialists. This could lead you to deduce that this is interesting but of little value in evaluating the competitive environment and its implications. Does it really matter whether the industry is dominated by specialized or multi-industry companies? I think it does. I believe the competitive character is significantly different. Let me prove my case.

First of all, industries dominated by specialists can be very competitive and even cutthroat when volume declines and share loss is at stake. The specialist has few options. Its survival depends on succeeding and making enough cash to stay liquid and solvent. Thus, it will either defend its position or even possibly try and gain. Its cash and capital will be vital, and it is worth knowing about its cash position. Cash flow will be the key measure, and though the specialist might like to maximize its earnings and investment, these will be less important. The multi-industry competitor has more options. It can stand and fight and use the resources from other businesses to sustain losses and even a negative cash flow, or it might decide to give up share or even exit. The battle of the specialists is obvious in the automobile market today. GMC, Ford, and Chrysler have all made their stand and are willing to lose millions, even selling off more profitable divisions, to hold or gain position.

The same fight is brewing in other industries where specialists dominate, including forest products, farm equipment, retailing, and television. In television, GTE threw in the towel and let Philips have its share. GTE had a broader portfolio and was not able to be a power force in consumer electronics.

The specialist-dominated industry may be tough when the market is growing or stable but not as tough as when volume is down. In fact during the audio-electronics growth, the specialist leaders were willing to sacrifice share and capitalize on the prosperity. In the multi-industry-led markets, the companies might be willing to be less aggressive and all share the rewards of the industry. This will depend on the options available to them. If this is a key ingredient to their portfolio, then they will fight just as hard as the specialists.

Another difference between specialist and multi-industry companies is the experience and expertise of their management. In the specialist firm, the leaders will normally be long-time participants who have grown up with the business or industry. They will know the ropes and have long-term relationships with the customers and intermediaries. This may mean that they will be marketing-focused and will be tough to prevent a loss of customers.

It may also mean that they will stress evolution or status quo rather than revolutionary change. The rewards of radical change will be low, and they will be the targets of those seeking to penetrate or gain market share. Specialists often have a longer-term horizon and commitment. The management team is also likely to be more integrated and have more continuity. This will all mean that they will know how to cut costs if the environment is stable and no major discontinuities occur. However, if there are major discontinuities, the team may not be able to respond rapidly. Further, it is likely that they could miss the significance of major innovations in technology or process. This may be the reason that many companies ignored new innovations outside their industry and were hurt, some beyond repair. For example, the steam-locomotive specialists (Baldwin Lima Hamilton and American Locomotive) missed the diesel and did not survive. The Swiss watchmaker industry ignored the digital and quartz revolution, and many fell by the wayside. The U.S. automobile giants were slow to accept the small cars.

Multi-industry managers may be quite the opposite. They may be transferred from other parts of the company and have little or no experience in the business. This can be both positive and negative. They will not be victims of the "folklore" and thus may be more willing to experiment. They will be more aggressive and have a shorter range of vision. Though customer relationships will be weak, they might try to use innovation as a means to displace the incumbent. Their lack of experience may lead them to make stupid errors and cause major disruptions that can result in significant losses. This is particularly true if they disturb the pricing structure or introduce products before they have been properly tested.

Even though businesses have many similarities, there are enough differences to require caution and deliberate execution of strategic change. Unfortunately some managers do not exercise this caution and deliberateness and move too rapidly. There are reports that Frigidaire's demise was partially a result of the continuing change introduced by management personnel primarily experienced in autos and not appliances. The same was true of GE's and RCA's unsuccessful computer businesses. "A manager can manage anything" philosophy has proved to be invalid, but yet it continues to be implemented by many multi-industry companies. The time horizon of transferred managers is short, and they will be highly opportunistic. This may mean that they will not wait for an upturn or will ignore the signals of a downturn. Often they use measures that may be contradictory or not fit the environment. Some markets are highly sensitive to fluctuations, and thus sudden stops or starts may be detrimental to all.

Before I move to the next characteristic, namely geographic focus, I wish to discuss the conglomerate. A conglomerate and a multi-industry company have many characteristics that are similar and a few that are different enough to warrant discussion.

Both the conglomerate and the multi-industry company are led by portfolio managers and thus can be more flexible in their response. Both are likely to use short-range plans and to transfer managers between and among divisions. The managers, therefore, may have less experience. Both will be opportunistic, but I think the conglomerate will be even more so than the multi-industry company. The traditional conglomerate will select the component because it will enhance its balance sheet, provide cash flow, and even be useful to inflate or stabilize the income sheet. The multi-industry firm will select the component primarily because it wants to be in the business, that is, the component complements its core business and is built on strengths. Of course, the financial characteristics of the component will support the decision. Because the conglomerate is more financially driven, it can often be more rapid. It may have less concern for the participants and the other stakeholders. Conglomerate management will tend to be financially trained and not technical-, manufacturing-, or marketing-oriented.

In today's world, the classifications of competitors must be reviewed periodically, since many changes occur every few years. I have already mentioned the automobile and consumer-electronics companies, but it is not restricted to this market alone. The airlines have refocused on their prime business, namely the operation of planes. Pan Am sold off its hotel and real estate properties. ITT has attempted to move from a conglomerate status to a more focused but still multi-industry company status. Westinghouse has concentrated on electrical equipment and broadcast and cable. The trend is to "de-conglomerate" and "de-diversify." NL Industries is selling off its traditional core to focus on oil field equipment and services. The reasoning behind these moves is a combination of financial necessity and a desire to focus on those industries that are considered to have the highest attractiveness. I will discuss this in more detail in the next two chapters.

Geographic Focus

Another characteristic I have found of use in evaluating the competitive climate is the difference between the domestically oriented versus the multinational firm. Some industries have been dominated by the multinational, while others appear to be domestic. I will demonstrate that this distinction influences the type of management, the objectives, and the flexibility of the firm as much as the difference between specialist and multi-industry companies. Further, the combination of these two variables makes it even easier to predict the response of a firm.

Some industries appear to be domestic or even regional by nature. This may be a function of the economics of the industry, perishability of the product, or culture and habits of the people. In the United States, appliances, banking and finance, building materials, food processing, food and lodging, and insurance have been dominated by companies whose primary concentration is on the home market. Appliances, food processing, and food and lodging have been domestic because lifestyles, food preferences, preferences in size and decoration of dwellings, and cooking and living habits vary from country to country, religion to religion, and region to region. Therefore, the winners are those that understand these characteristics, anticipate their changes, and are prepared to satisfy them. Thus, many of these companies have tried and failed to become multinational. Thus, frozen foods have been successful in the United States but not culturally compatible in Japan or Europe. Large appliances are suited to large dwellings—again a U.S. characteristic. Of course, the same point could have been made about small autos. The world is changing, and it is feasible that domestic industries will be required to become multinational. Eating habits are changing, and you now see McDonald's, Burger King, and Kentucky Fried Chicken in all major developed nations. In addition, the economics or technology may permit more world shipment. The Japanese proved it was economical to ship steel worldwide and became worldwide shippers as well as steel and automobile manufacturers. The substitution of electronics for electromechanics has made radios, computers, and industrial controls world products.

There are other industries that have always been global in nature and have thus been spearheaded by multinationals. Petroleum, chemicals, drugs, general machinery, and natural resources fall in this category. There are more that are moving in this direction—aerospace, financial services, autos and instruments, to name a few. In this situation, national characteristics do not appear to be as significant, and the economy of scale outweighs the local preferences. In addition, the companies themselves may be the driving force. The thrust of the giant U.S. oil companies like Exxon, Mobil, and Texaco made the oil industry multinational. Large chemical companies have always been multinational. At times the driver is the host government that recognizes that the domestic market is insufficient in itself, and so they urge exports and ultimately permit the companies to set up subsidiaries and local manufacturing.

Whatever the reason, it is useful to categorize the participants into three groups, domestic, multinational, and quasi-international. This classification can provide insights into the type of competitive management and their objectives and reaction to change.

Domestic companies are normally led by individuals who are narrow and are possibly uninformed about the international scene. They may be myopic and not recognize the changing international character of the industry or markets. They will be preoccupied with the internal workings of the company and unaware of political, economic, or other macroenvironmental forces. The diplomatic and political aspects of the job may be considered unimportant. Their objectives and goals will be consistent with that of the industry and local business conditions. This may mean they will be short- rather than long-range thinkers. They are surprised and shocked when a multinational or even a quasi-internationalist company (that is, one that is more export-oriented than global) makes a move to penetrate their home market. If they are strong financially and have a protectable position, they will stand and fight and may be very tough. If it appears that they are losing ground, they will cry "foul" and seek government aid. Rather than being aggressive, they will be protectionistic and seek import taxes. Sometimes they will move to third world nations where labor is less costly or where there are tax havens. If they are slightly visionary and strategic, they may put into place barriers to entry in advance of penetration. The pure domestic company has a limited life expectancy, since its markets will be small and it cannot achieve world scale. This is particularly true in small-market countries like Spain, Mexico, and Canada. In the United States, the market size may be sufficient to sustain the domestic-only firm, but the situation may be changing as the United States is targeted by multinationals.

The multinational is a different type of company. Normally multinationals are led by individuals who have a global perception and sensitivity to world economic and political conditions. If it is Japanese- or European-based, the multinational company (MNC) will develop this type of individual as part of its management-development activity. Philips, for instance, insists that its "high potential" executives have assignments in other countries. This is a "must" to get to the top. It stresses understanding the macroenvironment as well as the local industry differences. It recognizes the need to satisfy the needs of the host country and thus will take early positions in developing nations. With the multinational, the time horizon is longer, and the commitment is continuous not erratic.

Multinationals will be selective and will try to develop a compromise between world scale, the host country, and their own homeland. Unlike domestic companies, multinationals are more flexible and have many options. They tend to be more aware of changes and are not caught by surprise. If attacked, they will stand and fight if the country is vital to their grand plan, or they may wish to compromise and take a smaller stake. This may mean joint ventures or minority partnerships. Further, they may exit and move somewhere else.

In the next chapter, I will deal with another variation of the multinational company—the state-owned company. This new type of competitor is a composite of specialist and multinational. Therefore, I am going to deal with it as part of the in-depth evaluation.

The quasi-internationalist is a little like the conglomerate. It prefers to participate in its home market but is highly opportunistic in terms of international exporting. It focuses on economics and financial rewards almost exclusively. It will export when the home market is weak and it has excess capacity. In this case, "the filling of the plant" provides it with additional revenues to write off the fixed cost. Normally, the company will not add capacity dedicated to the export markets. At times the earnings and the risk from U.S. exports are less than those in the United States. This is often the result of government financing and guaranteed loans. The selectivity is high and the commitment short. Therefore, these types of firms can be in and out of the market.

There are other characteristics that impact the market and its profitability. The age and experience of the company and its financial stability or affluence can be important. Young companies tend to be more impetuous and willing to assume risk. Thus, they may do things considered impossible by the others. The more experienced companies will add stability and some planned evolution but will not be that dramatic. Wealth can also make a company more willing to take chances especially if it does not have many options to invest in growth. I have not used these characteristics as prime variables but rather as modifiers of the type of matrix that I am now going to recommend to highlight current and future demographics within an industry. I have used the degree of specialization and the degree of internationalization as the prime variables for plotting the demographics.

Plotting the Demographics

This matrix, like any other, is a visualization of what is happening, and it is useful in understanding the likely ground rules or factors that influence profitability. Let's look at the matrix, discuss the characteristics of companies in the various cells, and then illustrate what has happened in some well-known industries (Exhibit 5-1).

Domestic-only specialists are the most limited in strategic options and vision. They are vulnerable to cyclical swings, national policy, changes in the technology, and economic variables. Their management is skilled and resistant to rapid changes. If attacked, they will be tough and fight even if it means sacrificing short-term earnings. If not attacked, they will be benevolent. Cash flow and market share are prime measures.

Quasi-international specialists will export reluctantly and be very opportunistic.

Multinational specialists have regional options and are likely to seek world scale and standardization but permit the needed localization. IBM is my favorite example, but there are chemical, oil, and natural-resource companies that fit the same mold. Multinational specialists have flexibility in the countries selected but not in the product line. They know what systems are all about and can establish a worldwide network of parts, applications, and even research and development. They can have laboratories in various countries to provide incentive for host governments, but these laboratories are not self-contained, which would inhibit the host governments to nationalize them. Multinational specialists are led by industry-skilled, experienced executives but also have a global perspective. They can use the profits of one country to support another during its early development stage.

Quasi-specialists, or specialists with selective ventures, are slightly more flexible than their exclusive counterparts, and if they are multinational, they have the same advantages as I enumerated above. The companies in this category would include Pan Am, American Airlines, Mead, National Steel, and possibly Volkswagen. They have moved or are moving outside their core businesses but in a deliberate manner. If they do not like the results, they can retreat and, if lucky, use the profits or cash to enhance their current business lines. In most cases, their loyalties still lie with the prime businesses, and the new lines are experimental.

Finally, we have the multi-industry category, which is more complex and more difficult to track and anticipate. If a company is both multi-industry and multinational, it has the most choice—if it can manage the complexity and trade off rationally. The combination of diversification and

	Domestic Only	Quasi-International	Multinational Corporations
Specialist			
Specialist/Ventures			
Multi-Industry			

Exhibit 5-1. Competitive demographics matrix.

globality makes it difficult to know where the company's loyalty really lies. Such companies can move in a number of ways. They can harvest product lines, segments, entire businesses, and countries in order to provide the required revenues to support growth. They will tend to be impatient and to use short-range planning. Their self-evaluations will compare one part of the portfolio against another not against the competition. They will most likely focus on ratios like ROI, ROE, and ROS.

Since the management people are competing against each other, there may be considerable internal strife and gamesmanship. The top management will be forced to use a disciplined system or focus on the lower management. Trust and credibility will be the keys, since no one can be that knowledgeable across the entire firm. Because of this, there will be considerable focus on presentation, reviews, issues, and challenging assumptions. The value of diversity is that the company should be in a good position to reduce cyclicality, but in so doing, its growth is likely to be gradual and not dramatic. During the 1960s, diversity was the goal. Today specialization is once again desired. Thus, it is important to recognize the dynamics and have matrices which capture the past, the present, and, most importantly, the future. A few illustrations may be helpful.

Some Sample Matrices

The television industry in the United States shows the dynamics and also the impact of changes in competitor demographics. The information and communications market also is illustrative. A review of both can be enlightening.

The Television Industry

The television industry in the 1960s was dominated by domestic specialists and quasi-specialists (see Exhibit 5-2). Zenith and RCA were the clear share and profit leaders. The rest of the companies were marginally profitable followers. All of the companies were experienced, many having extended their offering from radio. RCA was the trend setter, and it had a complete system, including broadcasting and programming. Both Zenith and RCA were share-conscious and almost every year would have a fight to see which would be the winner. This lack of a clear leader and the price competition that followed made the industry marginally profitable. Sony appeared on the scene, and it was permitted to carve out a niche with small-screen, high-priced, reliable televisions. Clearly you chould characterize the industry in these ways:

- Television-oriented individuals were the managers.
- Cash flow and share were the major objectives.
- The leaders were highly reactive.

	Domestic	Quasi-International	Multinational Corporations
Specialist	Zenith Magnavox Admiral	Sony	
Quasi-Specialist	RCA Motorola		
Multi-Industry	GE GTE/Sylvania	Philips AEG	

Exhibit 5-2. The television industry—past.

- The industry was relatively status quo.
- There was a gradually evolving product, with competition on price features and distribution.

Today the game has changed considerably (see Exhibit 5-3). Zenith and RCA are still the leaders, but Zenith has moved into computers via its acquisition of Heath Kit. RCA has cut down on its diversified activities and appears to be refocusing on the television and its peripherals but still remains a multi-industry firm. Price competition continues, but there is more emphasis on innovation and making television a part of a broader information and communications entertainment system, with the addition of videotape, videodisc, personal computers, cameras, and cable.

Today, there are considerably more multinationals in the industry.

	Domestic	Quasi-International	Multinational Corporations
Specialist		Taiwan and Korean Brands	
Quasi-Specialist	Zenith		Sanyo Sony
Multi-Industry		RCA	Magnavox (Philips, Sylvania) Quasar (Panasonic) Hitachi GE

Exhibit 5-3. The television industry—present.

MNCs are dominant overall even though they are fragmented. The only remaining U.S. multinational is GE. The rest are either European or Japanese. Multinationals are more flexible and are willing to get out of the business if it does not succeed, though it remains a high-priority market for the Japanese and Europeans.

Today the industry appears to have different characteristics.

- Management is more oriented to video and information systems and consumer electronics than to traditional television.
- Innovation and change is more revolutionary than evolutionary, with the addition of new components.
- The focus is now more on total world share than domestic share.
- The participants have more options and are oriented more toward profitability than cash flow.

In the future, the definition of the market may change (Exhibit 5-4). Receivers may give way to systems. Software may become increasingly important, and competitors may become more diversified though focused. There may be more emphasis on innovation and less on direct price competition. It appears unlikely that a domestic-only company can survive, and there may be a need to be multinational. So within two decades, the type of competition has changed and the need for innovation systems has also increased in importance.

The Information and Communications Industry

The information and communications arena has also changed but in a different way. In the 1960s, the computer arena was clearly dominated by IBM, and all of the key participants were multinational (see Exhibit 5-5).

Because of IBM's dominance, the rest of the industry was focused on

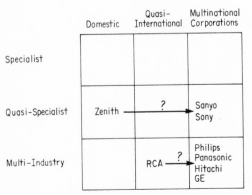

Exhibit 5-4. The television industry—future.

	Domestic	Quasi-International	Multinational Corporations
Specialist			IBM
Quasi-Specialist			Honeywell Burroughs RCA
Multi-Industry			Sperry GE Siemens Philips

Exhibit 5-5. The mainframe computer—past (1960).

survival, and competition was aimed at marketing and applications rather than price.

Today, the competition has expanded because of the advent of the MNCs and microcomputer companies (see Exhibit 5-6). All companies are still multinational, but many new names have appeared. The presence of so many multi-industry companies is a result of Japanese dedication to this industry.

IBM is still the leader, but its leadership is being attacked by different competitors on a segment-by-segment basis. The future is likely to bring other changes in the competitive demographics as new specialist giants enter the field and the definition of the market changes. Since they will not have to worry about many businesses, they will be very knowledgeable in their field.

If, however, they are multinational and focused, they might be willing to trade short-term for long-term profits. IBM has played a long-term-profit-horizon game. This was displayed by its willingness to lease computers rather than sell them outright. Leasing requires a consistently satisfied

	Domestic	Quasi-International	Multinational Corporations
Specialist			IBM DEC
Quasi-Specialist			Honeywell Futisu
Multi-Industry			Sperry Hitachi Siemens Toshiba

Exhibit 5-6. The mainframe computer—present.

customer, since those that are dissatisfied can cancel and go elsewhere. They are not trapped. IBM also illustrates another characteristic of a multinational specialist in worldwide production and total global system. It opened plants and labs in all major markets. This enabled it to cross borders and provide a balance of trade. Rather than making everything in one place, it made components in different countries and then assembled them where the market existed. This dispersed its risks and vulnerability to takeover. A worldwide sourcing network geared to capitalize on cost, materials, know-how, and governmental incentives is a powerful competitive advantage and is exemplified by the multinational specialist.

Companies in this category also have the ability to be the "technology" leaders in most markets, and it is the market leaders that can quickly follow when threatened. They do not want to be the innovative leaders, since they could displace themselves. They have more flexibility than domestic specialists and can trade off among countries. They have a portfolio of countries. Their management will be knowledgeable and skilled.

Summary and Strategic Implications

I have described how the characteristics of the competition can be useful in understanding the competitive nature of the market and industry. In a sense this adds to our understanding of the success factors. Some markets are more competitive than others because of these success factors, and your success or failure will depend on your ability to meet the requirements. If you are a specialist and are in an industry dominated by other specialists, it should be a battle of the wits and the ability to use your talents better than they. If, however, the key players are multi-industry, you might be able to make the industry unattractive to them and have them retreat or even exit. The opposite can also be possible. If you are multi-industry and multinational, you can use the resources of your other businesses to attack the specialists. But as we cautioned you before, be prepared for a reaction and a long, hard fight.

The Small Business Competitor Demographics

Thus far, I have described how a large or medium-sized company can use demographic profiling to understand its changing competitive situation. Since all companies are not large or medium-sized and do not have to worry about multinational giants, it is important to interpret how this might be used by the small regional manufacturer or retailer. The specialist category makes sense for this situation as well. Most retailers and small manufacturers are specialists. The multi-industry category is also appropriate. In the case of retailing, the department store or the multiproduct retailer would fit this category. The third category can be the conglomerate or part of a national or international chain. It could include franchises that are owned and operated by the chain store. Therefore, the concepts are quite similar, and the perception of change can be insightful.

On the horizontal axis, we can also use geographic focus or dispersion as the segmentation vehicle. First, there is the local producer or merchandiser. Next, we have regional chains, and thirdly, we can have national or international producers or chains.

Let's take an example of the retailer of audio and stereo products in a hypothetical situation. Exhibit 5-7 segments type of retail store along the vertical axis and geographic scope on the horizontal axis.

In this situation, we modified the vertical axis slightly to cover related-product retailers as well as department stores. The horizontal axis has not changed.

Suppose our hypothetical retailer analyzes the competitive situation in the past and records the major players. The merchant notes that a decade ago the major competitors in the area were the local specialty shops, since the product was concentrated on the top end of the product line. There were some dealers who also sold television sets and even large appliances, but they were stronger in the mid-priced area and not in the components segments. The department and full-line stores were weak competitors.

During the decade, the situation has changed. There are now a number of strong regional and national specialty chains that are major factors in the market, with either franchised stores or directly owned and managed

	Local	Regional	National
Audio/Stereo Specialist			
Related Products			
Department and Full-Line Stores			

Exhibit 5-7. Retailer segmentation for audio and stereo.

stores. Further, the related-products stores have upgraded their line and also their regional chains. Finally, some department store chains have opened boutiques and are competing directly.

So the switch has been made from small, locally owned specialists that competed primarily on service, selection, and quality to chains that compete more on price and promotion than on the other factors. Of course the strategic issues are what will happen in the future and whether this trend will continue. In other fields of retailing, such as soft goods, hardware, and even large appliances, the trend has continued. This has made the small specialists vulnerable and forced many of them to join cooperative buying organizations and/or to become franchised.

Review and Application

Step 1—Construct
Your Own Matrix

1. List all the competitors on a global basis that have competed or now compete in your industry.
2. Indicate the market share that each has and the segments that each competes in.
3. Classify each as to whether it is a specialist, quasi-specialist, or multi-industry company and whether it is a domestic, quasi-international, or multinational company.
4. Use the competitive demographics matrix in Exhibit 5-8 to plot each company.

	Domestic	Quasi-International	Multinational Corporations
Specialist			
Quasi-Specialist			
Multi-Industry			

Exhibit 5-8. Demographic competitive matrix.

Step 2—Analyze the Matrix

1. Describe the implications of this diagram in terms of the financial, market, and resource characteristics.
2. Identify the industry leaders and trend setters and note how aggressive or protective they are.
3. Determine whether its classifications will change (e.g., specialist moving to multi-industry or being acquired or merged into another category; domestic becoming multinational or vice versa).
4. Show whether the share or position of the leader will change.
5. Describe the implications of these changes: Will the industry become more aggressive? Will new resources be required? Will the changes invite new entries or force others to leave? Will the cost of participation change? Are there technological changes that must be anticipated and addressed?
6. Determine the success factors that can result from these changes.

Output

*   Listing of changes in competitive intensity
*   Listing of changes in success factors

6 The Competitive Strategy

In-Depth Analysis

Thus far we have stressed the need for understanding the total competitive environment in order to assess the nature of the game and how it is and will be played. The rules may change because the customer has needs and wants not being satisfied by the current competition. Or they may change because of new entries resulting from the backward integration of customers, or the forward integration of suppliers, or moves made by those on the periphery or even those from other industries that decide to expand their offering.

Regardless of the cause, changes may mean new opportunities or threats. In order to capitalize on these changes and develop operational and viable strategies, you must have an in-depth evaluation of the competition. By "in-depth," I mean a complete understanding of what makes the competitors tick and how they operate. Key questions to be answered are: What are their motivations and priorities? What are their biases? How do they view the future? What are the investment and strategic drivers for each of the segments, and what are the relative priorities?

In this chapter I will describe the ingredients of an in-depth analysis. The ingredients will depend on the type of competitor and the complexity will vary depending on the familiarity you have with the company and the industry.

Be Selective

Since you will be unable to study many competitors in depth, you must be selective. You should include the top two or three contenders, including the historical and future winners. As I pointed out before, the future winners may be different from the past winners because of a change in management, resources, or mergers and acquisitions. It may be helpful to include the major distributors, customers, and suppliers that may be motivated to move into the industry.

Degree of Complexity Will Vary

In terms of complexity and the type of evaluation, the multinational and multi-industry competitor will be the most complex and difficult to anticipate. As I emphasized in Chapter 5, this type of company is often the most flexible and has the most options. It can lose money in one market, gain share in another, and use still another to generate the funds. It may also be guilty of "dumping." This means protecting its home markets by tariffs or other barriers against imports, thus permitting it to make high margins at home and use these margins to price aggressively in other markets. In addition, the multinational and multi-industry company can trade profits between products and services in one market. Imagine trying to compete against these companies if they are willing to take huge losses in your markets with similar products. This makes it critical that you understand the relative priorities of the company. I will illustrate a few companies of this type, including a Japanese, a European, and a U.S. multinational. These companies will have similar characteristics but will be influenced by their host or parent country and, therefore, will have some different traits.

The second most complex type of competitor will be the geographically concentrated, multi-industry company. It will be complex because it will have a portfolio of products and services with which it can trade off. Thus it can lose in one business and finance the growth of another. This was the philosophy of the conglomerates in the 1960s. The plotting of the portfolio and not just one business is needed.

The simplest competitor is the single-industry, domestic-only competitor. It has only one business and thus does not have the option of trading off. You need only understand its one business and nation. This is like competing against Zenith, Maytag, or even a foreign competitor that serves only its home country. It may require analysis of the priorities between segments, but it is not as complicated as different businesses or nations.

Complexity is not synonymous with ease or the likelihood of winning in the competition. Some companies in the single-industry, domestic-only category are the toughest of all competitors. They will have fewer options, more commitment, often a more knowledgeable and decisive management. They will have no place to run and, if attacked, will be unable to respond rapidly and thus may be vulnerable. Or they may lack corporate commitment or the desire to persevere. When losses impact the corporate earnings, they may easily throw in the towel and get out even at considerable loss.

Evaluating the Competitor

I will deal with multinational, multi-industry companies, since they are the most complex. Some issues I discuss pertain only to these companies, but some issues pertain to all companies. When I discuss competitor analysis with CEOs or general managers, I ask them what is the most important question they want answered. Most of them will respond without hesitation that they would like to know the competitor's cost position. How do they stand in the cost game? Although I would agree that relative cost is important, I don't think this is the prime area that needs to be examined. Certainly it is one that I will cover in the next chapter, but it is not the place to start, as I will demonstrate in this chapter.

Determine the Competitor's Priorities

The first thing you do is examine the competitor's priorities and determine what they are in terms of where the competitor wishes to spend its money, and how they are changing. This priorization is called investment strategy: An investment strategy identifies which businesses in the company's portfolio will receive the most funds and which will receive the least. The top priority businesses may receive more than they can contribute on their own, in other words a "net-user" of funds. Others may be able to reinvest what they earn, while still others may be required to disinvest, not keep up with depreciation, so that the funds can be provided to the top priority. An investment strategy may be aimed at growth, defense, or harvest.

How a competitor makes investment decisions will depend on the type of competitor we are dealing with. If the company is multinational in nature, you must understand the extent to which the company is related to its government and how much control the government exerts on the company. If the parent company is strong and controls the competitor, directly or indirectly, you must understand the national priorities and the type of support the government provides to the parent company. Is the competitor vital to the nation's goals and ability to compete in the world market?

Let's take a few examples to illustrate how this logic may help in the development of strategic insights. I will use some real companies to show the approach but do so purely for illustrative purposes, and this is not meant to be an in-depth analysis of these companies. Since the Japanese are considered to have a strong national plan and to exert influence over their industrial giants, I will start with one of their large industrial companies. I have picked Mitsubishi. I think it is a myth that the Japanese government calls all the shots and their companies merely implement a grand strategy. However, the Japanese do have a successful set of national priorities that have been converted into specific industry priorities. They seem to have a system that permits aggressive competition in their home markets but fosters cooperation in the world markets. It is like having a play-off that anyone can enter and a world-cup competition that only the top few get a chance to enter. A review of the national priorities may help. In the 1960s, the Japanese backed consumer goods and provided an effective combination of home-market protection, financial and technological support, and favorable export incentives. They encouraged the licensing of the best semiconductor, integrated technologies they could obtain anywhere in the world and then encouraged applications of these technologies to the consumer-electronics markets. They did so well that today they are the clear leaders. They also supported the development of a steel industry and of shipbuilding. Again, the combination of a committed, dedicated workforce, access to capital at attractive rates and terms, and willingness to apply the best available technology has made these industries the best in the world, though they too are having problems with overcapacity and a depressed market. If you were in these markets at the time and were not equipped to hold your ground, you would be on the loser side of the ledger even if you had the best cost position in the world at the start. The cost position would change because of the factors I have cited. But the remarkable fact about the Japanese national priorities is that they are dynamic. They were modified in the 1970s and will change in the 1980s. A reading of publications of the Ministry of International Trade and Industry (MITI) is a must for any serious and committed businessperson. Here are a few ideas from their publication *The Industrial Structure of Japan in the 1980s.* They plan to focus on:

- Technologies for the development of alternative energy sources (nuclear, solar, geothermal, coal liquefaction, gasification, and coal-oil mixture)
- Energy-saving technologies, magnetohydrodynamics (MHD), and improved appliance efficiency

* Medical and welfare technologies and environmental protection
* The information industry and the aircraft and space industries
* New materials, including fine ceramics and biotechnology

The report identifies the trends and the implications of these technologies for specific industries. Thus, the Japanese have declared economic war on others in these industries, and if they follow their traditional pattern of operations, they will make the necessary commitments of funds, people, protection, and tax benefits and will encourage a combination of self-developed and licensed technological developments.

As I have urged throughout this book, you must ask, "So what?" Does all this really matter or are you merely dealing with interesting but not useful information? Suppose you are competing against one of the large companies in Japan. Will the national priorities influence the company and its strategy? I said I would use Mitsubishi as an illustration. Assume you compete against this large, diversified, and worldwide company. Mitsubishi had over $50 billion in trading transactions in 1980 divided up among different business arenas: fuels (23 percent), ferrous metals and related products (20 percent), nonferrous metals (8 percent), machinery (15 percent), foods (15 percent), chemicals (9 percent), general machinery (6 percent), and textiles (4 percent). If you compare the past and present national priorities with the portfolio of this company, you'll see that the priorities of the 1960s would be more supportive to Mitsubishi than those of the 1980s. But the situation is not all negative, since many of the products and services of Mitsubishi are vital to the industrial strength of Japan. For the sake of clarity, let me take this example even further. As you probe beyond the generalized headings, you realize that this company has a number of businesses related directly or indirectly to the technological priorities. For example, in the fuel arena, Mitsubishi is involved in a pilot coal-liquefaction plant that is integral to Japanese coal-liquefaction development. In its machinery business, it manufactures nuclear reactors, and it has a geothermal power plant in Kenya. Further, it produces aircraft and space and industry equipment. In the chemical arena, it produces fine and specialty chemicals and plastics materials. Using the research of the Battelle Memorial Institute, it has introduced extensive technical developments to Japanese industries, including flexible printed circuit board processors and solar energy technology, and it is developing alternatives to plastics. This clearly illustrates the need to probe deeply into the ways in which the company may be tied to the national priorities, which may not be obvious at first. I believe that if you probe, you will find that all of the major Japanese companies tie in in some way to the national priorities. This is true of Hitachi, Toshiba, Nippon Electric, Sony, and others.

A look at a European multinational will demonstrate other characteristics. In this case, we will look at Philips Gloeilamenfabrieken of Eindhoven, the Netherlands, commonly called Philips. First look at the home country, the Netherlands, which is quite different from Japan. The Netherlands is a small country with only 15,800 square miles and a population of 13.8 million people. It has four international industrial giants—AKZO, Philips, Shell, and Unilever. Although the government supports free enterprise, it also supports the major industries and their trading activities. The state owns and operates the railroads, central banks, radio and television, state printing offices, postal service, and telephone and telegraph. It participates in natural gas, state mines, airlines (KLM), blast furnaces, and explosives. Thus, the government has a multiple role. In essence, it does not have a grand plan but provides incentives to its industries in a variety of ways, including tax benefits, grants, and reserve accounts. Philips, as I already indicated, is a major corporation and thus critical to the country's balance of trade and payments. It produces home electronics for sound and vision (26 percent of sales), products and systems for professional applications (30 percent), industrial supplies (13 percent), lighting and batteries (11 percent), and domestic appliances and personal-care products (12 percent). It is truly multinational, with sales in a number of parts of the world. Sales are divided among many countries, including countries in the European Economic Community (EEC)(44 percent), the United States and Canada (17 percent), Europe (non-EEC)(12 percent), and Latin America (7 percent). Its home market, the Netherlands, provides only a small part of its total sales (8 percent) and is completely inadequate to sustain its size and profitability. This illustrates a very complex portfolio of products and regions. You can see that the EEC and home electronics provide the major portion of sales, and these must be considered if you compete in these lines in Europe against Philips. It should not be surprising that Philips does considerable research in integrated circuits, signal input and output devices, and optical techniques for information storage and transmission. Does this mean that Philips is less of a threat in the other lines and regions, or will it combine some of its talents to be even more effective in other geographic or product segments?

The third illustration is aimed at demonstrating that multinationals are not just restricted to the Far East and Europe. There are a number of U.S.-based companies in this category. Let's take International Telegraph and Telephone (ITT) as an example. I do not need to describe the size and magnitude of the United States, nor could I describe the national plans and priorities, because they change from year to year and administration to administration. However, this does not mean that U.S. companies are not given aid by their government. This aid may be in the form of tax incentives, research and development contracts, support of training loans for projects, or loans for developing nations. The Reagan administration has provided stimulants for savings and investments. Calvin Coolidge once said that the "business of America is business," and this was repeated several decades later by Charlie Wilson, Chairman of the Board of General Motors, who said, "What is good for General Motors is good for America," but still the relationship between the U.S. government and its multinationals tends to be adversarial. Certainly the facts of today seem to reinforce Mr. Wilson's opinion, since General Motors is having trouble in the 1980s and so is the rest of America. In addition, the Japanese model also reinforces the need for a cooperative agreement between the government and its key industrial enterprises. In the next decade, this reality may become accepted by society and there may be more cooperation and less adversarial attitudes among the major economic groups, including labor organizations.

I have taken ITT as my example since it has always been a multinational corporation deriving most of its earnings from outside the United States and particularly in Europe. ITT was an $18.5-billion revenue enterprise (in 1981), employing nearly 350,000 people worldwide. It is grouped into five businesses: telecommunications and electronics (30 percent of both sales and earnings); engineered products, including automotive products, industrial components, and semiconductors (26 percent of both sales and earnings); consumer products (16 percent of sales, 9 percent of earnings); natural resources (6 percent of sales, 9 percent of earnings); and finally insurance and finance (22 percent of sales, 32 percent of earnings). The tie between this conglomerate and its government is less obvious than that between the other two companies and theirs. ITT may not benefit directly from the government and its policies but it does benefit indirectly. Its federal electronics division has a role in the government-financed Defense Electronics Warfare (DEW) line in the Arctic. It is a contractor on the Voyager spacecraft. The deregulation of telecommunications may permit it to reenter the U.S. markets from which it was previously excluded. It is the largest telecommunications company in Europe, with over 50 percent of its revenue coming from this source. It is said that U.S. companies do not get support from their government and thus are competing against other companies that may have an unfair advantage. I believe that this is exaggerated. American companies have benefited from military and space explorations, from which foreign companies were excluded. They gained in foreign markets through funding of the Agency Industrial Development (AID) and export/import (EX/IM) financing, which were again exclusive for American companies. Of course, the other developed nations have copied these types of programs, and now U.S. companies may lack a truly competitive advantage. In addition, many companies did not use this aid to increase their product or technological strengths. Certainly ITT has been aided by its government, but it is not that obvious from externally available data.

Well! What is the point of all this? My point is that it is important to know what the objectives and priorities of the competitors are and that, in the case of the large multinational, they may be directly related to the government and its plans and needs. So why not start with this type of analysis and see where it leads? Also, recognize that the tie to the government and its needs may be both an asset and a liability. Philips is vital to the Dutch nation. It employs over 80,000 people in a small country and is a major exporter in a nation requiring export for survival. Because of this, it is inhibited from moving many of its manufacturing facilities to countries with lower labor costs; thus its production costs are higher than the costs of many of its competitors. Japan is locked into a growth-industry mentality, and this may be detrimental to the nongrowth industries and firms. Perhaps the companies with the real advantage are still the American firms that are more flexible and not as vital to the growth of the nation as individual companies. Everything has its pluses and minuses, and so you must be willing to understand both and not jump to conclusions before all the facts are available and analyzed.

Before I move on, I would like to review an emerging type of company—the state-owned and -managed company. This type of company is even more an instrument of the government than the others I have just described. There have been state-owned companies since the birth of the industrial revolution. They are normally formed to control and operate the natural monopolies within a nation. (Monopolies include water, electricity, railroads, airlines, telecommunications, radio, and television.) They are instruments for controlling profits and distributing the wealth to the nation. (This is different from the situation in the United States, where these types of services are regulated but privately owned, except in areas where the private sector refused to make the investment, such as in the Tennessee valley.) In the past, since state-owned companies were focused on certain specific industries, they did not affect other companies very much, except that it prevented some companies from participating in these industries. Often the private companies made the state-owned companies customers. As customers, state-owned companies would provide sales to the private companies, which in turn could use this leverage in worldwide marketing. But this has changed in recent years, and many of the state-owned companies have become owners of companies in traditionally private arenas. This has been a result of two factors: first, the policy of socialistic and communistic governments to own all of the industrial enterprises, and second, the desertion of companies by the private sector of that nation and of other nations. Thus there are now state-owned companies in automobiles, shipbuilding, chemicals, electronics, and even consumer products. They are looking at new and emerging markets and seeking acquisitions there. The Banque Nationale De Paris acquired the Bank of West in California. Renault, a state-owned company, has acquired a major stake in Mack Trucks, recently moved to take a major stake in American Motors, and simultaneously acquired Volvo's subsidiary in the Netherlands. Further, Renault is diversifying into machine tools and robotics and has opened subsidiaries in Austria, Mexico, Portugal, Spain, and the United States.

In Italy, the government controls a steel group, the national airline, four commercial banks, and an electronics company. There is speculation that it could take over other private companies, including Fiat, Olivetti, and Montefiore, if they have problems. In West Germany, the state owns 40 percent of Veba and Volkswagen. Veba has interests in oil, gas, nuclear power, electricity, aluminum, and petrochemical organizations. Volkswagen has diversified into electronics through its 1980 acquisition of Triumph Adler. Other state-owned enterprises include Salzgutter (engineering, steel, shipbuilding, and oil and gas) and Saazberg-gruppe (power plants). There are state-owned companies in Austria, the Netherlands, Norway, Sweden, and the United Kingdom. These nations own companies in aerospace, metals, machinery, automobiles, electricals, electronics, mining, petroleum, and steel. All of these industries are highly competitive and tend to have worldwide markets and competitors. They require world scale to be effective, and if borders are closed, loss of profits and position result.

The state-owned company is a reality in Europe and could become so even in the United States because of the troubled industries here. Is it conceivable that the U.S. government could own Chrysler or some of the airlines? This may appear unbelievable, but it could happen.

Some state-owned companies exist because of the need to save the companies that are key employers but cannot make it because they have lost a competitive advantage. If the companies were permitted to fail, the jobs would be lost and the workers might overthrow the government or vote the government out of office. Further, if the workers go on unemployment insurance, the cost to the government and society may be even greater than the cost of a government takeover. Or the industry may be considered important to the social good or the national defense. The government may take over the core industries, including aerospace and airlines. Or the objective might be merely to build prestige—the industry is more important to brag about than to make money. In such a case the government is investing in the embryonic market and hoping that it may ultimately be profitable. Thus the purpose is often not economic but sociopolitical, and this might make this breed of competitor tough to beat in the future.

Determine the
Geographic Portfolio

The next step in an analysis of a multinational competitor is to determine the geographic portfolio and priorities (this step, of course, is unnecessary with a domestic-only competitor). This analysis is required for the total corporation as well as each of its segments. In reviewing Mitsubishi, Philips, and ITT, it is necessary to outline the distribution of sales and earnings by geographic region. This type of data is provided in their annual reports—a sign of the true MNC.

You should look at how the data is arrayed and the statistics are provided. The way the world is divided may be insightful. If a company divides the world into categories such as Europe, the Far East, and Latin America, this may mean they are primarily exporters, because these are broad and nonimplementable groupings. If they use even larger categories, such as the whole of Africa or North America, this may indicate that these parts of the world are of little interest to them. If, however, they describe specific countries and are highly selective, this may be an indication that these are priority countries. We are interested in understanding the relative importance of their priority countries, the type of allocations being made, and the product and service strategies.

Information from the Philips 1980 annual report will demonstrate the type of data that is available from just one type of source. (Sources will be described and illustrated in Chapter 9.) Its home market, the Netherlands, represented just 8 percent of sales, a loss of 233 million guilders, 25 percent of assets, and 22 percent of employees. Its largest market was the EEC, which provided 44 percent of revenue and profits and accounted for 39 percent of assets and 40 percent of employees. Business in the United States and Canada was clearly best, contributing 24 percent of profits with only 12 percent of sales. Latin America provided 19 percent of profits and only 7 percent of revenue. You can see that the international markets were clearly used to support the losses in the Netherlands and the employment and asset base. Philips is clearly an employer in the homeland, and it is strong in the EEC. If you intend to attack it in these arenas, then you must be prepared for a tough fight. It could drop prices in the United States and Latin America, but this could erode profits, which in turn could force a change in the homeland position. This is not meant to be a detailed analysis of Philips, but it is an indication of the type of logic that these questions require. If you compete against Philips in electronics in the United States, you may become very aggressive and force Philips to make a choice between its home market and the U.S. market. If Philips is unable to respond, you may have a competitive advantage because of its tie to its government and the need to keep jobs in the Netherlands. This will be significant in competing against it in a third, neutral market such as Latin America.

Relative Attractiveness of the Countries

After you have completed an analysis of the geographic portfolio in terms of size, it is useful to evaluate how the company conceives the relative attractiveness of the country and its position in that country. This will require an understanding of the company's decision-making processes and the criteria used to select its priorities. These are similar to the criteria used to rank its products and services. The approaches may include simple financial and quantitative criteria, such as the return on sales and investment, assets, and equity, and more sophisticated evaluation of risks and rewards. Regardless of the criteria or the approach that is used, it is important to recognize that the key word is "relative." There is no part of the world, including the United States, that is free of risk or that is superior in all criteria. The question is: What does the competitor believe to be the relative attractiveness of the country and the region of the world?

Attractiveness will depend on the judgment of the top managers and, of course, may tie to their biases and objectives. Let's examine some of the factors that will be used to make this determination:

1. The size and growth of the region or market: Some companies are attracted to large markets, while others prefer smaller markets. Some prefer to participate in fast-growing markets, while others think that it is better to be in slower-growing markets. A company may believe that a country is attractive because it is small and has potential for the long haul and thus be willing to focus on it for the future not the current opportunity.
2. The nature of the competition: Some companies prefer to compete with small, domestic competitors, while others would like the challenge of taking on the large, multinational competitor. Some desire to join the competition and thus prefer markets that require joint ventures with local producers or distributors.
3. The profit potential and the need for investment: There are companies that wish to participate in nations that permit the expatriation of profits rather than in nations that require the reinvestment of funds in the country. There are others, however, that are delighted to leave the funds in the country, since it may be safer than returning it to their host country.

Combinations of these criteria help a company evaluate risks and rewards. For example, if a country is embryonic and inhabited by strong companies whose government is unwilling to permit the transfer of the profits, then the risk may be large and the reward small.

It is useful to step back and think about the competitors you are evaluating and determine how they evaluate countries and regions, and then it is important to determine how they evaluate their relative position or strength. This can differ from company to company. The question is: What does the company believe are the winning drivers (success factors) or combination of skills? And the answer may have an impact on the relative importance of geographic considerations. For example, there are some companies that believe that the key is technology, and they may believe that their technological superiority can win in any nation of the world regardless of its development and size. There are others that believe that marketing and sales is the key. Further, there are those that consider cost and manufacturing position or capability to be the vital difference. This may vary from product to product within a diversified company, but it may be more consistent than you realize. Thus, it is important to understand the priorities given to various factors and to determine how these will influence the decision-making process.

Determine the
Background of Management

Why do perceptions and criteria differ? The underlying cause of these differences is the background of the management team and the leaders of the institutions. Managers are likely to equate high attractiveness and key strength with the type of business they have managed in the past. If they have achieved success in rapidly growing markets of moderate size against tough, opportunistic specialists, then they are likely to see such characteristics as attractive. If they have made huge profits in small developing nations with an aggressive distribution network or if they have won in high-risk situations in unstable parts of the world, these are the types of environment they will seek out. This highlights the need to understand the background and experience of the top management of the competition.

Where do the managers come from? What are their educational backgrounds and areas of expertise? Are they experienced in the business in which they are participating, or are they new to the situation? What has been their work experience—marketing, technology, manufacturing, finance, planning, personnel? Have they been in line or staff positions? What is their reputation: Are they considered to be entrepreneurs, risk takers, administrators? Are they considered conservative or ruthless? I categorize three types of leaders—risk takers, caretakers, and undertakers. This may sound ridiculous and even cute, but it has more truth than fiction. Risk takers are those who are considered to be intuitive, opportunistic entrepreneurs. They thrive on rapid growth and creating something new. They prosper until the market matures. Caretakers are the administrators and professional managers. They can manage during the stable period and practice disciplined management. Undertakers can manage during the declining period. They know how to be "lean and mean" and reduce staff without destroying the business. The type of industry the managers are accustomed to—capital-intensive or labor-intensive; long-cycle or short-cycle—may also provide insight.

Past Performance Is a Predictor

Your reaction at this time may be that this is interesting but does it really help to explain and anticipate the actions, reactions, and priorities of people? I think it does. I was taught that one of the best ways of anticipating performance of people was to understand their past performance, starting back as far as we can go. People are "victims" of their past and their experience. They change slightly, but they normally do not change that much under normal circumstances. They tend to build on strengths and to replicate that which made them successful. If they were successful because they were good delegators, they will delegate. If they were successful doing things themselves, they will likely repeat this. I am not saying that people are robots and not adaptable, but there will be more consistency than inconsistency. Let's take a few examples and see what is likely to be learned.

There are companies headed by engineers and scientists. These companies tend to use technology-based strategies, sometimes successfully and sometimes not. Some strategies are clearly based on the genius of one person who dominates the company. Dr. Land invented the Polaroid camera and created the "instant photography market," even though others turned down his invention and said it would not work. Polaroid prospered because Dr. Land was correct and was able to get others to follow his lead. Of course, Polaroid's recent unsuccessful thrust into instant movies illustrates the fact that similar strategies are not always successful. Polaroid has changed management and will most likely be controlled by a different type of individual. The change in management may result in a change of direction.

Another company with a reputation for innovation and quality is Hewlett Packard, named after its founders. If you review the background of these two successful entrepreneurs, you will find that it has significantly influenced the company. Both Hewlett and Packard are technologists and have electrical-engineering degrees. In fact, both were graduated from Stanford University and maintain a strong relationship with the school, including establishing a laboratory on its campus. The management team is also dominated by people with technical degrees; eleven of the fifteen have engineering or scientific degrees. Does this mean that all holders of technical degrees will have a technology-based strategy? Obviously the answer is *no!* Some may have technical degrees but hate technology. They may have gone to an engineering or scientific institution but not have interest in the subjects they studied. This can be evaluated with further study. If they were successful technologists then they should be closer to the Land, Hewlett, and Packard illustrations.

There are other companies led by those who moved up in the organization because they were successful in keeping costs low, improving productivity, or innovating the production process. This was true of the majority of the great early American industrialists who were able to create the first mass-production system. Henry Ford was a genius in this regard, and his story is well known. But there are many illustrations in today's society. If you look at the background and personal philosophy of the managers of the Caterpillar Tractor Company, you will find a strong reason that this company has been able to become a premier manufacturing and service company. It hires individuals who are willing to work their way up from the factory and dedicate their entire career to the company. It hires directly from college and will not hire MBAs. Its top management has long experience with the company. The chairman joined in 1946, the president in 1938, the executive vice-president in 1947. The lowest service officer is the legal counsel, and he joined in 1963. Most of the top management moved up from manufacturing, including the president, Robert Gilmore. This will influence the options they consider, and they will most likely concentrate their resources on manufacturing and services.

Of course there are a number of companies that are controlled by the marketing organization. Most of us would immediately think of the packaged-goods companies such as Procter & Gamble, which hires and trains some of the best product and brand managers in the world. This company also has a philosophy of hiring directly from the college campus and then training its sales and management team to do it "the best way," which is, of course, the "P&G way." This is not meant to be a cynical or critical statement but rather a statement of the reality of the firm. IBM's management has the same practice, and you will find that this firm, too, has a strong, marketing-focused organization.

So what? The message is loud and clear. It is important to know the background, education, tradition, and culture of the top management team. If the members of the team have been with the company all or practically all of their working lives and the company has been well-managed and achieved its objectives and goals, then you should expect that the future will be a repeat of the past, with some adaptation. If they come from a specialized function, they will likely emphasize that function: marketing, sales, production, or finance. I believe this is what makes the

Japanese and Europeans so predictable. They have traditions that are difficult to change just as the companies I have used as illustrations do. But you should ask yourself some key questions. Has the company been successful and are the criteria suitable for the future? In the summer of 1981, the world was surprised at the aggressiveness of the new management team of DuPont. The team was headed by a DuPont veteran with a chemical-engineering degree. The new chief executive officer was Edward Jefferson. It appeared that he and his chemically trained management would continue the strategy of their predecessors, namely one of maintaining their niche, specialty products, and stressing development of the firm's potential in chemistry and the emerging life sciences. After all, DuPont was a triple-rated, global, innovative leader in its selected fields. It measured itself on return on investment, and it had an excellent track record. However, shortly after the retirement of Irving Shapiro, the new team behaved more like a hip-shooting, opportunistic firm than one led by a conservative technologist. It moved, over a weekend, to make a bid and ultimately acquired the stock of Conoco. This seemed to have been done with considerable speed and even the willingness to get into an auction with Seagram of Canada. Such a rapid change in behavior must force you to wonder about the change. Was it as dramatic a change as it appeared, or could it have been anticipated based on the history of the company and the background of the management? DuPont had noted in the past that it considered itself at a competitive disadvantage because it was not backward-integrated. The management had an interest in gaining its own feedstock. DuPont appeared to be willing to trade its heritage for a chance to obtain a resource-rich company to complement its major business and protect it against new competition. Thus you might be able to anticipate a systematic change even when it appears to be a major discontinuity from the past.

A second reason for change may be lack of success or concern about future success. If a company is in trouble and goes outside for a new management group, it is likely that the new people will change the decision criteria—possibly emphasize the opposite. There are numerous examples. Lee Iacocca was hired from Ford by Chrysler to be its CEO when the company was near collapse. Iacocca was known to be a strong marketing man and had been responsible for several winning introductions at Ford. He moved aggressively to change Chrysler from a stodgy, technology-based company to a stylistic and marketing-driven firm. He was even willing to sell off a number of the profitable, nonauto subsidiaries, such as the defense division and the credit affiliate, to save the nonprofitable company. Further, the company retreated into the domestic arena by divesting itself of the European businesses. His style, although different than the past, was predictable given the poor performance of the past. When Harry Gray assumed the chairmanship of United Technologies Corporation

(UTC) it was a narrowly focused company that was too dependent on its aircraft-engine and military businesses. Mr. Gray decided to use his skill learned at ITT and to diversify. He appeared to be interested in replicating his rival, General Electric, and added consumer, industrial, and energy offerings to complement UTC's defense businesses.

Determine the Competitor's Decision-Making System

Who Make the Decisions?

Thus far, I have emphasized the CEO and the top leadership. The one-person rule may make good feature stories for the business magazines and newspapers, but it is not that common in today's corporate world. Decision-making systems will vary from company to company, and it is important to understand how and by whom the decisions are made. In addition to the chairman, the board of directors are increasingly becoming a part of the decision-making process. This is because of the legal responsibility of the board, which can be sued for malpractice if the firm goes into bankruptcy. The large stockholders and even the senior managers can influence the final decision and also the implementation. If consensus management is in vogue, then the operating managers' stake and voice are larger. I have already mentioned the government. If the government is socialistic, then it will have a larger stake.

In recent years, management has had an increasing say in the decisions of their successors, even to the extent of removing the new people from office. In the case of CBS and ITT, we have witnessed the removal of the chairmen, not because they were losing money or damaging the company but because their apparent criteria of attractiveness and their vision of the corporation were different from that of their predecessors. In CBS, the former CEO was able to remove two of his successors and still remain the power in the company. In ITT, Geneen was able to remove L. Hamilton because he was trying to change the direction of the company.

This emphasizes the need to review the makeup and type of the board. This can change. I described how DuPont was able to beat Seagram to the acquisition of Conoco, but in so doing they inherited a new stockholder in the form of Seagram's management, which had been able to acquire a significant share of Conoco. Therefore, when the final deal was concluded, Seagram became owner of a sizable number of DuPont shares. It is still uncertain whether it will use its shares to override the DuPont management or force a change in the strategy, but it could happen, and if you compete with DuPont, this should not be overlooked.

There may be stockholders who have power even if they are not represented on the board. In the European and Japanese models, power is exercised by the government, the banks, and even the labor unions. In the United States, stock is owned by foundations, religious groups, and universities, among others. They have become more outspoken and have taken stands on company participation in parts of the world or businesses and even on strategies. Their stockholdings may be small, but they are vocal and can influence the voting of others. For example, some churches have taken a position on "human rights" and have forced companies to withdraw from South Africa, to halt production of atomic-powered devices, and to refrain from closing plants in certain cities. Increasingly, nonprofit institutions have become a more critical and outspoken stockholder group, and this can influence the behavior of companies.

Within a corporation there may also be powerful influences. In some companies there are specific divisions and groups that are so profitable that they exercise considerable influence over the top management. This may mean that the CEO is only a figurehead. I refer to these internal power-brokers as "warlords," since they remind me of the situation in feudal China and Japan. In these countries, it was the provinces that had the real power, and the central government could not control its own destiny. The central government would spend its time in making deals or warning against the warlords. During this period of internal conflict, the country was vulnerable to external attack. This was the reason the Japanese were so successful in conquering large portions of the Chinese mainland. But the same pertains to companies. If you find that the competitor is not unified, then you may be able to divide and conquer it.

What Is the Process?
In addition to understanding who makes the decisions, it is well to understand the process that is used to make them. Suppose that it is truly a consensus system, such as that which is reported to be used in Japan. This has both strengths and limitations. It is positive, since it expedites and strengthens implementation, but it takes more time to reach the decision in the first place. Some decision-making processes use sophisticated systems and even economic and business modeling. These too have pluses and minuses. They may look superior, but they are merely based on assumptions and mathematics that may not be well conceived. You need to know the criteria that are used and to understand how they will influence the direction of the decision.

Summary—
Competitor Evaluation

I have recommended that you examine the competitor's priorities, geographic portfolio, management background, and decision-making system.

In all of these areas we are concerned essentially with one issue—the commitment and direction of the competitor. If the competitor is a multinational, multi-industry competitor, then you must describe both the geographic and product priorities of the company. If it is only a single-industry, domestic company, then it would be vital to describe the priorities of the products alone. Priorities can be influenced by the government, the leaders, and the other stakeholders. Therefore, it is complex. It will all be summarized as a portfolio. Let's demonstrate with a few examples:

- **Company A** A U.S.-based multi-industry corporation:

   Highest priority—communications, information, and electronics (20 percent of sales and 15 percent of earnings)

   Second highest—specialty materials (25 percent of sales and 15 percent of earnings)

   Third highest—steel, aluminum, and other basic materials (50 percent of sales and 65 percent of earnings)

   Lowest priority—consumer packaged goods (5 percent of sales and earnings)

This corporation is clearly in a restructuring mode and is using the basic-materials businesses to finance its higher-priority segments. This means that if you are competing in the new lines, it may be tough going. But if you are in the basic materials, there may be an opportunity to gain share.

- **Company B** A U.S.-based multi-industry corporation that is opportunistic elsewhere:

   Highest priority—long-cycle, energy-related business that has been a long-term strength

   Second highest—industry products and services that are its areas of strength

   Third highest—consumer products that are less important

   This company favors long-cycle, technology-based business and capital-intensive services. It has had trouble in the consumer businesses and thus is gradually exiting them. It has some overseas businesses but prefers to be domestic. If it is your competitor, you can see where it will take a stand and where it will be willing to give up.

The Strategic Driver

Thus far in the in-depth analysis, I have been emphasizing the need to understand the competitor's investment priorities and strategy. But this is only part of the description of the strategy that the company is using. The next step is to describe the strategic driver for each of the major segments. The strategic-driver concept is built on the premise that there must be one thrust, more important than any other, behind each successful strategy. In the examples I used to discuss competitor evaluation, I indicated that innovation and technology was the driver of the three companies. Knowing the strategic driver is important, since it will permit you to determine whether the company has the resources to do the job and if the programs are internally consistent. This will be covered in more depth in the next chapter.

In my book *Strategic Alternatives* (AMCOM, 1979) I outlined each of the strategic drivers, which I called management strategies, and the conditions required for success. My purpose was to stimulate thinking about alternatives and recognition that it can be limiting, if not disastrous, to think that there is only one way and that it might be yours. One of the best ways to surface alternatives is to study competition and objectively determine whether other options could have value for you. It is important not to judge too early, since you may oversimplify your categorization of the competition as either "superstars" or "duds." Some companies may appear to be so strong that they are invincible, while others may appear to be able to do nothing right. However, even the strategies of the "duds" may be clever and creative and worthy of replication and more effective implementation.

I would like to list the key questions that will permit you to decide on the type of strategic driver that is being implemented. As I go along, I will illustrate some companies that are noted for implementing these drivers.

Product Drivers

Unique Products

Is the company noted for unique innovations and products? This is the driver that is used by the true technology-based companies such as the ones that I described earlier. In photography, it was a Polaroid strategy that was responsible for the creation of the instant-still-photography market. In consumer electronics, it was the Sony strategy that was responsible for the creation of the Betamax, which was the first videotape device, and the

Philips strategy that was responsible for the creation of the videodisc. In the office, it was the Wang and Xerox strategies that created the word processor and the dry copier.

Differentiation

Does the company have the ability to differentiate its product and add new and exciting features? This is the strategy of the Japanese camera companies that have created the computer camera and have added the ability to provide electronic flash, faster film, and professional capabilities at consumer prices. It is the strategy of the automobile companies that have added automatic transmission, power steering, power windows, and improved stereo radio. Differentiation may be a result of added features, improved styling, better performance, increased reliability, or longer life. It is often the secret to extending the life cycle of the business and making it more expensive to enter or even follow. The combination of barriers to entry and extended product life is highly profitable.

Standardization

Is the company known as the great standardizer that permits more applications, longer life, and less cost? This is the secret of mass markets, and it gives significant yields to those that are successful in having their products accepted as the standard. In cameras, this was the achievement of Kodak, the company that made the camera easy to use and available at a low cost and thus became the standard of the industry. This permitted them to sell film and developing equipment and supplies. In appliances, the name of Frigidaire became synonymous with refrigeration, the initials of RCA with color television, Motorola with auto radios, Gillette with the safety razor, and many other examples.

The strategy of Gillette became known as the razor-blade strategy. This highlighted the fact that you could literally give away the initial product to sell the replacement parts. Once the Gillette razor became the standard, then the company could make its major profits by selling the blades. The same could be said of Kodak. To some degree, this was the genius of the Xerox copier, since millions could be made on selling the paper and supplies as well as renting out the equipment itself.

Thus the driver options associated with the product are innovation, differentiation, and standardization. These may be used to grow new markets or share or to defend current position by creating expensive barriers. They can change as a product and a company mature. There are some companies that are the innovators, later become the differentiators, and finally become the industry standard as maturity is reached.

Marketing Drivers

Marketing can also drive or lead a business, as well as be a supporting strategy. There are certain things that can help you determine if a competitor is marketing-driven.

Creating Demand

Does the company have the reputation and track record to create or influence a significant increase in demand? As I mentioned before, this is the reputation of many of the packaged-goods companies. They have been able to take mundane, unexciting commodities and make consumers and users believe they are significantly different. This takes creativity and the willingness to expend a large amount of funds on advertising and sales promotion. Does one soap really wash better than another? Does one deodorant lessen perspiration more than another? Does one car ride more quietly than another? Some of the features can be objectively measured and are real differences, but others are merely perceived as differences. The distinction is in the advertising, the type of packaging, or the testimonial of experts or famous people. At times, the winners are lucky, having stressed the qualities that are in vogue at the time. In the 1960s, the automobile companies that stressed prestige items, such as real leather, vinyl roofs, digital clocks, and stereo radio, were the winners. Just a decade later, those that stressed economy, improved traction, compactness, and the like were the leaders in sales. The latter characteristics were more measurable and pragmatic, and so they tended to be more performance related than perceived differences. These were in tune with the reality of rising fuel costs and the concern for conservation.

Distribution and Sales

At times, the marketing thrust is driven by its approach to the market rather than its manipulation of perception or image. Does the company have a strong or unique distribution or sales approach that drives its strategy? This may be the barrier to the entry of others and the difference between success and failure. At one time, the secret to success was the ability to obtain and retain exclusive, high-class dealers or wholesalers. Until recently, the automobile companies combined perceived difference with exclusive, loyal dealers. It was difficult to obtain a Chevy or Ford dealership. If you had the dealership, it was exclusive for a town or even a county, and it was a guaranteed gold mine. The best prize was the Cadillac dealership, since Cadillac had a prestigious product and its clientele was not concerned with price and strongly wanted to own the car. At one time, appliance, housewares, television, and stereo dealerships were exclusive.

Today, the situation with these latter products has changed, and it is changing with automobiles as well. This was a form of franchising, but it has become even more powerful in the fast-food and new product areas. The fast-food chains have been able to go beyond other producers; they will provide a site selection, unique type of building, and the expertise of managing and operating the store. This system was pioneered by Howard Johnson's and Holiday Inn, and more recently McDonald's and Wendy's used it as well. This driver not only creates a unique way to get to the market, but it also enables franchisees to get started having low capital or using the capital and cash of others. The limitation is that it is difficult to maintain a consistent or high level of quality, which can have an impact on the reputation of the company or the brand. This, in turn, can reduce the desirability of the brand and the value of the franchise. If quality is declining, then it is a signal of the need to change the strategy. There are numerous illustrations of companies that have been forced to change from a franchise strategy to a strategy of creating perceived differences. This is what has happened to McDonald's, Howard Johnson's, Ramada Inn, and others. There has also been an increase of "factory outlets" operated by the manufacturers of products. The best-known illustration is Tandy's Radio Shack, but there are others, such as Dansk (a small supplier of dining accessories) and even several women's clothing manufacturers.

Geographic Expansion

At times, a company can grow by expanding its current product or services from one part of the city to another or to other states or even nations. Thus a company opens new branches or certifies new dealers in other regions. This has been one of the successful drivers of the Japanese. They protected and controlled their home markets, moved to other nations in Southeast Asia, and then targeted the United States and Europe. By protection and domination at home, they obtained a cost advantage permitting them to price aggressively in other developed nations. This has been the pattern in consumer electronics and automobiles and is now true in office electronics and computers.

Pricing

Is price the dominant factor? There are many who believe that pricing is the deciding factor and the major driver. I used to believe that this was a major driver, but in recent years, I have changed my mind, and now I believe it is a supporting strategy rather than a primary driver. It is probably more tactical than strategic, and it is based on some other uniqueness. It may be built on product innovation, low cost, or even distribution. There are many American businesspeople who believe that pricing is the primary reason that so many of the multinational foreign-based companies have been capable of gaining a quick position in the United States. I do not think this is true. Low price was combined with a strong product line, a willingness to lose in the short range, aggressive promotion, and a dealer network. Often price is the most apparent part of the equation. The premium price policy of Mercedes-Benz and Sony enabled them to create a prestige image, but their success was the result of many factors, including high-quality and innovative products.

Service

Is the company a leader in presales and postsales service, and does it back up its product with a long-term warranty? Service can be used to distinguish a product as much as a unique design can. This can be of importance when a product is complex and unfamiliar to the user. If the user has never used the product before and does not know what to expect or even what to look for, the aid received in making the purchasing decision and the confidence given in the product can be major contributors to the purchase. This has been true in the purchase of computers whether they be in the mainframe or in the mini, micro, or personal size. What will the computer do? Will it work? What happens if it does not work? Will I be able to get it repaired at a reasonable cost and within a reasonable time limit?

But there are other types of service that may be keys to the purchasing decision. One service may involve the financing of the purchase, such as the purchase of aircraft by an airline, locomotives by a railroad, or computers by an industrial company. Another service may be helping the customer to get a license to operate the product or to get necessary certification of the equipment. Services must be provided in a professional, prompt, and quality manner. Let's take a few examples of where the services have meant the difference.

IBM and Xerox both used services to gain a foothold in the office. American Express has achieved a quality reputation in financial and travel services. This has included making its credit card a premier card of the industry and its traveler's checks the most reliable and assured checks on a worldwide basis. There are companies whose whole thrust has been service. This is true of banks such as Morgan Guaranty Trust and brokerage houses such as Salomon Brothers and tax and accounting firms. On the popular level, H & R Block provides reliable tax-preparation services at a reasonable price. But service can also be important after the sale. The ability to maintain the equipment when it is operating may be crucial. This is important in the industrial sector, where the amount of downtime, that is, when the equipment is not functioning, may mean the difference between success and failure. Or it may be the ability to repair the equipment rapidly and have it on line in an efficient manner. The repair and maintenance of turbines for the electric utilities or the refueling of the nuclear steam supply reactors fit this category. The jet engines on airlines can also be the vital component in an aircraft.

Applications

Another powerful marketing driver concerns the applications of the product or the service. Sometimes this is as simple as advertising the product's applications and making the public aware of its uses. The genius of Arm & Hammer falls in this grouping. This company took a simple commodity, baking soda, and convinced the public that it could be used to deter odors in refrigerators or garbage cans or could be used as a sweetener. This was achieved by advertising and public relations. In recent years, makers of the diesel engine have proved that it could be used in a variety of ways ranging from propulsion to generation of electricity. The same is true of jet engines. Another example is the creative applications of integrated circuits and microcomputers. They have been incorporated into radios, thermostats, automobiles, laundry machines, microwave ovens, cameras, and computers. The whole emerging area of industrial automation has evolved from this technology. Strangely enough the innovators of applications have often been the users or the customers of these products and not the company that invented the devices. This is also the case with plastics and synthetics. The use of plastics has increased dynamically as the user has gained experience and has determined how they can be applied to their own products for beauty, styling, safety, and the reduction of weight.

Production Drivers

Capacity

Does the company use capacity as a weapon to gain or maintain position? This might mean adding capacity well in advance of demand in industries that require a long period of time to plan and build plants or processes. Capital-intensive industries fall in this category—metals, paper products, minerals, and oil and gas. If the decision is made to add capacity in advance of demand and the demand does not materialize or other major producers add at the same time, then there will be overcapacity resulting in a decrease in prices and ultimately in major losses. However, if the timing is correct and the company has the capacity to meet the demand when others do not, then it may be a bonanza. In these types of businesses the fixed cost and break-even point are so high that with high utilization, profits fall directly to the bottom line. With underutilization, profits fall when the break-even point is missed. Another capacity-based driver is the refusal to add capacity and run the facility at the high rate of utilization; in severe cases, a company may refuse to invest in the proper maintenance of the equipment.

Process Innovation

I have mentioned innovation in a few examples already. A company can be innovative in the products it offers, in the applications of the product, in the type of distribution or advertising it provides. But it can also be innovative in the way it makes the product. Does the company have a unique production and process? Such trade secrets or special formulas are vital in the production of chemicals, cosmetics, perfume goods, and so on, and the processes necessary for high yields and reliability are vital in the semiconductor business.

Productivity

A company may aim at being the least costly producer by reducing labor or materials or by increasing product reliability. Improved product reliability decreases total cost by reducing service and warranty costs. This is a productivity-driven thrust and is very important when a company has matured and the competition is trying to gain or hold its position by pricing. In today's world this is being achieved by the creative use and development of robots, computer-assisted design or flexible manufacturing. Often the creativity used to reduce costs simultaneously permits a company to improve its quality. An analysis of the Japanese experience demonstrates how such results can be achieved.

Supply

The guarantee of the supply of materials, fuel, components, and parts at reliable prices and timing may be the prime difference in the competitive arena and may be the strategic driver. There have been a number of companies that have backward integrated and begun making the components and parts or even the chemicals or petrochemicals. I have mentioned the move of DuPont to acquire Conoco in order to stabilize its supply of petrochemicals. But this has been the approach of the other oil giants, which moved into exploration and the "downstream" (backward-integration into chemicals and additives) in order to assure supply. In the automobile industry, the Big Three have moved into components and parts and have found them to be very profitable. Even my employer, General Electric, began to make its own motors and to control the supply of phosphorus and quartz in order to have more competitive cost positions. On the other extreme of this strategy there are some companies that have decided to make nothing at all on their own and instead to purchase finished products and concentrate on the marketing and distribution of them. This is called sourcing, and it is done to accelerate entry into new markets or to enable a company to follow the competition rapidly and with little risk. For instance, most of the American consumer-electronics companies source their videotape recorders from the Japanese and participate on a marketing level only. In the microwave oven market, this was the pattern followed by the

American companies that were late in the recognition of the market potential. In the automobile market, the Chrysler Corporation sourced small front-wheel cars from Mitsubishi, and American Motors did the same with Renault and General Motors is talking about joint ventures with Toyota and Suzuki. This strategy permits entry, but on the negative side, it increases the power of the supplier and may not permit the company to gain a product of its own.

Finance Drivers

Does your competitor have the reputation of being more innovative in how it finances or makes its deals than in any of the other criteria I have mentioned? The conglomerates that invented the financial-leverage strategy were more concerned with the balance sheet and the income growth than with the businesses they participated in. Today the opposite is happening, and companies are being creative in the divestiture of divisions. In either case, these are companies driven by finance and creative maneuvering.

Review and Application

Step 1—Evaluate the Competitor

1. Describe the entire portfolio of the competitor. You may wish to use a number of matrices depending on the nature of the company.
2. List the priorities of the competitor.
3. List the criteria that are used to make this prioritization, including the background of the management and the national priorities of the host country.
4. Describe the company's organization and decision-making process.
5. Record the objectives and goals of the organization and indicate how various groups influence these objectives and goals—stakeholders, groups within the organization, and others.
6. Record any other unique characteristics of the company.

Step 2—Identify the Strategic Drivers

For each of the competitor's segments, identify the major driver. This checklist may help.

Is it product-driven? If so, which of the following would best describe this thrust?

Unique Products   Creating an entirely new product segment by serving customer needs with a new technology or entirely different approach (e.g., Polaroid movie system).

Differentiation   Improving or adding capabilities to the current product; creating a differentiated approach or product (e.g., Polaroid SX-70, Japanese cameras).

Standardization   Moving product from specialized to more general use; making it easier to use; setting the industry standard (e.g., Kodak).

Is it marketing-driven?

Creating Demand   Changing sales by changing awareness and desire to use; implementation may be through advertising, promotions, demonstrations, and so on (e.g., packaged-goods companies, airlines).

Distribution and Sales   Changing sales by the use of strong or unique distribution or sales approach (e.g., automobiles, fast food).

Geographic Expansion   Changing demand by changing geographic emphasis—international to national to regional and so on (e.g., gas turbines, Coors Beer).

Pricing   Changing demand by raising, holding, or lowering prices, terms, conditions, or financing (e.g., L'eggs panty hose, major appliances).

Service   Changing demand by changing the services available or included with a product (e.g., self-service gas stations illustrate a thrust to reduce service).

Applications   Changing usage of a product or changing number of units sold by educating customers in applications (e.g., Arm & Hammer baking soda, IBM computers).

Is it production-driven?

Capacity   Adding capacity in advance of demand; utilizing capacity at maximum level; industries with high fixed costs usually employ this type of strategy (e.g., chemicals and other capital-intensive, long-lead businesses).

Process Innovation Developing a barrier of competitive advantage by having unique manufacturing capability (e.g., chemicals, forest products).

Productivity Automating and increasing productivity in either manufacturing or logistical areas (e.g., hardware coops such as True Value).

Supply Guaranteeing supply through backward integration (e.g., petrochemical companies); sourcing or purchasing rather than making finished product (e.g., audiotape).

Is it finance-driven? May include acquisitions, equity ownership, joint ventures, and so on.

Output

Throughout this book I have stressed the value of visualizing the output of your analyses. Such a visualization is helpful to communicate an output to others and enable them to assess its meaning and impact. I have found that

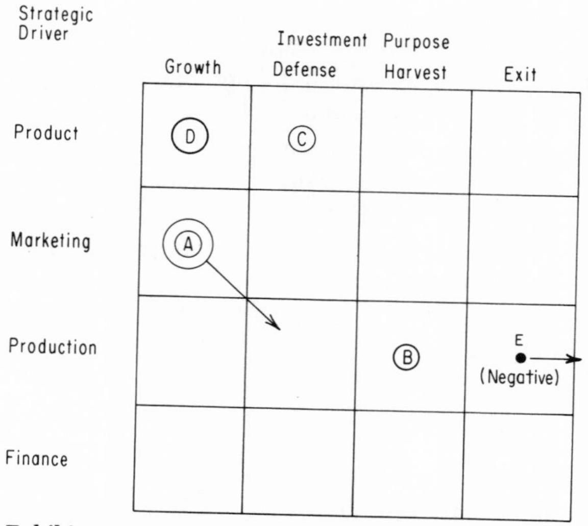

Exhibit 6-1. Investment/driver strategic matrix.

a matrix which summarizes the competitor's investment and strategic driver is equally helpful. In Exhibit 6-1 I've illustrated this type of matrix. The horizontal axis indicates the investment purpose of the segment. This purpose can be described as growth, defense, harvest, or exit. If you prefer, you may indicate the investment priority of the segment: high, medium, low, or of no value. The investment priority results from the analyses I described earlier concerning investment strategy. On the vertical axis of the matrix the strategic drivers are plotted, namely: product, marketing, production, or financially driven.

Using the matrix, you can plot the competitors' segments in their portfolios. If you refer to Exhibit 6-1, you can see that each segment is drawn relative to its contribution to either sales or earnings. In the exhibit, earnings are used because this permits a graphic display of the value of each segment to a competitor's profitability, and thus an indicator of how much effort he or she must exert if attacked or threatened. The larger the circle, the more earnings the segment contributes. If the segment doesn't make a positive contribution to profits, it will be displayed as a dot, with a notation that it is a negative profit segment.

Let's analyze Exhibit 6-1. Segment A is the largest contributor to earnings, representing 50 percent of the company's profits. Segment A is currently an invest-for-growth segment and is being driven by marketing. However, the arrow indicates that this segment will move to the defensive category and become a production-driven segment. Segment D is the second most important segment from an earnings perspective. It too is considered to be in the growth category, but it is driven by product. The situation portrayed is expected to continue, and it may be the reason that segment A is expected to move to defense from offense. Note that segment C is also product-driven, but for defensive purposes. The company is trying to balance its resource allocation by harvesting segment B and exiting segment E.

This matrix is intended to be another aid to your decision making. The matrix will be of significant help as you evaluate your competitors' implementation strategies and programs to determine whether they are internally consistent: the topic of the next chapter.

7 The Competitor's Implementation Strategies

After you have described the competitor's total portfolio and its investment strategy and strategic driver, you are in a position to probe deeper and specify the competitor's implementation strategies. It is important to do so to determine whether or not there is consistency and, if there is not, what can be done to take advantage of the inconsistency. In-depth evaluations should be limited to businesses or segments that are important to your business and that you are in a position to do something about. You cannot afford to do too many. As I describe the strategies, I will illustrate them and show how they fit various strategic alternatives.

Product Strategy

This focuses on how, where, and when a competitor's concepts, ideas, and products are developed.

Product Position

Leadership
Does the competitor wish to be the leader in product innovation? This may be real or perceived leadership. Obviously, if the strategy is product-driven,

it must have a consistent supporting implementation strategy and resource commitment. Has the competitor allocated the resources, including the financial, human, and physical resources? Where is this strategy being implemented? Does the competitor have centralized labs or decentralized labs? How successful has it been in innovating? What has contributed to its success? Can it continue to be successful in the future?

Some companies have had the reputation and thrust of being leaders and have had a tremendous track record. Many examples can be cited. Bell Labs is clearly an innovative organization and has made the U.S. telephone system the best in the world. A T & T has committed itself to innovation, and it has received a high return on its commitment. DuPont, Kodak, Xerox, and Polaroid all have built centralized labs and have had leadership strategies of varying degrees of success.

Selectivity Is Important

There are instances where companies lead in some businesses and not in others. This may be an indication that the product R&D is done on a local or business-by-business basis not on a centralized, corporate basis. Some companies excel in some lines and not in others; this is consistent with the portfolio concept. It is useful to understand why. Selection of priorities may be a corporate or local business decision. It could be the result of national funding. National priorities may emphasize some businesses or segments over others. It is also insightful to understand how the funding is made. Is it done directly through contracting or through subsidiaries?

Following

A company with a product-driven strategy does not need to be the leader. It can also be a follower. Following can be rapid or slow. Rapid following is difficult and can be very expensive. It may be more expensive and complex than leading. The key is timing. The company that can move rapidly is truly unique. You should probe to find out why a company has selected this approach and how it does it.

Why would a company elect a follower product-driven strategy? It might be because it has a lot to lose by being the leader. A company that is already number one will be interested in protecting its position and will not want to make the product they have obsolete. A strategy of following is a tough one to implement. It will take extraordinary competitive/market intelligence and research and development. The competitor must have knowledge of what the next generation of the product will be and also what the likely substitute products will be. It must be willing to invest in programs and projects in order to be prepared to introduce the product when the timing is right. Timing is critical. Following too early may mean reducing its own sales by substitution. Following too late can also mean lost sales. At times the competitor may be strong that it can get the customers to wait until it has the model or product that is already available from someone else. This was true in mainframe computers. When companies like Remington Rand, Honeywell, Burroughs, and Amdahl introduced bigger and even better machines, IBM announced that it was going to introduce the next generation soon, and since users already had their software and systems geared to IBM, they were willing to wait and not convert. Leasing also can work in favor of the strategy, especially if the attacking competitors would prefer selling.

At times, the problem is not rapidity but quality. The challenger must be capable of providing quality and reliability. If it is not capable of doing so, its challenge will not be successful. If the quick follower does not respond with quality, then it may accelerate its decline. General Motors followed Volkswagen and Mercedes-Benz in providing diesel engines at the peak of the oil crisis. This may or may not qualify as a rapid response, but it does illustrate the problem of not providing a quality response. The GM diesels were reported to not measure up. They needed more battery power than ordinary internal-combustion engines. They ran rough and had trouble with water seeping into their tanks. Many of these deficiencies were also true of the original entries, and it may have been wiser for GM not to follow at all. Quick following can be successful or unsuccessful, and it is not the only option for a follower.

Another option for a company is to follow at its own pace and when it is ready. This is the option traditionally employed, and it is especially suited for a leader. At times, this can be a successful thrust, especially if the innovator's product fails. But it can also represent significant risk, since the innovation may take hold, develop rapidly, and require a costly catch-up. For example, Kodak took over a decade to follow Polaroid in the instant-photography market. Polaroid is still number one, and Kodak has had to spend a great deal of money trying to catch up. Kodak did the same thing with the 35-millimeter camera and permitted the Japanese to gain a superior position. Even in photocopying, Kodak was a slow follower. Since it appears that Kodak consistently maintains a slow-follow strategy in its nontraditional segments, you might evaluate its reasoning. I have not studied Kodak in depth, but it may be that it has a strong "NIH," meaning "not invented here," attitude. It may have trouble admitting that others have better ideas or are capable of meeting customer needs better than it is. Or it may be that this is consistent with a strong desire to be the cost leader. There are many American companies that have adopted the slow-follow position. American auto companies have followed the European and Japanese companies slowly in the small-car field. American consumer electronics firms have reluctantly followed the Japanese in videotape players. RCA, which already had its own videodisc, waited until Philips had units on the market before it introduced its own.

Not Following at All

Some companies elect not to follow at all. It may be smart or dumb. It is smart if things do not work out, which is what happened with Mazda's rotary engine. No one followed, and Mazda discontinued. Gulf General Atomic offered a gas-cooled nuclear reactor, and no one followed. The design was not successful. Polaroid developed an instant movie camera, and no one followed. It did not succeed. Not following is dumb if it means missing significant opportunities and never being able to catch up. This is the hallmark of many losers—in steam engines, vacuum tube radios, electromechanical controls, and propeller-driven aircraft.

Approach to Product Development

Other elements of the product strategy involve how the product is developed. You will need to assess the competitor's ability to develop and commercialize products.

Self-Development

In the leadership role, the competitor may rely on its own developments and use its own proprietary and dedicated laboratory. This is typical of the companies clearly perceived as innovators and technology leaders. A T & T has its world-renowned Bell Labs, and IBM has its Watson Labs. Siemens, Philips, Xerox, Wang Laboratories, DuPont, and Union Carbide also develop products in their own labs. Many of these companies have combinations of centralized and decentralized labs. The centralized labs concentrate on basic, forward-thinking research and development, while the decentralized labs concentrate on the application and implementation of basic research. IBM, for instance, does basic research in its Watson Labs improving the state of the art in cryogenics to develop more powerful memories. Its division labs are located throughout the world. They concentrate on product development, but in some cases they do fundamental research as well.

If a company is both multi-industry and multinational, it might have product-development activities in many locations and permit competition to stimulate innovation and provide it with alternative R&D approaches. The 3M approach is a case in point. It encourages multiple solutions by making it difficult for a project to be killed. This enables an idea to flourish and protects it from being sacrificed at the whim of some manager.

How ideas are developed and what reviews they must pass are also important. If the review is made by lower-level managers who are concerned mostly about profits, it is likely that the ideas will be ignored if they take too long to turn a profit. If the ideas can reach the upper management for review and the company is healthy or considers innovation vital to success, then they have a greater chance.

Financing

The issue of financing is critical. If all R&D must be funded by the business unit, then it will be directly related to the prosperity of that unit. The rich units will fund, and the poor units will not. This is fine provided the rich are the long-term winners and have better opportunities than the poor. If, however, the poor units are in growth industries and cannot afford to capitalize on them, then it will be detrimental to total corporate health. Some companies have development funds that can be used "ex-budget," and in this case it is possible for the poorer businesses to get funding from other sources. But funding sources do not have to be restricted to inside the company. It is possible to obtain outside funding from the government or venture capitalists, or even to obtain it by pooling resources with competitors, customers, and suppliers. For instance, many companies seek out government contracts in fields of interest in order to gain a technology lead and use public funds. Some would argue that if it were not for the space programs, the microcomputers and minicomputers would not have been developed. This can be a tough way to fund, because it is restrictive and the patents often become public and thus available to the competition. However, if programs are smartly administered, this need not happen. It is possible to get some proprietary position or at least to have the running start on knowing how to make the product or mastering the key timing and scheduling problems.

Some companies separate ventures from the parent company and seek outside funding. Of course, this is typical for the emerging company, but it can also be used by the diversified or multinational company. Some Japanese companies separate their new ventures from the parent and then sell equity in these new companies. In Japan, most of this equity is owned by the banks. This permits some financing off the balance sheet and gives access to new sources of funds. Further, it can permit losses that will not reduce the return on investment or equity—a plus to financially oriented companies. However, it does have disadvantages because it may reduce the ability of the parent company to use the innovation and be synergistic.

Another way of financing is through joint venturing. If funding requirements are high or if the company is so weak that it cannot afford to develop on its own, this may be critical. In the race for developing the videodisc and its related software, many companies have joined together. Philips joined with IBM and MCA. GE planned to join with JVC and Thorne of the United Kingdom. By joint venturing, companies can bring complementary strengths to the development of a new industry. RCA on the other hand had done it alone. In the development of jet engines, there have been several joint programs, some in combination with airframe companies. In this type of venture it is important that the companies are compatible and that one of them is in a clear leadership position. Too many chiefs or incompatible objectives and talents will make a poor joint venture and will probably result in a loss for all.

Licensing

At times it does not make any sense to develop a product on your own, as a leader or a follower. Licensing another's design and using it can be extremely powerful if you have a clear strategy and the willingness to admit someone else may have the better idea. Some companies do this well, others very poorly.

The entire electronics age was born in the United States, and Bell Labs can be proud of its innovation. But it has not been the U.S. companies that have fully capitalized on electronics. Again it has been a clear strategy of the Japanese to be willing to use others' ideas and technology to gain industry leadership. At first, the strategy was one geared to using the initial product as is, but this was replaced by one geared to improving. Today the Japanese have become clear winners in many markets because they have not had a strong NIH attitude but rather have been willing to learn and improve. This attitude is crucial for the quick follower as well as the leader. If you can get licenses from the leader, it is smart to do so and then work hard at beating it at its own game. It is the use of the innovation that matters and not merely its initiation.

Companies may license from other companies as well as laboratories and universities. There are a number of companies that consciously seek out other sources by financing research at universities, hospitals, private labs, or even individually run enterprises. AMF finances universities to develop products even if it does not have complete control of the results. Hoescht has financed genetic-engineering work at Massachusetts General Hospital. Battelle Memorial Institute will contract to do company-funded exclusive as well as joint development projects, and several companies use this approach. I mentioned the Japanese companies' approach to this in a previous chapter. It may also be useful to establish a venture-capital organization to support innovation and then acquire the innovating company later. This has been the Exxon approach.

There isn't anything magic about which approach a competitor uses. It depends on its product positioning strategy, resources, and ability to capitalize on others' ideas. A leader may wish to protect its lead and not permit others to use its ideas. Thus, it may wish to closely monitor and tie up the innovators' right to sell to others or even disclose what they know. The use of approaches such as the direct funding of universities and private labs or the establishment of venture-capital companies makes the most sense. These approaches are geared to getting innovation at the lowest cost and the least risk. But there must be a willingness to fund for the long term. If you are a second- or third-ranked company, then the sharing of costs and results may be most advantageous. It is important to probe about the reasoning and approach used by competitors.

Degree of Selectivity and Scope

Having specified the desired product position and the means of funding and managing the outcome, you should now aim at determining whether the competitor is interested in being a specialist or a generalist in the marketplace. Let's have a look at the questions that will require answers.

- How selective is the competitor? Does it carry a full, partial, or minimum line?
- Does the competitor offer a wide variety for every style or model?
- Is this changing and why?

Breadth and Depth of the Line

A broad competitor will offer a complete line, though possibly only a single item or a few items of each style or model. Suppose it sells women's clothing. If it has a broad line, then it would sell all styles and fashions in a wide variety of sizes. This might mean selling contemporary, high fashion, and traditional clothing. If the competitor were selling automobiles, it might sell a full array of automobiles varying in size, price points, and so on to fit a multiplicity of needs and wants. The true generalist in a particular market is very broad and not selective. This is the philosophy of the mass merchant or discounter in the retail trade. If someone has a need, the company with this product strategy will fill it. This does not mean customization; on the contrary, it means being able to standardize some aspect of the cycle to be able to satisfy multiple wants with minimum modifications. For instance, in dress or women's clothing, the most economical way might be to be able to make the clothes in large volumes and to distribute widely. Auto companies might do this with critical components like ignition systems, batteries, and radiators—components that may not differ from one size auto to another. The true generalist will also probably have a very deep line as well—offering a wide variety for every model or style. In dresses, this might mean having an extensive coverage of colors, fabrics, and sizes—truly the "all things to all people" strategy. In autos, Alfred Sloane used this deep-line approach, supplying many styles, multiple brands, and many colors. In today's auto market, you can get almost any combination of color, style, accessories, motor size, and radio you desire. Thus, the auto industry has a very deep and broad line. Such a line normally fits the follower rather than the product innovator. An innovator is likely to be more selective and unwilling to be too extensive, at least at the beginning. This shows that many of the product-strategy elements do interrelate, and you should look for consistency. I will repeat this point in many places because it is critical. If the elements are inconsistent, the strategy will be ineffective.

A company may be fairly broad and deep—not quite a specialist but certainly not a generalist. This can be done by concentrating deeply on a moderate number of styles and models or by some variation of this theme. It is typical to find the companies in this category in trouble. They cannot provide the variety of generalists and do not have the reputation or power of true specialists. In autos, American Motors was in this category. AMC started as a full-line automobile company with the merger of Nash and Hudson. It elected to concentrate on the small car, featuring the Rambler. As it succeeded with this model, it moved into the intermediate line and has been marginally successful in some years and a loser in others. Recently, it added Renault to its offering, taking a broader position. Now, Renault has increased its ownership to become the senior partner in the deal.

The true specialist is narrow and deep and in a few cases may also be narrow and shallow. This is the entry strategy of many companies. They select niches that will permit specialization and, normally, innovation. Since a new company's product is untested and its resources limited, it keeps its offering narrow initially. Once it is accepted and its reputation has been made, it gradually increases in depth—providing more and more variations and then extending to other sizes and configurations. Sony originally was only a small-television company. They have now expanded into all sizes and have also added peripherals.

Volkswagen was the classic example of the narrow, shallow company. For years, it offered one model, the Beetle. This car was restricted to a no-frills status—no automatic, no power steering, no unique suspension. This was expanded slightly with the Super Beetle, which was semiautomatic. Today Volkswagen still concentrates on the small car but has a number of models and a more comprehensive line of autos, including high-performance models.

Consistency with Investment
Strategy and Strategic Driver

The question of consistency was raised earlier, and it is important to determine whether the product positioning, development, funding, breadth, and depth fit together. A product strategy that includes leadership, licensing, external funding, and a broad and deep line does not hang together. If this is your assessment of the competitor's strategy, you would be wise to probe as to why it is happening. Does the competitor have a "fatal" flaw that will knock it out? Does the situation indicate an inexperienced management team, poor organization, or confusion? Or is there something that is truly unique in this case? Many Japanese companies and nationalized companies have strategies similar to the one described above. They may seek leadership by using the technology of others. Licensing can be a low-cost entry, and if applications are intensive and even creative, a licensing firm can even outclass the innovator and creator. The funding might be through the sale of stock to institutions, individuals, banks, or even the government. Again, this is the Japanese model. Since aggressiveness is important, a full line may be vital to success. This is an example of how the elements of a product strategy can appear inconsistent but actually be consistent for certain types of companies. In the case of most American companies, I believe that such a strategy is illogical and probably will fail. I use the word "probably" because, with luck, it may work.

Leaders normally have a unique proprietary position that is not licensed. Further, they can seek outside funding but would prefer to fund themselves. Finally, the introduction of the product is normally focused narrow at first and broader later on. These are consistent with being a product innovator seeking growth and, if implemented as planned, will be successful.

The final questions about positioning emphasize how a company may wish to position itself in terms of degree of differentiation and how it may wish to differentiate. First of all, the company may elect not to be different but rather to be like all the other companies. This is standardization. There are some leaders that want to create the standard and have others replicate them. This will help to increase the organization's ability to learn and reduce costs. If everyone follows, then savings are produced and even licensing fees are generated. Philips of Holland created the audio cassette and licensed the industry. Unfortunately, the industry followers were more successful than Philips, and it did not gain the desired results. RCA standardized color television in the United States and was the leader in creating an industry. Kodak has standardized film in the United States and is the winner in a number of ways. But standardization may not be as preferred as differentiation. You can be different by providing unique features, quality, or styling. The video cassette game has been one of providing unique features, such as the ability to record at certain times, or the ability to record for a longer time. Personal computers are being differentiated by storage capacity, ease of use, and availability of software.

There are companies that distinguish themselves by reliability and quality. Uptime—that is, operating for long periods without interruption—guarantees are major selling points in many capital-intensive industries, including electrical generators, farm equipment, aircraft, and computers—the less maintenance, the better. In automobiles, time between tune-ups and oil changes is a key. Providing longer warranties or guarantees can also be vital and might provide a means of making a product standard. Styling and appearance can also be used (for example, the model-change game—making cars look more sporty, more affluent, and more sexy). Again there is not any one winning combination, and in any given industry different companies select variations. In cameras, Kodak emphasized standardization, Canon innovative features. Both are winners in their niches. Followers have tended to be losers—Bell & Howell is an example.

Product Strategy Work Sheets

The following work sheets may be useful in describing your key competitor's "product strategy" and in determining whether it is consistent with its investment strategy and strategic driver.

Competitor's Product Strategy

SELECTIVITY AND SCOPE
How selective is the competitor's line?
- Full   ( )
- Partial   ( )
- Minimum   ( )

What type of scope does the competitor try to have?
- Broad and deep   ( )
- Broad but not deep   ( )
- Deep and narrow   ( )

Is it increasing or decreasing its scope?

	Breadth	Depth
• Increasing	( )	( )
• Decreasing	( )	( )
• Holding	( )	( )

PRODUCT POSITION
How would you describe its desired position?
- Real leader ( )
- Perceived leader ( )
- Quick follower ( )   Note how quickly
- Reluctant follower ( )   it can follow
- Follows when it wants to ( )
- Doesn't follow ( )

APPROACH TO PRODUCT DEVELOPMENT
How does it obtain new or follow-up products?
- Uses its own basic research ( )
  with long-cycled develop-
  ment
- Uses others' research, but ( )
  innovates in design or
  applications
- Licenses ( )
- Joint develops ( )
- Copies ( )
- Other ( )

LOCATION
Where is product development done?
- In corporate labs ( )
- In business-centralized labs ( )
- In plant locations ( )
- Combination ( )
  Explain:

FINANCING
How are new products financed?
- From retained earnings ( )
- From other products ( )
- From external sources ( )

BASIS
How does it obtain ideas?
- Extensive consumer ( )
  research
- Marginal research ( )
- From competition ( )

- Primarily internal per-   ( )
  ception with little external
  research

EMPHASIS
What is its emphasis?
- Differentiation   ( )
  - Styling   ( )
  - Performance   ( )
  - Reliability   ( )
  - Features   ( )
- Standardization   ( )

Marketing Strategy

After you have completed the product strategy assessment, you should describe the marketing strategy that is used to support the product plan. You should consider the many areas involved in marketing, including the use of intermediaries, the salesforce, promotion, pricing, and service.

Intermediaries

Does the competitor go directly to the user or deal with intermediaries? If it goes directly, how does it do it? If it uses intermediaries, who are they and how loyal are they to the competitor? How many steps are there between the competitor and the user? Has this changed? Let's take a closer look at these questions and some of their strategic implications.

Companies that deal with intermediaries can do so in several ways. They can sell directly to retailers, which sell to consumers. Automobile companies provide a classic example. They sell only to authorized dealers. These have been exclusive, single-brand representatives—the local Chevrolet, Ford, or Chrysler dealer. This is still the preference of auto companies but has become difficult to enforce. Today auto companies continue to go through dealers, but the dealers may carry more than one make of car.

There are companies such as Zenith, Sunbeam, Sony, and others that sell to independent wholesalers which in turn sell to authorized retailers. This is called "two-step distribution." It is becoming increasingly difficult to maintain the loyalty and alliance of these independent wholesalers and authorized dealers because of the advent of "buying chains," which are comprised of retailers which join together and buy directly from manufacturers. This has been increasingly easy to do since there are manufacturers in Japan, Taiwan, and Korea that cater to this approach. There are some companies that have three-step distribution. Companies that make auto-repair parts sell to wholesalers, which sell to jobbers, which sell to garages, which install the parts in cars. Today the situation has changed somewhat, since Midas sells direct and others sell only to wholesalers, like NAPA. Some importers sell to agents, who sell to wholesalers.

Once you have determined the distribution strategy, you should probe to find out why this strategy is used and what its advantages and disadvantages are. Sometimes the reasoning is not very complex. It may be purely a function of tradition. It has always been that way. This can provide an excellent means of penetrating and attacking the leader. Some consumer market companies saw the advent of discounters early and joined them, while some resisted. It was the discounters that enabled imports to move in and destroy the traditional leaders. The numerous small, independent retailer was difficult to convert and had been a barrier to new entries. So was the exclusive auto or electrical-appliance dealer. The discounter provided an ideal channel for the new entry, since discounters purchased in volume, were willing to do their own inventory and floor planning, and this permitted the new entry to capture large segments with a few sales calls.

This is not a description of the relative merits of different retail approaches since they must fit the specific market. However, innovation is possible and worth probing. Does the competitor stress specialist or generalist distribution? This can have significant strategic impacts. Specialists are similar to the small independents, since they require personal selling and probably unique or high-quality products. The innovative competitor will focus on specialist dealers. These provide the presales and postsales required service. This is the current situation in personal computers ($3000 and up), where customer service is vital. Other computers lower priced ($1000 and below), however, are sold through traditional, mass-market generalists, since service is not important.

Salesforce

Regardless of the distribution, the approach to selling must also be probed. Does the competitor have its own salesforce? Where is it located? How large is it? Does the company use agents or representatives? How demanding is the company of those who sell?

There are firms that require technically trained, sophisticated salespeople. IBM salespeople are an excellent example, since they are smart and educated, make a good appearance, and are well-trained. IBM carefully selects and trains them. Not only do they know their equipment but also how it compares with the competition's. Other companies are less particular, and some let anyone represent them. Obviously, selectivity is both a means of success and an end in itself. Sometimes a salesforce can be overqualified, and this can be a disadvantage.

Organization

You also need to consider the organization of the salesforce. Organization can have an impact on the sales effectiveness and ability to respond to or anticipate change. Highly centralized organizations are unable to react rapidly; they have too many organizational layers to clear rapidly. Centralization is useful for maintaining control and might be effective for companies that sell large, high-priced equipment or those in which price control is important, but it is not helpful in rapidly changing environments. Decentralization of the salesforce by region, product, customer group, specialization, or price points can be effective under certain conditions. Some multi-industry firms are centralized in some markets and decentralized in others. What do your key competitors do? How do you compare? Do their skills match their organization? The higher the technological requirements the more centralized the organization is likely to be. If a firm is oriented to applications, it is likely to have a decentralized sales organization.

Rewards

How people are remunerated will have an impact on their behavior. If paid purely on commission, a salesforce will focus on what sells the easiest. This is good for the short range, since it is a system that responds to current customer needs. But it can have detrimental long-term consequences, especially if the strategy is to develop a new market or segment and gradually emphasize one over the other. A combination of commission and salary is an excellent approach to move the salesforce in the direction of the new line while encouraging support of the current line. This requires a willingness to make a few millionaires, especially in high-ticket items. Having successful salespeople motivates others, although those who have already made it may not put out to the extent desired. Finally, you can merely pay by salary. This is typical in situations that require team selling. It can also be effective, and the individuals can make out well.

What are the compensation approaches of your key competitors? How do they compare with the industry standard?

Training

In some situations, the nature and type of training the salesforce receives can separate winners from losers. How is the training provided by the competitor? Does it use outsiders? How often? What is taught? I come from a company whose tradition has stressed training, and the company has proved to be an excellent motivator, developer, and retainer of key people.

Promotion

The marketing strategy includes promotion. Promotion can be a main driver and key element of any strategy. It must be consistent with the overall strategic theme and image that is being created. If a company wishes to be the innovation leader, then it must make sure that the public and customers know about its inventiveness and uniqueness. Even if it is selling on price, it still needs a complementary promotional strategy. Some of the key questions to probe are: Is the competitor a large or small spender? How do its expenditures compare with the industry average? Does it spend more or less than you or the leaders? What is the emphasis of its promotion? Is it geared toward pull or push?

Pull advertising focuses on print, audio, and visual media such as newspapers, magazines, radio, and television and is designed to "pull" the customer into the store. Push advertising is aimed at communicating the merits of the product when the customer is already in the store. Some companies focus on national media, while others are selective and local. Some prefer to use print.

Another question deals with the continuity of the message in both timing and theme. Does the competitor have a strong monogram or label that is coupled with all products? General Motors and IBM have this. Is there one common message, such as GE's old "Progress is our most important product" or Panasonic's "Slightly ahead of our time"? There are other companies that use multiple brands and therefore have no corporate theme or identity. Beatrice Foods had no identity as such.

There is not any one approach that works in all cases. The key is to understand what is being done and then to determine if it fits the overall strategy and driver. I mentioned innovation, but promotion can also relate to other strategies.

Price

Closely related to the promotion strategy is the pricing strategy. What is the competitor's pricing position? Is it always on the high side, or always on the low side, or just about average? Does it lead or follow in price moves? How rapidly and frequently does it move?

Some companies are always on the high side, and this closely correlates with their reputation and product quality or innovation. There are instances where prices are maintained on the high side but the terms of purchase are very flexible and lenient—no discounts but 180 days of interest-free terms. This can be very attractive in high-inflation periods. Some nations support their industries by attractive financing—long-term, no-interest loans. This can swing the deal if the customer requires financing.

Different Pricing Strategies

You cannot stop after merely describing the situation, you must also understand how the competitor decides on the price it will charge. I will now describe some of the variations and indicate when they are normally used. The pricing strategy should correlate with the investment strategy and strategic driver for the business or segment, but it may not, and this indicates weakness or limitation.

Pricing can be based purely on internal factors. For instance, products may be priced to utilize capacity and "fill the plant." This is quite common when the industry or business has a high fixed cost and, therefore, every point of utilization above the fixed cost or break-even point has significant profit returns. Airlines offer specials because seat utilization is key and every seat filled over fixed cost is almost all profit. Hotels also practice this type of pricing. Thus, tours are priced for groups in this way to make it very attractive. Other industries that price to utilize capacity are paper, steel, copper, and so on.

Closely related to this approach is the total-cost or margin-pricing approach. Based on disclosures in the 1980s, it appears that General Motors priced in this way. It decided on the margin of profit it wished to obtain and then estimated the number of cars it would sell, along with total cost, and this became its price level. If volume started to fall, it responded with some factory-filling efforts. The results are well known. The average price of U.S. cars increased from $3900 in 1970 to over $8500 in 1981, and this permitted the Japanese to climb under the umbrella. This type of pricing normally yields umbrella pricing, and if it is not practiced with discrimination, it can have disastrous effects. This approach is normal for mature, oligopolistic industries in which one company seems to be the leader.

A third pricing approach is value pricing. The company attempts to determine the value of the product to the customer and then estimates how much it can charge. Value pricing is consistent with innovative products or services as well as those that denote prestige or status. The price has little to do with the company's cost. This pricing strategy can yield significant returns. For example, Mercedes-Benz and Porsche automobiles are status symbols just as Cadillacs and Lincolns once were. The price is set high intentionally, and the volume is kept low so that demand will be greater than supply. Companies making designer jeans, quality stereo systems, and prestige cosmetics and perfumes also use this approach. The worst thing that can happen is premature discounting or dumping. Therefore, this strategy requires a highly controlled distribution, with attention to "fair trade" practices—the manufacturer can decertify the retailer or distributor if it sells below suggested or advertised retail price. Often such a strategy includes a buy-back arrangement for unsold stock, especially in the seasonal businesses. This was the practice of Head Skis in the 1960s. The rationale is clear: Keep it selective, and do not sell exclusively on price.

The fourth approach is what is normally called learning-curve pricing. It is a common approach in embryonic industries where the stimulation of demand via pricing is desirable. This approach requires an understanding of how volume influences total costs or at least manufacturing costs. The relationship between these two variables can be plotted on log paper to deduce the slope. If the slope is at an 80-degree angle, it means that costs will decline 20 percent for each doubling of volume; if the slope is at a 70-degree angle, the costs will decline 30 percent for each doubling of volume; and so on. (Note the phrase "doubling of volume.") This curve is the experience curve, and it can be used for pricing. The approach starts with this type of analysis. Then, market growth is estimated and plotted on the line. If a company wishes to be aggressive and preempt the competition, it will price in a way that will enable it to expand the market and gain share, and it will assume the cost reduction. It is clearly the approach of the aggressor that believes that its product, combined with a low price, can make the market grow and that it can be the winner. This was the apparent strategy of Texas Instruments in calculators, watches, and home computers. Unfortunately, it won the battle and lost the war, since neither of these lines have been big winners; and in fact Texas Instruments has already exited the watch business.

Another popular approach is based on inflation pricing. This became popular when double-digit inflation became a reality in the 1970s. The concept is similar to the margin-pricing approach but is more forward-directed. In this approach, the company anticipates the inflation rate in the future and attempts to price in advance of the increase rather than after it. If done properly, this can reduce the number of times that prices must be raised and can actually increase margins. This approach is popular in long-cycle products where escalation can wipe out profits. At times there is a price reopener (that is, the price can be renegotiated at a later time), which can do the same job. The price reopener might be considered a commercial version of the old military and government "cost plus" contracts. It is very popular in the construction industry.

Lead Pricing versus Follow Pricing

Another dimension of pricing is positioning. A company may elect to merely follow the competition and not try and lead. It awaits the competitor's move and either responds immediately or has a delayed reaction. The delay may be to determine whether the price rise or decline will take. If there is a price rise, the company may monitor customer receptivity and see if the leader can hold share. If share falls, then it makes sense for the company to see if it can pick up the customers. If share holds, then it makes sense for the company to follow the price rise. If there is a price decline, the follower will wait to see if the leader can gain share. The issue is whether the action is positive or negative.

It may be useful to evaluate your competitors from this dimension and decide what it all means to you. In every industry there are numerous pricing approaches. For instance, in autos General Motors priced for margin, Volkswagen maintained prices and value priced, and Chrysler and AMC were followers and priced in response to GM and Ford. The Japanese have used a combination of pricing approaches, but they are always geared to increasing exports and capacity utilization.

Price Delegation

In addition, there is also the issue of control and delegation of pricing authority. Some companies reserve pricing authority to the top management of the company. It was reputed that when Thomas Watson was CEO of IBM there were weekly meetings to decide on pricing moves and strategies. If decisions had to be made rapidly, the top managers would meet and make the decision. This is not surprising when computers were large and expensive. Today, as computers have become smaller and cheaper, it would not make sense to have this type of top-down control.

There are companies where pricing control is reserved to the division or business-unit management, and others where it is delegated to the regional sales manager or even the local salesperson. Of course, in all cases there are restrictions, and no one has complete authority. The key is whether pricing is truly strategic or operational. In some products, one deviation from the norm can result in a precedent and even an unplanned price war. The OPEC decisions have had this type of impact, and thus decisions are now controlled by the nation that is the chief producer. In other cases, wheeling and dealing can be confined to the local area and not have a dramatic impact on earnings.

What is the norm in your markets, and how do the various competitors deviate? Where do you fit in this situation?

Service

A Means or an End?

There are many who argue that service is not strategic. I disagree because I have seen a number of businesses that have failed because the service strategy was not understood. The first question to probe is whether the competitor views service as a business or merely a support for a business. There are some companies that look at service as a business, in fact, the key business. They might be willing to give away the product to get the service opportunity. For example, it might be good business to price the jet engine on the airplane low in order to be able to service and provide spare parts later. Initially IBM and the other large mainframe computer companies viewed service as a means to sell computers. This has changed, and today services are sold separately. The question that can clarify the competitor's strategy is: How are the services priced? If they are included as part of the initial price or if they are only priced at cost, then you can assume that the competitor views service as a means, not an end. If, however, services are priced separately, then it would be fair to assume service is a separate profit center and is viewed as a business.

As with other elements we have discussed, there is no one correct approach. Whatever approach is used, it must be consistent with the investment strategy and the strategic driver and it must fit the market in terms of maturity. It is also worth probing the various profitability levels. This will also enable you to determine the type of services being emphasized.

Presale Services

Before the sale, you might help customers decide what they really need, what choices they have, and even how to finance their purchases. Normally, these services are considered part of selling. However, there are some companies that make this a business and charge a fee. The most obvious example is the architectural engineer who helps in the design of buildings and large projects like power plants. You should describe what the competitor's approach is now and what it will be in the future.

Other services are installation and training. A decision must be made on how these will be priced. Whether installation is included in the initial price or a surcharge is made for it is important with large, complex products or systems. How the operators are trained and at whose expense are also important.

Postsale Services

Then there are postsale services, which include maintenance and repair or even upgrading. Normally the customer takes care of these, but it can be a powerful competitive advantage if these services are provided at a fixed or guaranteed rate. This was the theory behind automobile, television, and appliance service contracts. RCA led the way in television, and Sears has pioneered in appliances. For an annual fee, like an insurance premium, the consumer would have a television, appliance, and auto "insured" for repair. The profit from this type of arrangement can be high if a company has its own service network, and this can be used as a load builder, that is, maintaining a steady rather than erratic work load.

How the services are provided has an impact on costs. If a company has its own trained service representatives, it is in a similar position with them as with its salesforce. Having its own representatives may increase expenses and ability to response, while using others' is less costly but less controllable. The issue is consistency. Does the service strategy fit the investment strategy and strategic driver, or is it inconsistent?

Service as a Barrier

I can remember that many U.S. companies believed that service was a major barrier, which importers could not overcome. After all, the Japanese and Europeans did not have the repair and maintenance network and thus could not penetrate the United States. Service was important because U.S. producers had a statistical quality-control mentality, and it was cheaper to fix the product in the field than to strive for higher quality rates in the factory. The uniqueness of the Japanese strategy was "zero defects." They decided that it was cheaper to have no rejects to fix than to set up an expensive repair service. Because of having defect-free products, they were also able to increase their warranty period, and they bundled service into the initial price. A barrier crumbled. The consumer feels more secure when a manufacturer will fix a product free of charge during a specified period of time. It makes them feel that quality and performance is assured. Thus "bundled" service has significant strategic value.

Marketing Strategy Work Sheets

Since the evaluation of a competitor is complex, it is worth applying the concepts as you proceed. Therefore, the marketing strategy work sheets are provided at this point for your use.

Competitor's Marketing Strategy

DISTRIBUTION

SELECTIVITY

How many steps in competitor's distribution scheme?
- Four ( )
- Three ( )
- Two ( )
- One ( )

Is the competitor changing steps?
- Increasing ( )
- Decreasing ( )
- Holding ( )

What type of distributors does it have?

	Wholesale	Retail
• Company-owned	( )	( )
• National chains	( )	( )
• Regional chains	( )	( )
• Independents	( )	( )

Does it seek dealers and distributors that carry:
- One brand   ( )   ( )
- Two brands   ( )   ( )
- Multiple brands   ( )   ( )

What type of a relationship is it trying to develop?
- Long-term   ( )   ( )
- Opportunistic   ( )   ( )

Are distributors or dealers:
- Generalists   ( )   ( )
- Specialists   ( )   ( )
- Full-service   ( )   ( )
- Partial-service   ( )   ( )
- No-service   ( )   ( )

READINESS TO SERVE

RAPIDITY
How rapidly does competitor meet customer needs?
- Has stock in advance of de-   ( )
  mand
- Responds more rapidly   ( )
  than its competition
- Meets competition   ( )
- Lags behind competition   ( )

LOCATION OF INVENTORY STATUS
- Primarily centralized   ( )
- Localized (own)   ( )
- Localized (intermediary   ( )

DEGREE OF CONTROL (Who controls inventory and how much power do they have)
- High   ( )
- Medium   ( )
- Low   ( )

PROMOTIONAL

POSITION
What is its promotional position?
- Leader   ( )
- Follower   ( )

EXPENDITURES
Does it spend:
- More than competition ( )
- About the same as compe- ( )
  tition
- Less than competition ( )

TYPE OF PROMOTION
How would you describe its promotion?
- Pull ( )
- Push ( )

What kind of media does it concentrate on?
- Print ( )
- Audio ( )
- Visual ( )

Is its promotion:
- Seasonal ( )
- Periodic ( )
- Continuous ( )

PRICING

BASIS
What is the basis of its pricing decisions?
- Maintaining plant utiliza- ( )
  tion
- Total cost ( )
- Maintaining a specific ( )
  margin
- Capitalizing on customer ( )
  value
- Maintaining a relationship ( )
  to inflation
- Improving learning-curve ( )
  position
- Meeting competition ( )
- Other (Specify) ( )

CONTROL
What kind of control is there over pricing?
- Central control ( )

- Restricted delegation   ( )
- Local control   ( )

POSITION

Are its prices:
- High   ( )
- Average   ( )
- Low   ( )

In pricing, is it a:
- Leader   ( )
- Follower   ( )

If the competitor follows, does it move:
- Rapidly   ( )
- Slowly   ( )

Rank the competitor on these aspects of pricing:

	Best	Average	Worst
• Terms	( )	( )	( )
• Conditions	( )	( )	( )
• Financing	( )	( )	( )

SALESFORCE

TYPE OF SALESFORCE

Does the competitor rely primarily on:
- Own salespeople   ( )
- Representatives   ( )
- Agents   ( )

QUALITY OF SALESFORCE

Does it require salespeople to have:
- Technical strengths   ( )
- Problem-solving abilities ( )
- Promotional skills   ( )

REWARDS

How does it reward performance?
- Salary only   ( )
- Salary and commission   ( )

How does commission work?
- Volume   ( )
- Share   ( )
- Margins   ( )

ORGANIZATIONAL EMPHASIS

Is salesforce organized around:
- Geography   ( )
- Product   ( )
- Application   ( )

TRAINING

What is the sales training situation? (of the salesforce)
- Periodic training   ( )
- Scheduled training   ( )
- Only if required   ( )
- No training   ( )

SERVICE

TIE TO PRODUCT SALES

Is the competitor's service:
- Bundled   ( )
- Unbundled   ( )

What is the purpose of its service?
- To enhance product sales   ( )
- To build customer confidence   ( )
- To generate income   ( )

What is the emphasis of its service?
- Presale   ( )
- Installation and training ( )
- Maintenance   ( )
- Repair   ( )

How does it control the quality and type of service provided?
- Provides its own service   ( )
- Uses franchised or authorized service agents   ( )
- Open-ended   ( )

Manufacturing Strategy

Now let's move on to the manufacturing strategy. This will include such issues as whether the company views itself as a producer or a provider, how and where the products are made, and the type of facilities, output, quality, flexibility, productivity, cost, and supply.

Producer or Provider?

The first issue is whether the competitor views itself as a producer or a provider. Some companies will only sell products that they make and are even backward integrated. This provides them with tight controls and, at times, with cost advantages. There are other companies that view themselves as providers of products. Thus they will purchase parts and assemble them or even source complete products for sale. IBM has different approaches for different products. In the mainframe computer arena, IBM has been a purist. It has used only its own products and software. It has been very integrated. This has often resulted in slow but strong response to competitors. In the personal-computer segment, IBM has viewed itself as a designer and a provider not a producer. It has sourced and assembled the integrated circuits, the printer, the cathode ray tube (CRT), and even the software.

How and Where
the Product Is Made

You should consider the following questions:

Location
- Is the product made in single-product or multiproduct plants?
- Is the product made in the United States? If so, in which states?
- Is the product made outside the United States? If so, where?

Type of Facilities
- Are the plants modern or antiquated?
- Is the plant expensive or inexpensive to operate? Why?

Capacity Strategy
- What is the state of processes, work flow, and so on? How often has full capacity been achieved?
- What is the level of capacity utilization desired?

Some companies are in a harvest mode and will run the plant above the desired level, often ignoring maintenance. This is a short-range approach but may be consistent. Building capacity in advance of demand and not worrying about maximum or even optimum utilization is another option. This is particularly powerful in long-cycle businesses where a quick follow is not feasible. It is like having money in the bank, ready when demand materializes. It is also powerful when inflation is high and replacement costs are rapidly accelerating. Quick response is the preference of others. This is a tough strategy to implement and can be impossible in long-cycle situations. Normally it can be done in industries that are not capital-intensive. Finally, you can lag demand. This ties with a harvest strategy and high capacity utilization.

Flexibility

Related to capacity is the degree of flexibility. At one time this was difficult to achieve if the desire was to maintain high volume levels. In the past, automation decreased flexibility while it increased fixed costs and raised break-even points. This has changed in recent years as programmable control systems have been installed. Robotics will also permit a trade-off between volume and flexibility. The Japanese have proved the feasibility of this approach.

Quality

Earlier I mentioned how quality affects the marketing and product-development elements of strategy. I mentioned how it must be considered when thinking through the nature and extent of provided services. There is no question that quality must be maintained at a certain level. The minimum is related to the users' expectations and needs. Further, it is related to the price and value of the product. Given this minimum, the question is whether the competitor is attempting to merely meet or exceed this.

If the competitor wishes to exceed the minimum, the question is by how much. If it has a goal of being the best, then the probing should move toward the means it has selected. The quality may be a result of its product design, the manufacturing processes it has selected, the nature and quality of materials and components, or its willingness to trade volume for quality. I have described the zero-defect approach used by the Japanese. This approach adds expense to the manufacturing process, since it forces a reduction of volume if quality standards are not being achieved. Further it may require closer tolerances in production and efficient, reliable, and cost-effective vendors. But all of this can be compensated by reduced failures and service calls in the field. As the reputation for quality is earned and known, the company may be able to demand a premium price or, if it desires, to increase share and volume.

Another means that has become common today is the use of automation and robotics. This was once perceived exclusively as a cost-cutting device and associated with productivity improvement. But it has proved to be equally powerful as a means of improving quality. Robots can be used in areas that are traditionally considered to be boring or hazardous. Boredom or fear have been major contributors to low productivity, high absenteeism, and poor work performance. Again, automation may have higher initial costs, but it can have lower total costs in the long haul.

Another quality strategy may be training- and development-oriented. The competitor may assure quality by having a well-trained workforce. Further, it may invest heavily in training the customer in order to improve satisfaction and quality of use.

Productivity and Cost

What is the competitor's relative cost and productivity position? This is an easy and logical question to ask but a tough one to answer. In fact, this is even tough to answer about your own company. It may be sufficient to merely know relative standing—high, medium, or low. Precise standing will be costly to determine. You can also consider the cost and productivity objective or goal of the competitor. Does it want to be the lowest-cost producer or is it satisfied with being average? Or perhaps cost doesn't appear to be a concern. Not being concerned may be okay for the short term, but as maturity occurs, such a position will not be viable.

You must also consider how cost position will be achieved. Will it be achieved through labor reduction, material substitution, process upgrade, improved yields, or moving to low-cost countries? Do these make sense in light of the total strategy and resources?

Supply

Where does the competitor stand with regard to supply of materials, components, or labor? If the answer is that is has obtained its own suppliers, in other words, that it has backward integrated, then you must ask why it has done so and whether this presents an opportunity or a threat. A common theme arises: Having your own salesforce, distribution, and so on is more expensive initially; potentially it could be less costly and could increase control. The same is true of supply. Relying on others can have advantages and disadvantages. On the positive side, a supplier may be more skilled and have the advantage of volume. On the negative side, there may be a risk of not getting prompt and timely delivery or a supplier may raise prices. If a component is critical to quality and price and availability is uncertain, backward integration makes sense. Normally, competitors have multiple approaches, with a combination of ownership and purchase.

Inventory and Readiness to Serve

Related to supply is the competitor's approach to inventory of in-process and finished goods. Some companies have extensive warehousing facilities and maintain large quantities of finished goods; this is expensive but can be effective if quick response is required. Warehousing can be particularly powerful when a market is growing and demand is high. Often it is the company with the product at hand that can gain share and increase sales. "Stock-outs," that is, not having the supply on hand when demanded, can be costly since the competitor may take and hold the share.

Key Questions

- Does the competitor have an extensive in-process, subcomponent, and finished goods warehousing network?
- Does the competitor try to have high, medium, or low readiness to serve?
- Is such action consistent with the company's investment strategy and strategic driver?

Financial Strategy

Now that you have a snapshot of the competitor's product, marketing, and manufacturing strategies, it is worth probing into how the competitor funds and controls expenditures and investments. Financial strategy includes the understanding of the mix between debt, equity, and retained earnings. Does the competitor rely on short- or long-term debt? Who are the debtors? What is the cost of servicing this debt?

In recent years, the rate of debt servicing has dramatically increased, and companies with large debts have had a mixed blessing. The cost is high, but they have paid off in inflated dollars. Some companies were fortunate to have lower-cost debt because they borrowed at favorable rates or had access to low-cost government loans or benefits. Other companies have decided to keep debt low and rely on equity or earnings. This is an excellent decision for a growth company that has high price earnings multiple (i.e., price of stock divided by earnings) and pays no dividend. In the past decade, a number of Japanese companies have spun off their growth businesses and financed them separately. This was a low-cost method of financing growth while retaining control. Of course in Japan the owners of stock tend to be financial institutions, and they will behave differently than the private and institutional buyers in the United States.

Equity has its advantages and disadvantages. The stockholder can be fickle, and the price/earnings ratio (P/E) can drop below the book value, thus making equity offering unattractive. There are a number of companies that have been buying up their stock and paying off debt, thus becoming semiprivate rather than public companies. This protects them against takeover and provides more flexibility, since they don't have to deal with the Wall Street analysts, who appear to be almost manic-depressive at times. Understanding the financial strategy can help to explain what may be seemingly irrational moves. For instance, if a company has decided to maintain a low debt/equity ratio, it may forgo growth and refuse to make investments for the future. If a company is seeking to raise its P/E and assumes that P/E is based on consistent earnings growth, it too may harvest rather than grow. However, it may also be considered a good risk, and when it goes to the debt market, it will get preferential treatment and terms. Of course, these are useless unless they will be used.

There has been a lot of work done recently to analyze the financing strategies of foreign-based multinationals. It has been found that they differ in a number of ways from their U.S. counterparts.

1. Since they are often owned by banks, they seek longer-term, consistent returns and this permits longer-term perspective and payoff.
2. They can set up reserves for contingencies, which reduces their tax rates.
3. They have access to pension reserves for reinvestment.
4. They spin off and finance growth businesses while maintaining control.

All of this impacts their hurdle rates (i.e., the percent of return expected in order to make the investment attractive) and expected rates of return.

Another part of financial strategy is the type of accounting that a company selects. For instance, does it use LIFO (last in first out) or FIFO (first in first out) to value inventory? LIFO deflates earnings but reduces taxes. FIFO has the opposite impact. Does it repatriate earnings from foreign affiliates or let them accrue?

Dividend policy is also important to track. Some blue chips will pay out 50 percent after tax and even borrow occasionally to do so. The venture companies have no payout. They retain all earnings. What is the method of payout? Is it in cash or stock?

People and Climate Strategies

The most important asset of any company is its people at all levels. Retaining, motivating, and developing key people may separate winners from losers. There are a number of options to the people strategy. Some companies have a "womb to tomb" mentality and policy. They will hire people directly out of school, train them, and seek to retain those who are vital to success. This has been the philosophy of a number of U.S. leaders like IBM, GE, GM, and Caterpillar. This is similar to being integrated, and it has similar rewards and risks. Other companies have a "hire and fire" mentality. They hire when needed, paying whatever they must and expecting no long-term loyalty. When things get bad, they "fire" again as a matter of course. This is like sourcing a product. It is highly temporal and lacking in permanence. What is the people policy of your competitor in the managerial and professional ranks?

Hourly workers are another dimension. They can either join or refuse to join a union. Again, there are a number of attitudes toward unions. Corporations often view unions as enemies and fight them continually. They resist unionization in the first place, and if decertification is possible, they will take action to deunionize. At times, unions are embraced and coexistence or peace is sought. In this case, the company believes that peace will support higher productivity and quality. The selection of these options will depend on the nature of the union and the industry. Some industries have aggressive unions, and contention is the only choice. This has been traditional for the auto and steel industries. There are some unions that are so dominant and some companies that are so weak that the situation is peaceful but expensive. This is often the situation in companies where the workers are represented by the Teamsters. These situations change but normally only because of unusual circumstances. Auto and steel unions have become more cooperative because of the significant losses imposed on the companies from competitive forces and market changes.

Another dimension of the people strategy is compensation and rewards. I mentioned this earlier in connection with the salesforce. But the issue is broader than that. How are employees paid at all levels and in all business aspects? People are motivated by pay, and the generality is to pay well as a reward for performance. But this is a generality, and again practices vary. Some companies base salaries on longevity. Certainly this is the Japanese model. Some pay considerable portions on bonuses. Bonuses can be paid on meeting specific business objectives or sales targets, meeting ratios like ROI, ROS, RONA, and so on. Some companies base salaries on position level in the organization. Workers often have a combination of base pay and incentive. There is not just one way. There is not just one answer.

Whatever system of compensation is used, it must be related to total strategy. Pay should relate to the business. It must be competitive, and the rules must be known. You cannot pay everyone in the same way if you believe in differentiated strategy. Growth through product innovation is a longer-term proposition. It is more risky, and so the people who work for such a company must be compensated differently. The question then is whether a compensation system makes sense for a particular company.

Development and training are other factors to consider. What is the long- and short-term commitment to the training of people? Certainly, a "womb to tomb" policy requires a continuous, planned development of people. It may be accomplished by having formal career planning, in-company schools, and even management or technical institutes. It may be contracted to others. It cannot be haphazard or unplanned. The "hire and fire" approach is different, and it will not require the same attention or investment, since a company with this policy will buy talent when it is required and discard it when it is not.

What I have been highlighting can be summarized by one word— "climate." What is the climate in the company? Is it one of fear and repression? Is it one of a benevolent dictatorship, or is it positive and understandable? Some companies prosper under all three climates, but each takes a different toll on the workforce. Fear and repression can work in businesses that are focused on cost and operations. They will not encourage creativity or risk taking. This is not a pleasant climate, and cooperation and trust will not be apparent. The benevolent dictatorship also works, but again it will inhibit openness and questioning. It is dependent on the skill and know-how of the dictator. If he or she is skilled, creative, and lucky, it will succeed. If not, the whole organization will go down together, often not knowing what really happened. The positive, open, and even to some degree contention-oriented climate is good if the market environment can permit mistakes, internal conflict, and to some degree entrepreneurial spirit. We need to ask the same questions here. What is going on, how well does it work, and will it change?

External Strategy

The final implementation strategy deals with the competitor's external policies and attempts to influence its environment. It may try to influence local, state, and federal governments, industrial leaders, and public opinion leaders. There are several approaches available. A competitor might be the leader and be very outspoken on certain issues. It might do this directly through print, audio, and visual media. For instance, Mobil Oil placed advertisements in all major newspapers articulating its stand on energy and other national issues. The use of institutional advertising is another popular approach. Lobbying is common among large companies and national institutions like the National Chamber of Commerce and, recently, the Business Roundtable. There are also trade and industry associations. In foreign countries it is quite normal for governments and companies to work closely in setting commercial and business policies. On the local scene, companies influence the community through sponsoring educational and cultural events and encouraging their executives to be active in organizations like school boards, the Red Cross, the United Fund, the Boy or Girl Scouts, and athletics. This promotes the image of businesspeople as concerned citizens. Of course other companies maintain a low presence or no presence at all. Participating in or giving to institutions or getting involved in government is not recognized or encouraged.

What are your competitor's policies in this category? Does it really matter, or is it of current or strategic value to be active or visible? Does it represent an opportunity or a threat? This latter question deserves some elaboration. Taking a stand or becoming a spokesperson can help build a positive image and can support a total strategy if the stand is well-conceived and implemented and also if it comes across as constructive and not defensive. The publications of the oil companies were construed by many as being self-serving and counter to public good. This may not have been true, but this type of action is related to perception, and it must be planned from this perspective. Thus, it may be dangerous if it is not effective. Taking a stand on an unpopular, controversial issue can have a major impact on a company. It could result in boycotts or open hostility. This kind of action can be lasting.

Review and Application

Asking these questions and describing your competitor's strategy will be of limited strategic value unless the evaluation is documented and analyzed. Further, each competitor must be compared with other competitors and with your own company.

The following illustration can be used to describe your competitors' strategies and your own. You can check the best descriptors and then provide supporting data as well as evaluate internal consistency.

Investment strategy and strategic driver			
Question	Competitor X	Competitor Y	Your company
What is the investment strategy?	Growth	Defense	Growth
Strategic driver?	Marketing/Distribution	Cost/Productivity	New product development

Product strategy			
Question	Competitor X	Competitor Y	Your company
Position?	Quick follower	Reluctant follower	Leader; evolutionary features
Where and how?	Own centralized development labs	Outside labs and other firms	Decentralized labs
Quality and reliability?	High quality and reliability	Satisfied with being the industry average	High quality and reliability
Where ideas come from?	User- and customer-focused	Internally oriented	Exensive research; anticipates users
How financed?	Business-unit financed	Business-unit financed	Corporate-financed
Selectivity and scope?	Highly selective in both depth and breadth	Selective; narrow but deep	Tends toward broad line; broad but not deep

Product strategy (*Cont.*)			
Question	Competitor X	Competitor Y	Your company
Degree of differentiation?	Tries for differentiation in appearance	Standardizations	Differentiated in performance; weak in styling
Evaluation:	Looks internally consistent, with possible exception of scope; may be too narrow for a distribution growth strategy and centralized labs may inhibit quick follow.	Consistent but vulnerable; a major innovation could route them.	Consistent, but may be too broad and not sufficiently deep.

Marketing strategy			
Question	Competitor X	Competitor Y	Your company
How sells?	Direct and some intermediaries	Intermediaries	Direct only
Retail?	Franchised, controlled retailers	Not controlled; only one can sell	Wholesale-focused; some selective retail
Size of salesforce?	2,000; 15 regional offices	50; no regionals	2,500; 25 regional offices
Type?	Technical background; extensive training	No training	Periodic training
Organization?	By region	By distribution	By region
Compensation?	High salary; no incentive	Incentive only	High salary; some incentive
Promotion?	Primarily local and coop ads; 5%/NSB; uses personalities as endorsers	Low budget; 1%/NSB	National and coop; 7%/NSB; product-focused.
Price?	Competitively priced	Cost-priced; desires high capacity utilization	Value-priced
Control?	Regional manager	Corporate-controlled	Corporate-controlled
Service?	Full service; incrementally priced	No service of its own; relies on dealers	Full service; incrementally priced; separate business unit

Marketing strategy (*Cont.*)			
Question	Competitor X	Competitor Y	Your company
Warranty?	120 days; parts and labor	30 days; parts only	90 days; parts only
Evaluation:	Strong approach; very tough and expensive approach.	Weak and more consistent with harvest than defense.	Expensive; training may be weak; look at warranty; could be vulnerable.

Manufacturing strategy			
Question	Competitor X	Competitor Y	Your company
Makes or sources?	Makes product	Makes product	Makes most; sources low end
Where?	Single-product plant in U.S.	Multi-product plant; not very synergistic	Single-product plant in U.S.
Type of plant?	Modern processes; old facility	Old processes and facility	Ultramodern; very efficient
Capacity utilization?	70% of 5,000 units; running at break-even	95% of 3,000 units; excess of break-even	60% of 8,000 units; underutilization intentional "in advance of demand"
Flexibility?	Not too flexible; locked into hard-wire automated system; run in lots	Inflexible	Flexible; use of robots
Quality?	Uses statistical quality control; "fix-later" mentality	Not quality-oriented	Seeking zero-defects; good standards
Cost/Productivity?	Lowest cost position	Low cost but volume sensitive	Highest cost but could be lower if volume achieved
Supply/Integration?	Highly integrated; no external suppliers of critical parts	No integration; multiple vendors; quality problems	Semi-integrated; tends to single-source
Inventory/Readiness	Extensive warehousing Strong inventory in advance	Few warehouses Stock-outs common	Moderate warehousing Conservative inventory

Manufacturing strategy (*Cont.*)			
Question	Competitor X	Competitor Y	Your company
Evaluation:	Consistent but vulnerable in flexibility and quality.	Consistent but vulnerable; could be problem if volume is lost.	Consistent but vulnerable in supply; needs more volume and must review inventory practices.

Financial strategy			
Question	Competitor X	Competitor Y	Your company
Debt/Equity?	80/20; highly leveraged	50/50	20/80
Debtors?	Large banks; long-term loans and bonds; 8% average interest	Mixed; short-term, high-interest (15%) loans	A few large banks; high-interest (15%) loans
Accounting?	LIFO	FIFO	LIFO
Evaluation:	Strong even though leveraged.	Moderate; high interest could be a problem.	Moderate; high interest could be less of a problem than for Competitor Y.

People and climate strategies			
Question	Competitor X	Competitor Y	Your company
Philosophy?	Hire young; train own; seek retention	"Hire/fire"	Mix between "womb to tomb" and "hire/fire"; has been changing and moving toward "hire/fire"
Hourly workers?	No union	No union	Some union but not militant
Compensation and rewards?	Seeks to reward for performance; salaries mostly above industry average	Not consistent; will buy talent when necessary but also will not raise salaries unless necessary	Highly incentive-oriented; Pays for performance, but it is "what have you done lately"

People and climate strategies (*Cont.*)			
Question	Competitor X	Competitor Y	Your company
Development and training?	Extensive training; excellent career planning and development	No training	Good training but relies on outside institutes
Evaluation:	Strong but expensive; might be too inbred.	Weak and highly vulnerable.	Moderate; not sure it is best case for growth and production-innovation strategy.

External strategy			
Question	Competitor X	Competitor Y	Your company
Position?	Not visible; does not take stands on issues	Reactive and at times has had problems; very antigovernment and antilabor	Selective; trying to develop a dignified image
Approach?		Lobbies; uses publications	Strong local support of cultural activities
Evaluation:	Inconsistent; you would expect more public image building.	Highly vulnerable.	Consistent; good image builder.
Overall evaluation:	Strong competitor; has a few weaknesses that could be targeted but will fight hard.	Weak; could be knocked out; won't fight too hard.	Needs to correct some inconsistencies.

Other Uses

This type of analysis can surface the inconsistencies of the competitor. The marketing strategy may not fit the investment strategy and the strategic driver, and so that strategy and its implementation may fail. Through analysis you may find a means of taking advantage of the inconsistency. You can also use this analysis to spot the industry standard in each functional area and see how you compare. Suppose everyone else sells directly and you use manufacturers' representatives. You may be providing more flexibility and an opportunity to increase share at little expense—a competitive advantage at little cost.

8 Strategy Review and Development

Throughout this book, I have urged you to apply the concepts immediately and determine the strategic implications. If you have followed my advice, you will have a number of useful insights, but your overall view may still be unfulfilling and incomplete. In this chapter, I would like to review the various techniques and then pull them all together to clarify, reinforce, and demonstrate how this system can be of use in reviewing and developing strategies.

Review of the Techniques

Battlefield and Users' Analysis

The first analysis reinforces the need to understand your product's users, the individuals, institutions, or groups for which your company exists and without which it will be unsuccessful. I am not talking about consumers unless you sell directly to users. Customers may be intermediaries, and these were discussed earlier. The strategic questions emphasize the needs and wants of the user and emphasize that these may change. What is the function provided by the product for the users? How satisfied are the users? If there are deficiencies, what are they? Do they vary from one user group to another? Do your direct competitors or your indirect competitors do a better or worse job than you? Are there emerging technologies or approaches that do a better job now or could do a better job in the future?

All these questions require you to define the competition in the broadest possible way so you won't get lost in the middle too early. They encourage you to think about indirect competition and new substitutes and to construct a "battlefield" map. And the concept of life cycles for businesses forces an often reluctant recognition of temporalness—that is, that all products and services grow old and can be replaced.

Total Industry Analysis

The next analysis, the total industry analysis, forces you to make an assessment of what is going on around you. It requires a look to the sides, to the aft, and to the fore, and the results give you a macroview of the industry. In essence, total industry analysis probes what you know about the objectives, goals, strategies, and needs of those that sell to your customers, of those that supply the components, parts, and materials, and of those that are your intermediaries, retailers, and distributors. It is normal to underestimate the threat from some of these groups and just consider them as allies or associate participants and not as real or potential competitors. This may lead to surprise and, if completely ignored, may lead to disaster. The strategic questions are: What are the current objectives and strategies of your suppliers and distributors or of those that serve the market with complementary products? How well are these companies doing? If successful, how will they continue to grow? If there are few growth opportunities in their own situations, then what is necessary to determine the options that are open to them? What are the economics? Who makes the most money, you or them? Are the success factors changing, and does this help them or you? Have there been a lot of mergers? Have the demographics of competition changed? Are these companies undervalued and therefore targets of the greedy? Do your strategies or strengths threaten them?

These questions force a recognition that reality can change, that is, that today's friend or ally may be tomorrow's foe. After analyzing the situation, you may decide to become more integrated yourself and to increase your scope and product offering—major changes in strategy!

Analysis of Competitor Demographics

In the next analysis, you move more closely to your direct and existing competition. First you become a "demographer" not only of customers or users but of the competition. You identify the specialist and the multi-industry companies and the local and the multinational companies. Life cycle is important here, too, because as the industry matures, the demographics often move from specialist to generalist to specialist and possibly from domestic to multinational to domestic.

The strategic questions are: What has the nature of the competition been in the past? What type of company has dominated? What is the current situation? What will it be five years from now? Ten years from now?

These questions are geared to anticipating changes in the rewards, risks, and overall aggressiveness of the situation. The nature of competition influences expectations, defensiveness, the ability to finance and participate in growth, and the success factors.

Analysis of
Winners and Losers

You now move to an analysis of past, present, and future winners and losers. You need to determine the criteria to be used. The multinational will have a different set of criteria than the pure domestic competitor; the multi-industry, than the specialist; the conglomerate, than the single entrepreneur. Having determined the meaning of success, you now sort out and categorize the winners and losers. When the listing is complete, you ask: Why did some companies succeed while others failed? Was success a result of resources, initial position, management, or chance? All of these characteristics can influence and separate winners from losers. What is likely to change that will make tomorrow's listing different from today's? This change may be a result of interaction between different parts of environment, change in resources, or the result of harvesting or not replenishing the resources. The output is a listing of past, present, and future success factors.

Success factors are the variables for measurement and are important for comparison of current and potential competitors with each other and with you. How well do you compare? Are you stronger or weaker in technology, marketing, production, and finance? For each firm, do the strengths outweigh the limitations? Will these continue to hold? Are limitations or weaknesses fatal flaws? If so, is this recognized?

In-Depth Analysis

This assessment leads to the final assessment, namely an in-depth description of the competitor's strategies and programs. What is the key competitor's investment strategy and strategic driver for each part of the company, that is, its portfolio analysis? What are the implementation strategies for the segment that competes directly with you? This probes into the supporting programs in marketing, production, finance, product design and development, and management. Inconsistent or unrealistic strategies are the key reasons for failure. Saying one thing and doing something else or not having the resources to follow the game plan results in failure.

So what I have prescribed is a total look at competition. If properly used, this will help you:

- Avoid surprises
- Develop options
- Surface real strengths
- Identify inconsistencies that may ultimately cause defeat for the competitor

Case Studies

Enough review and preaching! Let's turn to some cases that can be used to assure complete understanding and improved applications. I will use a variety of cases to do the job. First, a look at a machine tool company that is small and that is in a long-cycle, traditionally cyclical, and matured market that is undergoing changing competition and that has the potential for significant growth. In the second case, we will look at a local bank that is strong in its traditional market but is facing significant changes and must evaluate its position in a bigger but more risk-prone market. In the third case, we will focus on an exciting growth market—personal computers. In the fourth case, we will deal with a local retailer.

Each case will be hypothetical, though the environment and competitive moves will be realistic. My objective is to show how you can take all of the analyses I have just described and use them to test what you are doing and what needs to be changed. I am using hypothetical situations to avoid the problem of arguing about specific companies and their internal environments. This would be counterproductive.

CASE I   Worldwide Machine Tool Company

This company manufactures cutting and shaping tools that are used by many steel and metal industries. It is located in the Midwest, is family-owned, and is traditionally very profitable. It has a nonunion workforce and has been highly paternalistic. The company has been specialized and niche-oriented. It has sold both to other equipment companies that have incorporated their products into large systems and directly to large user companies. The company's traditional assets have been customer relations and a strong reputation for quality. It has never been an innovator, preferring to be a follower that improves on new features, which enhances its reliability. It never has dealt with distributors but does have its own service organization that responds quickly when in need. Thus, the situation has been very benign, and the company is content with its performance. There is no apparent desire to change. Sound familiar? Success is often a tranquilizer.

Now let's assume that you have been hired as the new strategic planner or, if you prefer, that you have just returned from a management seminar. You figure that it may be worthwhile to think about the competitors.

Users

You start thinking about the user of your equipment and the function the equipment provides. You are in the "hole making" and "cutting/trimming" business. The equipment you sell enables the automobile and appliance companies to make holes in metal and then shape and trim the pieces. Precision is not that important, but it is important that the equipment perform well. You know the major users well and have discussed their problems with them. They find the equipment satisfactory. It does the job, and the equipment you sell is among the best. However, the users say that they would like to increase speed and that the drills and shapers are often inhibitors to increasing speed. Thus, if you had a chart, you would note, "Increase speed" as a desired objective. But this is not new, and it has not inhibited growth in the past. However, it does make you start thinking about new technologies that could do a better, faster job. Lasers and ultrasound come to mind. There are laser guns that can drill and shape very fast and that use a lot less energy and power—another concern of the users. Lasers are not new, but there have been a number of new systems, and it has been a major technology priority for the Japanese and Germans. Another item to note would be, "Laser is a potential substitute." You now ask yourself if there are other external factors that could make the use of lasers more attractive. Yes, there are several you recall. Both major user groups are under considerable pressure to improve productivity and quality. The U.S. auto manufacturers have been losing share in the United States and in Europe. The Japanese have been able to increase productivity and quality while making design and performance improvements. Partly this is because they have invested in modern equipment, including robots, which are used for the routine, tedious jobs like drilling, shaping, and turning. There has also been an increased use of laser and sonic machines. Thus, you have additional confirmation that new technology is likely to be accepted by your customers. The appliance industry has not felt the onslaught of the MNC's aggressiveness and penetration, but this is expected to happen. They are striving to improve productivity and quality because of increased U.S. competition and continuing inflationary increases that cannot be recouped in price.

Another factor is changes in the tax investment laws. The U.S. government has increased depreciation schedules, thus encouraging more replacement. Further, the ability of financially strong firms to buy and then lease back to those unable to buy on their own encouraged even the profitless and struggling companies to replace obsolete equipment. The need for increased productivity and quality combined with a more favorable tax climate has made the machinery markets highly attractive and has stimulated growth. But it has also encouraged the entry of MNCs and companies pushing the more innovative, state-of-the-art equipment. You make a notation: "Grow top of line." A counteractivity also comes to mind, the increasing movement of U.S. producers to manufacture offshore rather than in the United States. Many of your U.S. customers have decided to move to lower-cost countries. This has reduced the size of traditional U.S. markets and has positioned the Japanese and, recently, the Koreans to be able to gain share. You make another notation: "Declining growth in traditional markets."

Finally, as you think about customers, you recognize the inevitability of increased concentration. There will be fewer but larger companies in the auto and appliance fields. Mergers will continue between offshore and U.S. producers. This will change the location where products are produced and will be supportive of the offshore movement noted before. But there is another aspect—namely, a number of the auto and appliance firms in Japan and Europe have subsidiaries and are affiliated with machine tool companies. This is the first sign of a customer that will potentially become a competitor.

This illustration demonstrates how an assessment of users can lead to a number of insights about the need to change the product offering, the entry of new competition, and even the decline or growth of segments.

Macroview

The supplier is a second group to analyze from a competitive view. There are two groups of suppliers worthy of analysis—the control manufacturers and the suppliers of cutting materials. Your evaluation of the major companies in both of these categories results in a recognition that they are constrained in terms of growth. They are thinking about moving from the component-supplier status to the total-systems position. They are being driven by the desire to offer more value and to provide solutions to problems. This is supported by the users' preferences to deal with one company and have a solution-oriented supplier. The foreign manufacturers are already in this position.

Notation: Suppliers are likely to forward integrate.

Distributors, on the other hand, are not a threat, even though they also recognize the need to offer total systems. The reason for the lack of a threat is that the distributors are small, undercapitalized, and historically weak.

Notation: Distributors are unlikely to backward integrate.

Even though you have thought about substitute technologies and the potential forward integration of suppliers, there is the need to evaluate other new entries. In this case, it is companies that sell communications and data-processing equipment to the offices of your customers. It is another system offering that may permeate your markets. Companies selling these systems are acquiring factory-equipment companies in order to sell compatible equipment that will permit them to move from the office to the factory.

Notation: The threat is mergers and total office and factory systems.

Demographics

Armed with the type of analysis I have just described and the notations, you can now draw your demographic profile. You should use three separate diagrams—one for the past, one for the present, and one for the future (Exhibit 8-1).

You decide that the most meaningful split would be component supplier, systems supplier, and multi-industry firm for the scope and focus, and U.S., foreign, and multinational for the geographic perspective. This is different than what was described in Chapter 5, since it is designed for this company's industry. The systems supplier category is very relevant and may be the key to future success, since it appears to couple with user needs and the strategic thrust of new and existing competition.

An analysis of the demographic profile charts in Exhibit 8-1 demonstrates the changes we just described. In the past, the competitors were all component and subsystems companies, with the largest share controlled

	Component Supplier	Systems Offer	Multi-Industry		Component Supplier	Systems Offer	Multi-Industry		Component Supplier	Systems Offer	Multi-Industry
U.S.	A,B, C,D				A,B	D			You 15%		
Foreign	F				G,H						
Multinational	B B					C	E				E,I,J 85%
		Past				Present				Future	

Exhibit 8-1. Demographic profile—past, present, and future.

by the U.S.-based component specialist. These companies were family-controlled, highly focused on quality, and not very innovative. Each company carved out a niche and was content to stay within its confines. Each was highly reactive to threats, and when competitors invaded, the company beat them back. Customers were content with this situation, and the environment was peaceful and benign.

The second chart shows the current situation. The major share of the market remains within the control of the two largest U.S. producers, of which you are one. Competitor C has become part of a multinational systems-oriented company. Foreign Competitor D has also increased scope and now provides a systems offering. Competitor E has become part of a multi-industry conglomerate that also makes autos, and it has become both an internal supplier and a more aggressive worldwide competitor. It has also picked up considerable strength in electronics and is now recognized as an innovator. Competitor F could not make it and has exited from the U.S. market, having decided to concentrate exclusively on Europe. There are two new companies that have started to penetrate (G and H), but both appear to be unprepared and primarily opportunistic. A little later I will discuss the implications of these changes on the success factors.

The third chart illustrates the future projections—an entirely new situation. All of the components companies, except your company, will either provide systems or be part of multi-industry conglomerates. The forecast is even more disturbing, since 85 percent of the market will be controlled by multi-industry and multinational companies, and you anticipate your share will decline to 15 percent of the available market. Further, because all except your company will provide systems or be part of a multi-industry company, they may have a way to trade off more profitable components or businesses to compensate for losses in your market or component. You will also recall that a combination of foreign or multinational with multi-industry can result in a very flexible, even cavalier, type of competitor.

Notation: A tougher competitive climate will materialize, and it may be less profitable.

Winners and Losers

Determining the characteristics that distinguish the winners from the losers will yield insights about strategy and about how you might wish to change. It is clear from the assessments you have already made that in the past the winners were those companies that specialized in components. They developed strong relations with the original equipment manufacturers. These companies were skilled at providing electromechanical controls and quality tools and bits. They were not interested in systems. The success factors continue to be the same in the present, but they will be quite different in the future. The market leaders will clearly be those that are in the direct-marketing situation and that are willing to be in total systems. But there will probably be room for one or two specialists. This is based on observations of other companies in other industries. Specialists can survive even if all the others become systems suppliers.

In-Depth Analyses of Some Competitors

Competitor C— A Multinational Systems Supplier

This company has been in the business for over fifty years. It started as a smaller manufacturer of tools in Germany, and after World War II, it started to move worldwide. It uses joint ventures, manufacturing associates, and licensees and is very strong in Europe and increasingly aggressive in the United States. It moved into the systems business via its own development and a few selective acquisitions. It is proud of its reputation and is dedicated to being a worldwide leader. Its strategies can be summarized as follows:

Investment Strategy
Aggressive growth (particularly in the United States).

Strategic Driver
Systems innovation and increased application.

Implementation Strategies
Production Strategy Innovation and applications extension via its own self-development and in its own development labs. Has opened productivity applications centers in Europe and the United States.

Marketing Strategy Direct selling, with its own well-trained salesforce. Will provide extensive front-end and follow-up services. Prices for value but will bundle all services. Committed to making machinery system work.

Production Strategy Builds the majority of key components in a modern, automated facility outside Berlin. Has fabrication and assembly plants in many countries.

Financial Strategy Family-owned and not concerned with stock market fluctuations. The family has been willing to reinvest in the business and to take its rewards by developing its net worth and providing good-paying jobs for family members. It has strong governmental contacts and has used government incentives and funds when available. In its worldwide developments, the company has used partnerships in order to gain acceptance and also to capitalize on the host governments' interests and incentives. In the United States, the company has used its own funds for the most part. Though exact data is scarce and not easily available, it is considered that the company is financially strong and will continue to be so.

Management Strategy Highly paternalistic, and the top job could be described as nepotistic. The family, however, has been willing to accept changes. It uses professional consultants and has sent the younger generations to the best business and technical schools.

Summary—Competitor C

Positive	Negative
• Has commitment	• But may be too inbred
• Innovates	• But may be too internalized
• Has marketing strengths (applications)	
• Has financial strength	• But may be too conservative

Notation: Will continue to be tough but may be vulnerable in its desire to remain in complete control. May provide a model for expansion.

Competitor E—Industrial Equipment Division of a Multi-industry, Multinational, Japanese-Based Company

This competitor is part of a multibillion-dollar company, or *zaibatsu*, that includes mining, steel, autos, electronics, and industrial equipment. The *zaibatsu* has a number of separate companies, but they are interlocked and centrally controlled. It appears to have a major interest in focusing on electronics and specialized marketing. It is deemphasizing steel and autos but has no intention of getting out or harvesting. Industrial equipment has been mostly focused on providing innovative equipment that can enable the other companies in the *zaibatsu* to improve productivity and quality. About ten years ago, over 90 percent of the sales of the industrial equipment division were made to the other divisions. As the division began to increase the use of electronics and offer robots, the percent of sales to companies outside the *zaibatsu* has increased, and today only about 50 percent of sales are internal within the multinational corporation. It appears that this trend will continue. The strategies of the industrial equipment division can be summarized as follows:

Investment Strategy
Aggressive growth.

Strategic Driver
Electronics-based innovation.

Implementation Strategies

Product Strategy It continues to innovate, using the know-how of its electronics division and its own robotics capability. It makes customized equipment for other parts of the *zaibatsu*, and when the equipment is perfected, it then offers it to other companies. This assures high quality and also a strong cost position. The timing may lag as much as five years. This has not been a disadvantage in the past, but could be in the future, since developments are moving rapidly.

Marketing Strategy It uses its own applications and marketing teams, which include salespeople, technologists, and industry experts. It is highly focused on auto and steel but is moving into other industries. It uses a trading company that is part of the *zaibatsu* to sell in other parts of the world. This permits it to trade goods as well as sell directly. It does not have a consistent pricing practice. It will price or develop any terms that it takes, if it wants the order. It will use independent service companies as well as other partners.

Production Strategy All factories are in Japan, and products are assembled there. The company is planning some U.S. production, but this will be focused on robotics alone. It has a strong but not militant union. This has resulted in good wage settlements but without strikes. Quality has been good. There is excess capacity, but this fits their desired utilization rate of 80 percent.

Financial Strategy The parent company has a strong financial position and has ample purchasing and debt capacity. This specific division was a spin-off specialist company and is listed on the national stock exchange. This has permitted growth without an erosion of the total company's rating.

Management Strategy The management of the division is skilled in the industrial electronics market and is knowledgeable about the type of customers and the needs and problems they have. The managers are long-service employees and are highly regarded by the corporate management team. The reward system has permitted them to gain personally but also to take a long-term perspective, which is typical of the Japanese.

Summary—Competitor E

- Strong commitment
- Highly aggressive
- Electronics and robotics know-how
- Dedicated marketing
- Tie with trading company
- Modern efficient manufacturing (but union could become militant if profits decline)

EXHIBIT 8-2 Worldwide Machine Tool Company

Current Situation and Strategy:
- A specialized, niche-oriented company
- Sells to other equipment companies and some large users
- Follower but improver—emphasis on reliability and quality
- Has its own service organization

Analytical techniques	Notations	Strategic implications
User assessment Automobiles Consumer appliances	Current equipment satisfactory. Would like more speed. Laser and ultrasound are possible new approaches. Need productivity and quality improvement. Change in investment tax laws encourage modernization.	Opportunity to become leader. Possibility of licensing. Develop "top of line." Erosion of market share inevitable. Concentration inevitable.
Supplier evaluation Control manufacturers Suppliers of cutting materials	Suppliers recognize they are constrained in growth.	Suppliers will forward integrate. Must be prepared.
Distributor evaluation	Small, undercapitalized. Will become obsolete.	Distributors will not backward integrate. Likely to decrease in importance.
Substitution/new entries	Office communications/information companies are moving into the factory, making acquisition.	Systems are vital and will become part of an office/factory interconnection.
Demographics Systems category is vital to assessment	Was specialist-dominated industry. Will be a systems, multi-industry, multinational-dominated industry.	Anticipate share erosion. Your company will be only specialist. More competition, less profitability.
Winners and losers	Past: Specialist that sold to OEMS. Present: Specialist still OEM-oriented but changing. Future: Direct, user-oriented, provides systems, but there may be a place for one niche-oriented component specialist.	Changes forces questioning of the viability of remaining in the components, domestic-only category.
In-depth analysis Competitor C	Will be tough. May be vulnerable because of desire to remain in control.	
Competitor E	Strong, dedicated, committed to market. Will gain share.	Might be a way to tie with Competitor E to hold or even gain share.

- Flexible financing
- Long-term management
- Rewards in tune with strategy

Notation: A strong, dedicated competitor that is committed to this market. Will do whatever is necessary to gain share and be the winner.

Strategic Implications

Now that you have assessed the total situation and all aspects of the competitive scene, you can determine how and to what degree you need to change your strategy.

All the analyses agree that in the future it will be a systems market and that unless this is included in the total strategy, it will be a "no-win" situation. The current strategy does not seem viable unless alliances are formed with either the suppliers or one of the multinational, multi-industry competitors, such as Competitor E. There is an opportunity to license, joint venture, merge, or sell out. Harvesting is only a short-term solution, and timing is important. If the company waits too long, its position will be eroded and it won't be able to sell off.

Obviously, there is more to strategy development than competitor analysis, but this illustration should demonstrate without a doubt that it is vital to assessing current strategy and identifying options. The illustration (Exhibit 8-2) is generic, and I have not tried to use one particular company, but it represents what is happening in a number of markets and industries. Consumer electronics has a number of similar examples. The television set is moving from being a self-contained entertainment system. The television receiver companies recognize this and are moving to tie in with videotape, videodisc, telephone networks, and personal computers. The office typewriter and copier are no longer stand-alone components but are now part of a word processor and duplicating system and will ultimately be tied in with electronic mail systems. How does this situation compare to yours? If it is similar, have you examined your strategy and determined if it will continue to be viable?

CASE II   Mid-American National Bank

As I pointed out in an earlier chapter, financial institutions are experiencing a revolution and most are unprepared. The old game plan of obtaining funds at low rates and loaning at high rates was completely changed in the 1970s. The traditional savings and loan associations and mutual savings banks were shocked to find themselves having large portfolios of long-term, low-interest-bearing mortgages and being forced to pay high interest on many new instruments like certificates of deposit. Inflation and competition have taken their toll, and the end is still not in sight. The FDIC and state regulators have been forced to merge weak banks with stronger banks.

Let's assume you are the chairman or chairwoman of the board of a medium-sized bank in Detroit. The bank is over seventy years old and has a solid reputation. It has been well managed and is conservative. The managers have developed an excellent rapport with customers and been good citizens. The bank has expanded the number of branches and responded to changes in the federal and state banking regulations. It has had a strong portfolio, and it has been traditionally split about 50 percent for business, commercial, and industry and 50 percent for consumers. As with most banks, it has paid low salaries but has been able to attract and retain a number of skilled people.

Users

The major business clients have been the automotive companies and their hundreds of suppliers. The situation these suppliers are in is similar to the situation the suppliers of the Worldwide Machine Tool Company are in. They are going though a long-term cyclical downturn and have low profits. I won't elaborate on the changes that have been occurring, except to say that the customers have had significant financial problems and have required extensive loans that have become increasingly risky. Our hypothetical bank has been forced to participate in the consortiums that were formed to save Chrysler and to provide liquidity for Ford. Both of these giants have been good customers and have had a policy of spreading their funds around. The major problems have been the suppliers of smaller parts and components. Many of these have gone bankrupt and have been merged with other companies. These traditionally low-risk customers have also been forced to borrow from other companies, including insurance companies, and to obtain municipally backed bonds.

The results of all these changes have been a new risk profile and a much more competitive climate. In addition, the business user has required more global services. This has been a result of the increased manufacturing offshore and the coupling with international suppliers. This need has provided an opportunity for a number of foreign banks to get a share of the auto and auto-supplier banking business—another competitive change. As you examine the future, it is apparent that your bank must be able to finance, obtain letters of credit on a global basis, and make high-risk decisions rapidly. This is not a very pleasant forecast.

Notation: Business clients are demanding more favorable terms on a global basis. Foreign banks are a threat.

Another significant user group is the local merchants. They include large department stores, discounters, and numerous small, independent retailers. These customers have also changed in the past decade. In the 1960s, they were locally owned and in many cases family-owned businesses. The key to success was having a strong relationship that included personal as well as commercial banking. In the 1970s, many of the businesses were merged with national chains and taken over by more aggressive, nonlocal merchants. Loyalty declined, and decisions were based on purely economic grounds. This meant quick decisions to provide hundreds of thousand dollar loans or lines of credit and at highly competitive low interest rates. Personal financing was separated from commercial, and the friendly bank image declined as an asset.

The merchants allied themselves with the "bank card" syndicates, and the bank was forced to have both a MasterCard and a Visa credit card affiliation. Both were unprofitable and resulted in new losses and more automation. The "debt" card is coming, and if the bank wishes to keep these accounts, it will also be required to have banking machines in the merchants' stores. This is expected to be expensive and will require more "funds-transfer" equipment and personnel.

Notation: All of this raises the issue as to whether this group of customers is worth keeping.

A related group is the individual consumers, who want checking and savings accounts as well as mortgages, personal loans, and auto financing—a large, expensive group to serve. Consumers have required full-service banking with an emphasis on convenience. This has resulted in increased banking hours, more branches, more "automatic tellers," a multiplicity of accounts, and increased frustration as the percent of over-withdrawals and mortgage defaults has increased. Teller turnover has also been a problem. In addition, the consumer has been more willing to transfer accounts and use "nonbankers" to provide savings and financial services. These have included Sears, American Express, Merrill Lynch, and numerous mutual funds. I will discuss these types of competitors in more detail later.

As you look at the future, individual consumers will have more sophistication and be increasingly tough to deal with. They will want to do more banking, shopping, and investing at home. This will require even more technology and will cause associated problems. It will enable more companies to get into the savings and credit business and permit more movement of funds.

Notation: Consumers will be tougher and more costly to serve. The barriers to entry will decline while the cost of participating will increase.

A review of all the user changes may make you wonder whether it is really worthwhile being in the financial service business. The key is financial services versus banking services. The market will force you to become a financial services company not a banker.

Macroview

An analysis of suppliers may seem to be unnecessary because the supplier of funds is either the customers I just described or the federal government. However an analysis of these areas can provide some additional competitive insights. There are many new sources of funds that have developed over the past decade. These are highlighted by the funds from the oil-rich countries, like Kuwait and Saudi Arabia, that are seeking ways of investing huge sums of money. These countries could become competitors, given the globality of the market and product competition. These countries may acquire banks or initiate new institutions or means of providing funding. However, in this illustration you might not wish to deal with this issue or trend unless one of the large customers like Chrysler was acquired by a foreign government. The federal, state, and local governments are also competitors for funds and for customers. This has become obvious as the debt and the debt requirements of the government have increased interest rates, and many banks have keyed their interest rates to the treasury note rates. Thus, an understanding of the government may be vital to future success. Again, however, let's assume it is beyond the bank's planning needs.

Notation: Many new sources of funds. How can the bank get its share?

Demographics

Even though we are dealing with a service, it is relevant and useful to use such categories as specialist, multi-industry, and conglomerate to describe the product and service scope, and regional, national, and global to differentiate the geographic scope. This would not have been the case a decade ago, since banks were regional and were isolated from the competitive moves of the conglomerate or multi-industry company. These profiles are only meant to illustrate the use of the concept in identifying competitive moves (Exhibit 8-3).

The profiles reinforce what we have described earlier. Just a decade ago all the competitors were in the regional bank category because of regulations, and they had a more unique role than different types of financial institutions. This has already changed slightly as banks have moved from a regional to a national basis. Bank E was merged with another institution because E was on the verge of going into bankruptcy. As you think about the future, you can forecast that Bank D will go out of existence and five new larger financial institutions will become major competitors. K and L are both foreign banks that are moving into the region. This is a result of the changing nature of the automobile industry and some of its key suppliers. As the companies are merged or acquired by their multinational competition, the foreign banks will have direct access to the U.S. market— a phenomenon not clearly understood within the industry or even by the state and federal regulators. Two additional competitors will be national, multi-industry companies, such as American Express, Control Data, and Sears. There will also be conglomerate-type competitors, such as Gulf & Western. Note the inclusion of insurance companies, a piano company, major retailers, loan companies, an aerospace company, a computer company, and even a steel company.

What does this mean to our hypothetical bank? First of all, the way business will be conducted in the future is likely to be very different. It will be much more aggressive and tough-minded. The foreign banks will have different sources of income and will be willing to make loans in order to increase share and gain a stronger foothold in the United States. Further, they will have an excellent capability of exchanging worldwide currencies, rapidly granting credit in remote parts of the world, and, through their trading companies, even providing third-party or direct bartering.

The multi-industry companies may also provide financing in conjunction with and to support product sales. They may also be able to use tax credits or trades to enable them to justify credit or loans, which a traditional bank may find unacceptable. The conglomerate may not be in the game for the long haul, and if things get rough, it may dump.

Notation: Need to be able to participate worldwide and offer global financing. Need to track the multi-industry competitors to determine their profit objectives.

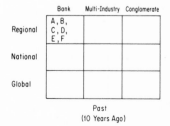

	Bank	Multi-Industry	Conglomerate	Bank	Multi-Industry	Conglomerate	Bank	Multi-Industry	Conglomerate
Regional	A, B, C, D, E, F			A, B, C, D,			A, B, C		
National				E, G			E, G	H, I	J
Global							K L		
	Past (10 Years Ago)			Present			Future (10 Years Ahead)		

Exhibit 8-3. Business and industry segment—past, present, and future.

Winners and Losers

As I mentioned, the successful banker in the past was the one who was tied into the local community, had good contacts, and could be decisive in a timely manner. This was particularly true in the commercial, industrial, and business segments. The government regulated the industry and thus limited competition to the way the services were packaged and sold. The consumer segments were more dependent on convenience and a feeling of personal concern and security. Profit was made by getting cheap funding and selling it as high as possible. The industry was genteel and dignified.

The deregulation of the industry and the entry of new types of competitors, including retailers, have changed the success factors and will likely change them further in the future. In the business and commercial segments, the winners are likely to be those that can provide a full array of services on a worldwide basis. Timing has become more crucial and is often achieved by having a sophisticated information and communications network that permits the business user to instantaneously evaluate its financial position and options, to borrow or repay funds, and to keep the earning power of its assets at a high level. If the business needs to transfer funds on a worldwide basis, then it is important that this can be done efficiently and rapidly. In addition, the business user is looking for expertise in how to invest or use funds in the optimum way. Obviously, the packaging of the deal and confidence in the financial institution remain important but less so than in the past.

Although the consumer still wants convenience, security, and concern, his or her expectations of speed, accuracy, and availability of options will increase. This means you will need the ability to provide more banking and investment services at home and at the consumer's convenience.

Notation: This analysis emphasizes the need to be innovative and technology-oriented so as to be able to allow users maximum flexibility and the ability to make informed choices.

In-Depth Analyses of Some Competitors

In this case, you decide to focus on those competitors that are not well known to you. First you look at one of the national banks—First Bank of the East. Next you study and highlight one of the large multi-industry companies—the retailer turned financier. Finally you review the multinational bank.

As before, you will focus on those strategic characteristics that may force or permit a change of strategy. Your intent is to decide if you must change strategy or if you can merely use your current approach in a different way.

Further, you may be able to use one or several of these competitors as allies rather than adversaries.

Competitor E—
First Bank of the East

This is a bank with multibillion-dollar assets, and it is one of the ten largest banks in the world. It has focused on very large companies and even participated in grant loans to foreign governments. Since regulations have changed, the bank has moved into many states and has made several acquisitions. It was able to increase its presence in your region by making an acquisition of a relatively weak, overextended bank. In fact, the state banking commissioner was instrumental in closing this deal.

Investment Strategy

Aggressive Growth Has clearly stated that it wants to be number one or two in the nation by 1986.

Strategic Driver

Regional expansion via acquisition and merger. Has made several acquisitions in the past three years.

Implementation Strategies

Primarily focused on marketing and acquisitions. There is nothing unique in its products or ability to supply funds. Has a very well-known chief executive who is also strong in national politics. He has been a driving force in several business institutions and serves on the board of one of your large accounts.

Notation: A strong competitor, dedicated to enhancing its position in the region. No way to become an ally.

Competitor H—A National Retailer

This is a company that is one of the largest retailers in the United States, with revenues in excess of $20 billion and assets over $25 billion. It is Midwest-based and has been a customer in the past. Starting in retailing, the company began in the financial services business through liability and auto insurance to consumers and in small businesses via its retail stores. It moved into life insurance and securities and acquired a savings and loan and, recently, a brokerage house. It has not been in international or U.S. commercial banking or leasing, but it appears headed in this way as the regulations change.

Investment Strategy

Prime thrust is in the consumer financial services, but it has a secondary thrust aimed at the commercial and industrial services area.

Strategic Driver

Combination of aggressive marketing and full-service offering. "Convenience—one-stop banking" is its theme.

Implementation Strategies

Product Strategy A full offering of financial services to all users includes securities, cash management, investment management, underwriting, savings and loans, credit cards, foreign trading exchange, property and casualty insurance, life and health insurance, mortgage insurance and banking, and real estate development and brokerage. Currently missing are commercial banking and leasing and data processing services, but it is anticipated that these will be added in the immediate future.

Marketing Strategy Primarily consumer not commercial and industrial. A direct, company-owned salesforce works in retail and small outlets. Company permits the salesperson to sell everything. Pays for performance (a low salary but generous commissions).

Financial Strategy Goes to market periodically and gets funds through a self-contained affiliate.

Management Strategy Believes in self-development and promotion from within.

Summary—Competitor H

Positive	Negative
• Full array of consumer services	• Not strong in the commercial and industrial segments; focused on small business
• Strong consumer marketing	
• Good credit rating and asset base	
• Good management	• Not skilled in the commercial and industrial segments

Notation: Major threat to the consumer segment. Probably won't be strong in large commercial and industrial accounts for some time.

**Competitor K—
A Multinational Bank**

This is a major Japanese bank with a multibillion-dollar asset base that is part of a Japanese *zaibatsu*. It came to the United States to provide financial support to the Japanese auto company's development of its own factory network in the United States, but it has developed close ties with a number of large regional banks. It has a mixed portfolio but is relatively weak in the U.S. consumer segment.

Investment Strategy
Moderate to low aggressiveness in the United States.

Strategic Driver
Supportive of other divisions of the parent company. It is not a prime
business thrust.

Implementation Strategies
Product Strategy A full array of services in Japan, but limited offering
in the United States.
Marketing Strategy Works through other institutions but will offer
long-term financing if required to sell equipment or build the plant.
Financial Strategy The primary source of funds is the parent com-
pany. Has some ties with Bank of Japan on worldwide financial deals.
Management Strategy Japanese managers, even in the United States.

Summary—Competitor K

Positive	Negative
	• Limited offering and need to tie with the manufacturing affiliates
	• Poor marketing
• Strong source of funds	
	• Japanese management only

Notation: Possible ally. Could be a means to strengthen world thrust.

Strategic Implications

In the summary illustration, Exhibit 8-4, I have highlighted the insights
gained through each of the analytical techniques. Even though we have
assessed the situation from several different perspectives, we find a few
factors being repeated. Certainly, being global and providing rapid "lines of
credit" are emphasized. You can deduce from this that unless you have
incorporated these into your strategy, you will not be a future winner. In
fact, you will likely lose position and may not be able to survive. It is
apparent that these are current weaknesses and must be corrected. The
notations and implications indicate how this may be achieved. You may be
able to tie up with one of the multinationals that want to participate to
support their industrial-client thrust. This is a nice situation that, if properly negotiated, can help both parties. In addition, it is also apparent that
the consumer segment is becoming unattractive for you. This is the
targeted area of the national retailer competitor, and this may enable you
to get out with a positive rather than a negative impact. This is not bad,

EXHIBIT 8-4 Mid-American National Bank

Current Situation and Strategy: A medium-sized regional bank, with a portfolio split between commercial business clients and consumers. Positive loyalty toward bank—on the part of both the employees and the customers. Not a leader, but willing to follow at a methodical and risk-aversion pace.

Analytical techniques	Notations	Strategic implications
User assessment Business (local companies)	Demanding more favorable terms and global financing. Foreign banks are a threat.	Need to provide global terms and conditions.
Merchants (a variety of store types)	Conditions are forcing a raising of the issue as to whether this is a group worth keeping.	May get out of this segment if possible.
Consumers	Will be tougher to serve. Barriers to entry will decline, and cost of participating will increase.	Need to evaluate worth of participating.
Supplier evaluation (source of funds)	Many new sources. How to get your share?	Can you develop contacts that will permit the bank to get a share of this new source of funding?
Demographics	Need to be able to participate worldwide and offer global financing. Need to track multi-industry competitors to determine their profit objectives.	Reinforcement of need to be global.
Winners and losers	Past: Maintain reputation and relationships to keep depositors and source of funding. Present: In business segment, increased need to provide rapid financial services on a global basis. Action, cost, availability of service more important than personal relationships. In consumer segment, convenience and one-stop service. Future: More of present. Very competitive. Will require quick decision making and willingness to take increased risks.	Need to be innovative and technology-oriented and to provide customer with maximum flexibility and a chance to make own choices.

163

EXHIBIT 8-4 Mid-American National Bank (*Cont.*)

Analytical techniques	Notations	Strategic implications
In-depth analysis		
Competitor E	Strong, dedicated competitor. Will move to enhance position in your region. Won't be an ally.	Need some way to neutralize thrust. Can you become aggressive in its region?
Competitor H	Strong threat to your consumer position. Not that strong in the commercial and industrial segments.	How about selling it your consumer business?
Competitor K	Possible ally.	How can you cultivate an alliance to strengthen your global financing ability?

since two strategic changes can permit you to increase the probability of success.

In the first two cases I have focused on illustrations of companies that are mature and have a relatively strong position. These companies are conservative and wish to continue to hold their position but are being threatened by a number of new competitive forces. The competitive analyses were able to highlight a number of changes that have to be addressed, as well as to provide insights on how to address them. In the next case study, I will describe a company that is small and aggressive. This will demonstrate how a new entry can use the same techniques to identify the cracks in the armor of the current leaders.

CASE III Personal Computing, Inc.

Our hypothetical company is a small firm that is embarked on creating an exciting new market and industry. The product is personal computers, and the company will be called Personal Computing, Inc., or PCI. PCI was founded only two years ago by a group of technical people who left the major computer company because they were dissatisfied with the attention being paid to this new growth market by the larger, dominant computer company. The company has developed a small personal computer that is modular in design and sells in the $2,500 to $3,000 range if completely equipped. The major element costs about $1,200, and then it requires either one or two disk drives, a monitor or a converter for the standard television, and also a printer. The base unit has 48K memory and 8 bits.

The thrust has initially focused on the small businessperson who would like a small computer to take care of inventory control, billing, payroll, tax accounting, and other critical and labor-intensive activities. PCI has established a nationwide sales and distribution network. Sales have grown rapidly, and the workforce is doubling every two years. The company's strategies can be summarized as follows:

Investment Strategy

Aggressive growth to create a new market. Current focus is on the small business segment, but the company hopes to be able to penetrate the home computer market within the next three to five years.

Strategic Driver

Applications-driven. Working to increase the operating and applications software especially in the financial and business management areas.

Implementation Strategies

Product Strategy Company focuses on the main computer, which can be added to inexpensively and easily. Currently sources all of the key components and peripherals. No intention to backward integrate, but availability of the chips and LSI circuits is a concern. Printers and disk drivers are sourced from Japan. Has a small applications laboratory. Software is developed under contract to precise quality standards by small California- and Boston-based software shops. PCI has a quality-auditing group to make sure that software is reliable and memory and operations are efficient.

Marketing Strategy Uses a combination of heavy local and national advertising in conjunction with its large retail structure. Has aggressively franchised all that have the apparent financial viability to make it. Franchises have been successful and are currently owner-operated. There has also been a strong effort to support the growth of user groups and publications that reinforce the applications. There is a small national sales-force, and there have been some recent moves to increase sales efforts in New York, Boston, Los Angeles, San Francisco, and Dallas. There is no offshore salesforce, though this is being considered for Europe.

Production Strategy All PCI-made equipment is produced in a small but expanding facility in Southern California. The workforce is young and dedicated. Production workers can share in profit growth. There is no union. Equipment is relatively modern, though some is second-hand. There is a small purchasing group in the Far East, with offices in Hong Kong and Japan.

Financial Strategy All capital has been provided by venture capitalists and the equity of the management team. The company is privately held, but it will go public within the next three years.

Management Strategy Highly entrepreneurial, risk-oriented, and willing to invest time and capital to grow. Low turnover, but it is too early to tell. Rewards have been commensurate with risks.

I have described the strategies and characteristics of PCI in detail so that you can see how the company must change in order to continue to be successful in growing both the market and its share.

Users

The users of personal computers are small businesses, professional firms, and hobbyists. The small businessperson wants something that is easy to use and can be applied to solve problems. He or she is not interested in becoming a programmer. Reliability and ease of operation are of prime importance, but cost is also important. Lawyers, doctors, and other professionals are also not interested in becoming programmers; they are more interested in applications. The third user group, the hobbyists, is the exact opposite. Hobbyists are more interested in sophistication and are not disturbed by complexity or the need to do their own programming. Cost matters, but it is not critical. As time goes on, there will be an increasing number of consumers who will be more like the small businesspeople and professionals than the hobbyists. Price will become more critical then, since the average individual consumer is very price-conscious. These consumers will require more front-end sales help than small firms do. PCI will need a strong service network, since repair and maintenance will also increase in importance.

Notation: Primary users will continue to demand ease of operations, large selection of applications programs, and lower prices.

Macroview

Suppliers

The major suppliers are the giant integrated-circuit (IC) companies that make the electronic components. These companies are primarily in the United States and Japan. Each of them has attempted to forward integrate at some time, and several make minicomputers. They have the ability to design and produce small personal computers, but they have had trouble marketing the end products. It is assumed that when the market grows to a significant level, they will enter but will not be able to make a long-term total business commitment. Therefore, they may damage profitability, but they will not be long-term winners.

The suppliers of printers and other peripherals are not likely to provide total systems. They will be content to offer a full array of existing components. The European and Japanese suppliers, however, have a close relationship with the small-computer manufacturers and systems suppliers, and thus, they are indirectly competitors. This can impact the availability of the printers and other peripherals, since suppliers will satisfy their major customers first. It could also effect the cost of the product, since they could favor those that purchase in the larger quantities.

> *Notation:* IC and LSI producers are likely to forward integrate, but it is unlikely they will succeed in becoming the real long-term winners.

Distributors
In recent months, a number of major retailers have joined the numerous franchised specialty computer stores in the offering of computer services and systems. These firms include one of the largest retailers in the world, which is opening up specialty retail outlets. This retailer normally develops its own unique line of private-label merchandise, especially on big-ticket items. In this case, it has tied up with the largest computer producer, whose name is synonymous with computers.

There are several retailing companies that are evaluating the opening up of computer stores, but these will probably serve the traditional retail and distribution role and may not be considered major competitors.

One of the major consumer electronics retailers is also in the process of developing its own unique line of personal computers, even to the extent of designing and manufacturing them. It too will acquire the peripherals and the components necessary to package a total offering. All of these retailers are first targeting small businesspeople and professionals—the same customer groups that are prime on your list.

> *Notation:* The retailers and distributors that have traditionally sought their own private-label merchandise have done so in this field also and are already key competitors. As the consumer market grows, it is predictable that more will follow this model.

Substitution—The Battlefield View
In our other cases, we either evaluated the threat of other ways of satisfying the same function (machine tools) or did not consider it that important (banking). In this case, your company is providing substitutions. First of all, your company is counting on substituting for the other ways of providing information processing and retrieval. The traditional ways include using log books or ledgers to record accounting data or maintain records; the use of files to keep track of correspondence, invoices, and inventory; and the use of manual inventory controls. Other modes that are being targeted are the use of "batch processing" operators who will do the key punching,

use large mainframe computers, and furnish data processing sheets or even finished reports and the use of "time-sharing" companies that permit remote access to computers and that will provide the consulting or applications software to do the job.

Thus, the question in this case is whether your company will be able to change the habits and loyalties of the users. You will be successful if you can provide the right combination of price, ease of operation, and availability.

> *Notation:*   Will the personal computer have sufficient advantages to enable you to get users to convert from printed media or other computational services? How long will this take?

Your company is not the only one offering substitutes. Simultaneously with the advent of the personal computer, there has been the development of other ways of providing information processing and retrieval. Communications is also changing dynamically, and there is an increasing number of communications devices that are providing digital services. These include mobile communications, cellular systems, new sophisticated telephone systems that utilize land transmissions, and even satellites. Individuals and businesses will have use of remote computers to process business and personal data and to gain access to very large data bases. These systems may complement the personal computer or may substitute for it.

> *Notation:*   Strategy must include monitoring of the communications technology as well as the current and future on-site computer systems. It will be particularly important to track A T & T, ITT, and GTE, as well as a number of other multinational communications companies.

Demographics

In this case, we observe a different type of demographic profile than in our prior two cases (Exhibit 8-5). We can see that the present and the future (next five years) profiles are the same, whereas in the other cases, they were significantly different. The newness of the market and the anticipation that it will not grow very rapidly during the forecasted period make the difference. If you were to plot the decade, you might see some change but none as significant as in the banking and machine tool markets.

Since five of the eight players in this industry are either foreign or multinational and all except two are very large, we can see that the opportunity is clearly global and will require significant and long-term commitment of resources. The electronics industry is among the most transnational, and industry standards (e.g., codes, legal requirements, etc.) are not barriers to entry. Another unique feature of the profile is that we are using communications and information companies as a special category, since these will be the primary competitors. This means that you will be playing against large, well-managed, well-funded giants—companies that have profits in the billions and that have access to a powerful combination of technology and capital.

Notation: Winning won't be easy. The time horizon will be long, and the resource requirements will be very large.

Winners and Losers

Since the industry is in its infancy, it will be difficult to contrast the winners and losers to identify the current and future success factors. There is, however, a technique that may be helpful. You can make analogies with other industries that have similar characteristics and that are old enough to permit an assessment of companies that won and companies that lost to determine what distinguished them from each other. The stereo industry may be useful, since it has some similar though not exact characteristics. On the similar side, the stereo industry is electronics-based and the equipment is modularized. Further, success is dependent on the availability of economical, reliable software in the form of records, tapes, and broadcast transmission. Among the differences is the fact that stereo systems are sold primarily to consumers and not to large commercial and industrial users.

From a competitive point of view, there are several interesting insights that can be drawn. First of all, the initiators of the systems were not able to survive once the market grew large. Their failure was a combination of a

	Small Specialists	Large Communications/Information Companies	Multi-Industry
U.S. Only	A, B	C	
Foreign		D, E	
Multinational Corporations		F	G, H

Present and Future (5 Years Ahead)

Exhibit 8-5. Demographic matrix.

failure to innovate and a failure to provide sufficient capital for the long haul. Many of them refused to recognize, or recognized too late, that it was a global business and that components could be sourced and shipped on a worldwide basis. Many of the companies that were strong in associated markets like records or broadcasting tried to enter but were unsuccessful. In addition, segmentation occurred, and it was important to make a choice and focus on one or two segments and not try to be a full-product participant. If this analogy has enough similarities, then you may deduce that winners in the personal and small computer market will be companies that are (1) global, (2) willing to source worldwide, (3) different from those that are in the software business, and (4) selective (concentrating on one but no more than two segments).

This discussion of segmentation may be worth pursuing further. The winners in the stereo business were either those that focused on the high end and specialized in one or two key components (such as the turntable or the speakers) or those that offered a full line of low-price, moderate-quality products. This may also be true of the personal computer market and may be very pertinent for PCI.

Notation: How to segment and which segment to focus on may be major strategic issues.

In-Depth Analyses of Some Competitors

Competitor B— A Small, Domestic Specialist
This company is quite similar to PCI. It was founded about three years ago by a number of engineers who became disenchanted with a large, rapidly growing IC producer. These individuals recognized the potential of the personal computer and were working on a special project to develop one. They made a prototype, but their employer decided to discontinue it. So they left. Their product has a good reputation and is clearly one of the quality leaders.

Investment Strategy
Moderate to rapid growth in the high-price end.

Strategic Driver
Innovation and solution orientation. More product than marketing.

Implementation Strategies
Product Strategy
Hardware: has a high-quality, state-of-the-art offering that is made in its own facility. High value added to the product (thus high degree of

integration). Small but very competent research and development organization.

Software: Has its own software development organization, and is credited with developing reliable, efficient software. Company is solution-oriented. Will contract with subject matter experts to design useful software and systems; often the industry expert or the reputed leader.

Marketing Strategy Small, dedicated safesforce with programming and systems background. Some distribution but very selective. Recently signed agreement with the largest retail chain, but kept strong control over how and to whom systems will be sold. Concentrates on its own high-end niche.

Production Strategy All production done in its own, single, highly automated facility. Has no affiliation with outsiders, but will acquire high-end equipment if it meets company standards.

Financial Strategy Favorable, long-term debt from large banks. No venture capital money. Offers some public stock but is highly restrictive. Public stockholders cannot vote; private stockholders have all voting power.

Management Strategy All top managers are owners and have complete control. All have technical backgrounds. Chairman is forty-five; rest are under thirty-five. Hires from top schools and has low turnover. Offers very liberal salaries. The organization is solution-oriented and "matrix" in nature, which means individuals have two managers, one functional and another project focused.

Notation: Clearly the high-end leader. Will be willing to sacrifice profitability to build reputation. Good model to follow for solution orientation. Track potential problems with retailer. May lose quality image.

Competitor C—A Large U.S. Communications and Information Company

This competitor is one of the largest corporations in the world, regardless of the category, and is by far the largest telephone company. It consists of a large research and development lab, its own equipment-manufacturing plants, and over a dozen regulated telephone companies. Because of federal and state regulations, it was not permitted to participate in the data processing business, and it was not able to capitalize on a number of its major electronics developments. In the past five years a number of regulations have been changed, and the company has now organized itself into a nonregulated as well as a regulated component. This change alone could make it a formidable competitor for PCI. In addition, Competitor C has targeted the small computer as one of its major growth segments. The strategies of its home information division can be summarized as follows:

Investment Strategy

Aggressive growth aimed at simultaneously creating a new market and positioning itself as the clear share leader.

Strategic Driver

Company is synergistic, and will take advantage of its unique position in the home as a means of creating a new business. It already has a strong position with consumers and small businesses with its telephones. In recent years, the telephone's sophistication has been greatly enhanced, and it has become a major communications linkage. The strategy is to offer more devices to hook up with the telephone, including an intelligent terminal, storage disks and tapes, and memory devices. Users can plan their own computer systems and make them as simple or complex as desired. Further, they only have to pay for exactly what they want, and they have the option of renting, leasing, or buying.

Implementation
Product Strategy

Hardware: Uses its corporate labs to develop its own unique equipment, and supplements with others' equipment if necessary. Would like to prevent other manufacturers from developing compatible equipment and has refused to license them.

Software: Is developing extensive software to cover all business and consumer needs. Has arranged a licensing approach that permits individuals, including their own employees, to work on their own time. It will pay them a flat fee or a royalty percentage. Software is considered to be of high quality.

Data Bases: Since company has an extensive network, it offers access to large specialized and generalized data bases. These include legal, financial, investment, and medical data bases that have been produced by large publishers and data-base companies, including *The New York Times*, McGraw-Hill, Prentice-Hall, and Dow Jones. The cost for subscribing is nominal, though usage fees can be expensive.

Marketing Strategy Utilizes its telephone company affiliates, as well as its own small business and individual outlets. In states where other companies own the telephone system, it licenses the distribution rights or has company-owned outlets. It refuses to use individual stores or national retailers. It has a special, highly trained, consultative-type salesforce that can help clients, on a fee basis, to apply the system to solve their unique problems. Its pricing is very competitive, and it will provide special discounts for volume or nonprime-time usage. National, regional, and local advertising is extensive, and company also obtains the advantage of the regulated affiliates' corporate advertising.

Production Strategy Uses its own U.S. facilities, which are highly automated and have a nonunion workforce. This is unique to the total company, which has a national, militant union. Because of the close ties between divisions, the company is highly integrated and can do almost anything it wants to technically.

Financial Strategy Uses parent company's funds and has no debt of its own. Cash and capital are available.

Management Strategy A mix of long-service, telephone-oriented individuals and some newly hired computer-oriented individuals. This appears to be a mixed blessing and is probably their major limitation. The company is a slow, methodical, conservative institution.

Notation: A major, tough competitor that will increase the cost and risk of participation. Will be toughest in the small-business segment. Need to develop compatible equipment that will permit piggybacking on its efforts.

Strategic Implications

Again, we can use the summary of our assessments to identify whether a change in strategy is needed or desired. The fact that the competitors are all aggressive and, in most cases, well-managed, is an important insight that needs to be dealt with. The demographics clearly reinforce the need to be focused and selective and to aim at segments that provide PCI with some competitive advantage. We have indicated that one competitor is clearly focusing on the high end and has a commitment to excellence. PCI will have a tough time competing in this segment. The large communications and information company is also seeking uniqueness and will provide a total system. PCI will most likely do best if it concentrates on the low- to medium-priced segment and is flexible and adaptive. Its designs are modularized and this enables consumers and small businesses to add at their own will. The issue of software compatibility is important and cannot be underestimated.

Thus far I have illustrated a machine tool producer being attacked by multinationals and new systems suppliers, a regional bank being pursued by a dynamic change in the financial services industry, and a small computer company trying to compete with giants while simultaneously growing a new market. Each of these cases dealt with large- to medium-sized institutions in large national or multinational industries. To round off our illustrations, I would like to use a small, local business that is participating in a small market. Even though some of the techniques may not yield as much here as they did in the other cases, I think they will still prove to be worthwhile.

CASE IV   A Local Retailer

The retailer firm is in the appliance business, selling refrigerators, ranges, laundry equipment, and dishwashers and also a complete line of radio, television, and video and audio peripherals. It has revenues in excess of $5 million and is owned and operated by a single family. The family has been able to develop a strong company image as a value-priced and service-oriented firm. It has been profitable during its thirty-five years of operation. It has had a simple strategy and is interested in maintaining its position in a slow-growing period. Let's examine the competitive scene.

Users

Individual consumers are not likely to get into the appliance business, but it is worth understanding their needs, wants, and desire to acquire quality products at reasonable prices. They will price shop and have brand preferences, but overall they will consider the full offering, which includes price, availability, and confidence in the product and the dealer. There has been an increasing desire on the part of consumers to buy conveniently, and this includes a willingness to shop at home via catalogues and, most recently, through electronic media, especially cable television.

> *Notation:*   Need to think through the impact of shopping at home on the competitive scene. It may permit manufacturers or wholesale distributors to offer products directly to consumers without the services of retailers, which could be a major threat.

Macroview

The retailer buys directly from the manufacturer, but there are a number of wholesalers that currently sell direct to consumers or are planning to do so. These wholesalers will focus on the low end and will not provide services. However, since they will strive for volume, they could erode the profitability.

The manufacturers themselves could decide to forward integrate into retail and sell directly to consumers. Several of them already have their own wholesalers, and the next step could be easy and profitable. The growth of shopping at home, whether via catalogue or electronic media, could encourage this move and could have a significant impact on the traditional retailer. There are also indications that some of the large multinationals are considering having their own franchised and company-owned retail outlets.

Notation: It is very likely that the wholesalers and manufacturers will continue to forward integrate and will become a major threat to traditional retailers. They will go for the volume segment and stress price. Service will be limited. This will be one of the key things differentiating the offering. However, two manufacturers have large service organizations that will provide quality service at competitive prices.

Demographics

The profiles in Exhibit 8-6 have been adapted to fit the retailer's needs. There are a few attributes worth noting. First of all, we have divided the specialists into local and national. Further, we have included a multiproducts category while combining the multi-industry and the conglomerate categories. We have included a multinational category, but this may not be necessary at all, since none of the companies are multinational. However, this may only be a temporary situation and may change in the future. Any foreign competitors could also be placed in the multinational category.

An examination of competitive demographics yields some observations. Several companies will disappear from the local specialist category. Some will either go out of business or be merged, and others will move to the multiproducts category. There will also be a number of new additions, especially in the national specialist category. This means that the resource

| | Specialists | | | Multi-Industry and |
	Local	National	Multiproducts	Conglomerates
U.S. Only	A, B, C, D, E, F, G	H, I	J, K	L, M
Multinational				

Present

| | Specialists | | | Multi-Industry and |
	Local	National	Multiproducts	Conglomerates
U.S. Only	A, B, C	H, I, N, O	J, K, F	G, L, M
Multinational				

Future

Exhibit 8-6. Demographic matrices—present and future.

requirements will change and the purchasing power of the larger companies may become a problem for you.

Winners and Losers

The historical winners have been those companies that were operated by local merchants who catered to the needs of the local consumer. They provided personal selling, product knowledge, and most importantly the service. The total offering and packaging was vital to success. This has changed, and in recent years the winners have been those companies that could provide the lowest prices and generate large volumes. Service and product knowledge have become less important, since the manufacturers offered service and the product quality has reduced the number of service calls and failures. In addition, the products have fallen into the commodity status, and with the exception of a few new products, consumers have been able to determine their choices without much presales help. Even the new products have had enough promotional instructions to guide the consumer in the selection process.

> *Notation:*   Volume and pricing have become the most critical success factors.

In-Depth Analyses of Some Competitors

The Buying Pool

In this case, there are a number of small local specialists that have joined together to form a buying pool, which has permitted them to combine their traditional selling and service with lower prices. These companies have multiple brands and in many cases multiple locations. This puts them in direct competition with you. They have become more aggressive and are seeking share.

> *Notation:*   Can you join this buying pool? If so, what are the advantages and disadvantages?

Competitor A— A Specialized National Retailer

This company is a major national retailer that specializes in appliances and consumer electronics. It is one of the largest accounts of two major brands, and the manufacturers provide it with excellent prices and also high coop-advertising allocations.

Investment Strategy
Aggressive national growth.

Strategic Driver
Marketing and sales promotion.

Implementation Strategies
Product Strategy Sells national brands and special economy models on a private-brand basis. Has a special purchasing organization in the Far East to acquire products made to its unique design.

Marketing Strategy Has a combination of three types of outlets: (1) its own store, (2) leased space in several large discount outlets, and (3) franchises in remote locations. Has its own advertising group to develop copy and fliers. Is experimenting with some electronic media for shopping at home.

Production Strategy Does no manufacturing, although it does own equity in a few of the vendors. Has four large warehouses and does its own trucking.

Financial Strategy Public-owned company. Listed on the American Stock Exchange. Highly leveraged. Is a strong negotiator with vendors, and gets a lot of indirect financing from its vendors.

Management Strategy Top managers are veterans of Sears and have excellent knowledge of consumer-durables retailing. Company is noted for training and does a good job in retraining its top people.

Notation: A tough competitor. Has grown rapidly and provides good service and pricing.

Strategic Implications

The competitive environment will force you to become more aggressive in pricing and, therefore, to get the product more cheaply. You will either have to join the buying pool or become affiliated with a national chain. Current strategy will not permit holding current position, and you must either become more aggressive or sell out while there is still something to sell.

Chapter Summary

In this chapter, I have illustrated how the various analyses can be used to identify strategic issues and the need to make strategic changes. In each case, I highlighted the competitive situation. Notations were made and integrated into areas requiring the attention of the top and operating managers.

9 Sources of Competitive Intelligence

I must emphasize that you need to be practical and not make this activity too laborious or an end in itself. Competitive analysis is a means to evaluate your business's current strategy effectively and to determine the need for making changes. The most common reactions I hear when I discuss competitive analysis are that it is too difficult and too unreliable. "After all," someone may say, "no company is going to disclose its strategy to the world, and if it did, I would be very suspect about its reliability."

In this chapter I wish to dispel this myth and demonstrate that you can obtain a fairly realistic assessment of the competition and its strategy. I won't dispute that a competitor isn't going to clearly spell out its strategy in great detail, but I will prove that with the application of the thinking processes reviewed in this book and with sound intelligence gathering and review, it is possible to learn a great deal about the competitor.

Intelligence Isn't Just Collecting Data

The Funk and Wagnall dictionary defines intelligence as "the faculty of perceiving and comprehending meaning." The word *meaning* reinforces the points that I emphasized; without meaning the effort is worthless and isn't justified. Intelligence activity requires that you seek out data from every possible source and then put all the data together to develop a hypothesis that can be tested. It is an ongoing process and not an annual exercise. It is not just a hectic or periodic scurrying around for data and filing it in a file drawer. Competitive intelligence is a way of thinking. It will require many people who will know what to look for and when to report it. It stresses a willingness to become aware, to collect, and not to judge or discard too early. A delicate balance is required. A good intelligence network must be selective, since it can't be overloaded with trivia. It is more than a clipping file or a folder that has so much in it that it is unusable and won't be analyzed by anyone. But as I just pointed out, the trick is to be selective but not to overlook parts of the puzzle that by themselves don't appear to be relevant but will fill in the gaps or reconfirm what is known from other sources. Intelligence gathering is both quantitative and qualitative, dealing with instincts, intuition, and hard, cold facts. A good intelligence system will utilize individuals from a variety of backgrounds and types of training. It will have financial, manufacturing, marketing, technical, and even general managers. These people will not be full-time spies nor will they spend hours just reading or interviewing others. The ideal team will consist of professionals who know enough to recognize what is meaningful and then convert it into strategic intelligence that is meaningful to the business.

Throughout this chapter, I will describe information sources and then indicate how they can be useful.

All intelligence comes from two types of sources—that which the competitor provides about itself and that which is provided about the competitor by third parties. These sources can be further segmented by the group that the competitor addresses or the group that describes the competitor. For instance the competitor may be communicating to the external public or the professionals in the industry, or it may be trying to explain its actions or abilities to the investors or their representatives or even to the government. In addition representatives of these various stakeholders may be reporting or interpreting what they know or hear about the competitor. These sources are normally public and not proprietary in nature, though they may require some further interpretation by those who are knowledgeable. This type of information is called secondary research by the professional market researchers, but it is a prime source. I will take each of these types and examine it in depth, elaborating and illustrating as I proceed. If you follow the guidelines and are creative, these inputs can be woven into a story line about the competition that will be helpful in developing and evaluating your strategy. I will start with those competitors that are already in the market, and the logic and approach can be applied to your current competitors and suppliers as well as those that serve the same customers with different groups of products and services.

Investor Sources

What the Competitor
Tells Its Investors

This first set of sources is provided by the competitor to communicate to those who hold its stock or are owners of the company. These documents are required by the law and are part of the public domain. The same type of documentation is difficult to obtain for the privately owned company, and so in these cases you will have to rely on other sources of information.

The most obvious place to start is with the annual report. This source is often overlooked and underestimated as to its content and value. In recent years the annual report has become more and more elaborate and has become a significant instrument of the CEO to tell the world about the company and its vision of the future. I have found that it is important to obtain and study past reports as well as the most current annual report. Go back at least five and possibly ten years and analyze what has evolved over the period.

Start at the very beginning of the report, with the letter from the chairman or chairwoman. In this letter the top management and chief strategists will often explain what they believe to be the most important achievements or problems of the past year. This will include whether they are satisfied or dissatisfied with the financial and market results. It will communicate how they measure their own performance. Look to see if they stress sales or earnings growth or both or if they are more interested in the return on sales or investment ratios. They may try and explain the performance of the total market or of significant segments. Are they satisfied, and how do they think the situation will change in the future? Often there will be indications of successes and failures as well as the targeted opportunities or threats. Thus with one or two pages you may benefit from the observations of those who really count in the firm and who make the strategic decisions. These perceptions will be invaluable as you compare them with what others say and believe about the company or the markets in which it participates. Note the word "perceive"—we are dealing with the perceptions of others, and such perceptions may not be true statements of the facts. The top men and women may or may not know what is really going on even if they think that they do. It isn't rare to find that their perceptions are out of sync with the rest of the world and even their peers.

They may be so enamored with their success that they believe that they are infallible, or they may be so egotistical that they can't admit they made a mistake. Sometimes they will act on what they want to believe rather than what the market or the world really tells them. This is very important to know; you must not think that everyone is objective. If a company isn't tuned with reality or is deceiving itself, it may create long-term problems for itself and everyone else in the industry. This is particularly true if the competitor is the leader and everyone else takes their signals from it.

As I said, it is interesting to compare the letters in the past annual reports with the letter in the current one. First you can note whether there has been a change in the leadership. Next you can see if the message is the same or different. There are many cases in which the message is quite different from year to year. This is particularly true of companies in crisis. These companies will most likely have had a change in management, and each CEO may have had a different view of the company's strengths and the future course it should take. Also determine if the problems are repeated year after year and if the solution is depicted as being just around the corner. Problems are often rationalized with a dream of a happier, more successful tomorrow just around the corner. Most of the time, it is nothing but a dream and a promise, and the problems get worse. Even if the company is healthy, there may be considerable differences in the perceptions of the top management. We will examine the annual reports of the currently troubled Chrysler Corporation in the 1975 to 1980 period as our example of a company in crisis. We will review the annual reports of A T & T, our healthy but changing company, during the same period to determine similarities and differences between these two types of companies. As we examine these reports, it is important to ask whether the earlier reports would have enabled an analyst to predict the changes in strategy and results.

Let's begin with the 1978 A T & T annual report and the opening comments from the chairman of the board, J. D. de Butts. He began with an analysis of his record in earnings growth. He measured his performance in two ways: first, in the earnings-per-share growth rate, and second, in the dividend record. He then discussed the major trends.

- Usage of the telephone had grown at an 8 percent growth rate per year since 1971, and the number of long-distance calls had doubled.
- The information age had begun, and Bell Telephone system was prepared to participate in it.
- The system strengths were in its networking. Further, the world was entering the age of the intelligent network that would handle data and be suited to the specific needs of the customer. (This provided a clue to the desire of the company to move into data processing and transmission and was repeated in several sections of the report.)

The subsequent comments dealt with the changing world and the need to restructure the company to meet the challenges and the opportunities. Both of these emphasized the company's need and intent to become more marketing-oriented and less function-oriented.

The remainder of the 1978 annual report elaborated on these points and provided data to support them and to illustrate the type of moves being contemplated by the company. From this data base, the analyst could start to build a theory about A T & T's plans to become an information rather than a telecommunications company.

A review of the 1980 annual report permits an identification of the similarities to and the dissimilarities from the 1978 edition. The first difference was the chairman himself. The president had assumed the chairmanship. This illustrated the management planning and succession planning of the company. Since the company was wealthy, you would expect that the story line of 1978 would be similiar to that of 1980. In 1980, there was emphasis on the earnings growth of the company, but it was less specific. The information-age theme was continued, and the new chairman reemphasized the commitment to transform the company from a telephone company into a complete information company. In addition a new dimension was added to the change. The company was determined to become global in scope instead of merely national. In the past the company had been prohibited from participating overseas, and so the management was assuming that the government would permit a change in status and scope. There was more stress on technology, and the company emphasized that it was the inventor of the transistor, which helped to create the electronics age. The subsequent paragraphs described the restructuring, with the same emphasis on marketing and the separation of the regulated from the nonregulated components of the company. This was reconfirmation of the creation of American Bell, later named A T & T Information Systems ("Baby Bell"), and its separation from "Ma Bell."

Next there was a description of how the enterprise would use faster depreciation, since there would be less concern to keep the cost to the individual customer as low as possible and more concern to become a truly world-class competitor. Again the report elaborated on each point and provided the data to support the theme.

This is an excellent example of how the annual report can be used to develop a theory of the competitor's strategy and direction that can be validated from other sources. A T & T was (and remains) a well-managed company, and therefore its publications communicated in advance what it wanted to do and the strategy and organization it would follow.

Now let's look at the opening letters of a company in crisis, or at least in a major unpleasant transition—Chrysler. I will contrast the same two years, 1978 and 1980. In 1978 the chairman of Chrysler was John J.

Riccardo. The report began with the bad news. The company had lost money, sales were down, and it had lost share in its main markets in the United States and Canada. It was almost everything that a leader of a company would rather not discuss, especially with its owners and investors. There was some minor good news. Profits were reported from the secondary parts of the company—the credit and military segments. The third section dealt with the strengthening moves. These included the use of innovative financing to provide capital for needed modernization and new products. There were moves in Europe, Japan, Brazil, Australia, Mexico, and South Africa that permitted Chrysler to have a small equity position in these emerging markets. There was also a strengthening of the management team, including the appointment of Lee Iacocca as president. Since Iacocca was coming from Ford, it could have been assumed that he would replace Riccardo when he retired. This is what happened, and it was predictable.

As you read the letter, you clearly get the message that many things are wrong and the company is in trouble. Management was striving to be optimistic, but all of the positives were related to the peripheral not the core businesses. The report attempted to blame the problems on government regulations and the burden these placed on the "small" company. It is worth noting that Chrysler at the time was a $10 billion company.

Two annual reports later, you find a similarly troubled and unprofitable story. As with A T & T, Chrysler had a new chairman but for entirely different reasons. Iacocca had become the chairman of the *new* Chrysler Corporation. The word "new" provided a clue. What was new? Chrysler had reduced its fixed costs by over $1 billion, but it continued to lose in the same key segments as before. Facilities had been upgraded, and heavy investments were made in new, award-winning, front-wheel-drive cars. At least there appeared to be more emphasis on fixing the problems with the core businesses; little attention was given to the secondary markets or subsidiaries. This indicated a commitment to remain an automobile company and not sell off the core business and focus on the subsidiary businesses.

What can you learn from Chrysler? You can clearly see that the company that is constantly making excuses and that tries to find something to brag about at a time when its survival is threatened is most likely to become even sicker and possibly die. The management may have lost touch with reality, or it may be so overwhelmed that it can't function properly. The entire annual report in 1980 was a dull collection of numbers.

Enough about the beginning of the report. Let's explore what else we can learn from the annual report. Again I'll use A T & T as an example. In 1980 there are statements about the current size and the forecasted growth of the information market. The company estimated it to be in the $200-billion range in 1979 and estimated that it would triple within the decade. The company said there would be more intelligent networks, and in fact there are pictures of the equipment. There were descriptions of the anticipated new business services that the company planned to offer and of several of the experiments it had already tried. Home-communications trends were also included. All of this was valuable information for competitors or even new entrants. It permitted a comparison of their assumptions with those of the current leader. Certainly it wasn't the entire story, but it provided a hypothesis upon which to build.

The graphics in the financial section were also informative and useful to study. These showed the rate of growth of sales, the research and development funding, and the price performance of the company in relation to inflation. The rest of the financial section provided in-depth data about the company's performance over the decade as well as its debt and liabilities. Most of the critical financial ratios were already calculated and ready for analysis.

You can evaluate the type of directors and officers that the company has. The mix between outside and inside directors is worth noting, since it may indicate how much control the CEO has over his or her own destiny. The background and tenure of the directors is also useful to study. By comparing the past annual reports, you can highlight turnover and may be able to determine the reason for the changes. If the turnover is constant, it may indicate that the management team is in disarray and can't agree on the course of action for the future.

The annual report provides still more information, namely the analysis of the business lines, which is an important analysis for the multi-industry firm. This part of the report may provide understanding of how the competitor segments its businesses. It may also enable you to deduce the company's priorities and how they contribute to the total sales and earnings. A comparison of changes in this mix may be insightful to determine if the priorities of the company have changed. Suppose a company obtained 80 percent of its revenues and earnings from one line in the early part of the decade and this has now dropped to 40 percent. This will force you to identify how the mix has changed and whether the company is more vulnerable in its traditional line. The way the company defines its segments is also useful. If a company defines its segments very broadly, it may be merely a means of preventing the type of analysis I have been describing. Broad definitions don't permit the investor to know precisely where profits are being made. However, it may also indicate that the competitor has a very broad perception of its mission. It may also indicate that the company may be planning to make acquisitions or move into allied areas. For instance, suppose a company describes itself as an energy company and has an energy group. Upon examination you note that it is only in the petroleum refining business and doesn't have any other natural resources. It is worth making a note that the company may be thinking about expanding and worth looking for this in other documents or sources. A company with a narrow definition may also provide some clues about the future. It may lack vision or be so highly specialized that it will decline when the market declines. Regardless of how the company segments the businesses, it is worth examining the following:

- How much of the company's earnings and revenues come from each of these segments, and what has the trend been?
- How have the capital and cash flows of each segment changed?
- What does the company think of each of these segments, and do its opinions conform with what you or others in the segments think? This is an indication of the relative attractiveness of the segments.
- What are the company's opinions about its relative strengths and limitations?
- Examine the pictures that depict the segments. What is emphasized?

Each of these analyses provides insight about the priorities of the company and its dependence on its segments. In our Chrysler example, I mentioned that in 1978 there was a discussion of the non-U.S. markets and even the nonautomotive segments. This was almost completely absent in the 1980 report. These facts may have permitted you to anticipate that the new management would consider and even act to sell off the foreign equities and the nonauto segments to save the prime line—autos. This is exactly what happened, and the Chrysler watchers may have had the nonauto competitor looking to acquire the Chrysler assets or aggressively moving to take the share.

Annual Meetings
The annual report is merely an introduction to the competitor. Relative to this report is the annual stockholders meeting and special prospectus. Many underestimate the value of monitoring these meetings and their related documentation. The CEO may use this opportunity to brag about accomplishments and to explain further about the problems and their solutions. There may be presentations by the chief technical, financial, and marketing officers and possibly by the major operating officers. These presentations may be supplemented by written material. There may be questions from the stockholders that identify current problems within the company or potential and emerging problems. Watching how the officers handle themselves under pressure and how candid they are will also be helpful to understanding the type of people running the show. Often it is the unrehearsed portions that are the most helpful.

When a company is making an acquisition or being pursued by another, it is very likely, if not required, to submit reports on its businesses and their health. This may include an in-depth explanation of why the management supports or protests the merger or acquisition. These reports may be a summary of the entire strategy and the future direction of the company. In recent years a number of unwelcome pursuits have been made, and those being pursued spent time and money explaining the reasons to reject the bid. In some cases, it led to a change of direction and even management. Conflict can be very instructive.

What Investors Say
About the Competitor

Investment companies and stockbrokers prepare extensive reports on companies and industries to guide their clients in making investment decisions. Some of these reports are very comprehensive, and I will illustrate their content in the next few pages. These documents are often prepared by individuals who have been following the company and the industry for a long period of time and thus have a first-hand knowledge of the management, including their past successes and failures, as well as the major opportunities and threats that appear on the horizon. It is important to note that the experts will vary from firm to firm and industry to industry and that the experts on the electronics firms may be in one investment house and the experts on chemicals may be in another. Thus you must do some research to find out who the experts are. This may be achieved by looking at the industry interviews in publications like the *Wall Street Transcript* or in the major business publications like *Business Week.* Your own investment banker can also be of help in the selection of the reports you study. As I will stress throughout the chapter, the key may be to obtain a number of sources and not lock yourself into any one report. The analysts are human, and they will also have biases and thus not be entirely objective. A lack of objectivity can result from a personality conflict with the leadership of the firm or from investment disappointments.

For illustrative purposes, I will take a few examples of the types of reports that may be available from analysts. First I'll discuss a small, high-technology, growth company. This company designs, develops, manufactures, and markets a small business computer. The report begins with a summary of the analyst's perceptions and recommendations. The company's distribution, product line, pricing, and targeted customers are summarized. The report asserts that the company's past success can be attributed to its distribution network. There is a description of the forces that have contributed market growth in the past and may do so in the future.

The key competitors are outlined, and a comparison is made between the company and its major competitors. This is followed by an in-depth analysis of the entire product line, including the key components and the vendors of the components. This material covers several pages, and there is a section on the market shares of each of the competitors. The company's distribution and sales networks are outlined. This includes the number of employees in each category. The report closes with a summary of the financial issues and the key financial statistics.

This report, combined with other sources, can contribute to an understanding of the key characteristics of the company. A complete analysis of this report and others about the company can help you to identify the overall strengths and limitations of the competitor. You clearly see that the past success has been attributed to distribution, and you must challenge whether or not this will continue in the future. As I said, some analysts are more bullish than others. In the case of this small growth company, the reports were all positive and they recommended the purchase of the stock. But this isn't always the case. Analysts are similar to all critics. They are trying to tell the story the way they see it, and they aren't doing a public relations job. These individuals are rewarded for picking winners, and their reputations are on the line. Professional investment analysts will use a number of sources to obtain their information, and they may be the same sources you will use. But they will also have a direct connection with the company management on a personal basis. The company may grant individual and group interviews and presentations. Investment analysts may interrogate lower and middle management or, at times, individuals who have left the company. Further, they will talk to all the companies in the industry and thus have a complete picture of what is happening. Investment firms have so much at stake that they may also hire market research firms to do special studies and provide proprietary information. Their information is current, and they will try to anticipate changes and the impact those changes may have on the industry and the company. You will find reference to the opinions of experts in the field, and these may guide you in determining what other sources to probe. These additional sources will be discussed later. In short, the investment analyst is an investigative reporter.

Let's take another example. Unlike the first example, the firm under study is a multi-industry company and, therefore, more complex. In this case, there is an overview of the entire company and all of its lines. Each of the lines of business is described, and its contribution to the company's sales and earnings is evaluated. Thus the consumer business is depicted as contributing 25 percent of the sales and only 15 percent of the earnings. The industrial division is a major contributor of earnings, over 50 percent, and its contribution has been rising. There are several smaller divisions that are marginal in the sales and earnings picture for now, but the analysts believe these are the future growth segments. The rest of the report examines each of the segments and discusses the company's relative strengths and limitations. In addition there are insights into the trends in the industries that the company focuses on. The report enables the reader to obtain some idea about the company's ability to maintain its share.

As I've discussed in the prior chapters, there is a need to understand the diversified company's total portfolio even though you only compete in one or two of its segments. In the case of this company, the health of the industrial sector must be understood, since it is the prime source of earnings and cash and the company may be invincible if this sector gains in strength. If it has problems and its earnings are impacted, the company may be forced to reduce its moves in other segments. This may be an opportunity for the adversary. The divestiture by AMF of its Harley-Davidson motorcycle business is a case in point. The parent company found that it didn't have the funds to invest in this division and still grow its industrial sector. Thus it sought to sell the business to another company, but because of the division's weak position and the aggressive competition of the Japanese companies, no other company was willing to make the acquisition and invest the funds required to turn the division around. The division was sold to its employees, using a "leveraged buy-out" arrangement. This approach permits the employees to buy the company with a minimum of funds, because the company finances the purchase and the employees expend their sweat and effort to make it work. In this example, the parent company decided on its priorities and removed one of the cash-draining segments. If you were a competitor in the motorcycle business, you would also be facing a different, possibly more aggressive and committed but financially vulnerable competitor. The key would be to anticipate this move in advance and develop a strategy to deal with it.

Industry Studies

Earlier I mentioned that the investment houses may hire market research firms to analyze the characteristics and dynamics of an industry. These companies are a valuable source of data about industries but also the key players in the market. There are dozens of companies that follow certain industries. I have used research reports of Stanford Research Institute (SRI), Arthur D. Little, Inc., and Creative Strategies International. These firms are professional and expert in the fields that they follow. Some firms specialize in the high-technology, electronics, communications, and biotechnology fields, while others specialize in the mature fields. Their reports include the same type of industry material that the investment analysts cover. At times there are reports on major companies, such as Sony, IBM, A T & T, GM, and Exxon, but most of the time they will focus on total markets and the major participants. The industry study is an excellent starting point to obtain share estimates. You can also get an indication of the small, innovative entrants that may become the future leaders or may be merged into the other, larger companies—mostly, companies already in the industry, but also those considering entry. This is a major difference from the analysts' reports, since they concentrate on companies that are on the stock exchanges. The smaller companies may be private and not listed on an exchange.

You can subscribe to the complete service of the market research firms or merely buy the reports when and if they are of interest. In addition you can hire these firms to do proprietary or semiproprietary research. I must repeat what I said before: The quality of these reports will vary, and the individuals will have biases. It is worth contacting the firm after you have studied other sources and have developed a hypothesis about the industry. It is important to read past reports to ascertain the style and depth. Take the opportunity to talk to the individuals who did the reports and to probe into their background, experience, assumptions, and biases. Some of the firms hire outsiders on a freelance basis, and others have full-time, experienced individuals. Regardless of the imperfections, these studies are valuable and very cost-effective. They provide insights that may be useful in filling in the gaps and completing the puzzle. One of the most useful aspects of this source is that it gives you an overview of the total industry with the competing technologies. Technology may be very critical, and in many cases it is difficult to obtain a nontechnical description of what it does and how it fits into the total offering. You may retort that these evaluations should only be done by those with a technical background. I haven't found that this is true, since quite often technologists will not be able to see the forest for the trees and will become so critical that they don't think in terms of the total situation.

Credit Reports

As I mentioned, industry studies are often focused on the new, high-technology industries and not on the mature, nontechnical businesses. For mature businesses, you may have to resort to another source—credit reports. These reports have many limitations and are primarily designed to determine the creditworthiness of the firm. Therefore, they focus on the historical financial stability and viability of the firm. They contain information about how the company views itself and often have comments and quotes about the company by the officers and suppliers to the company. The most useful part is the biographical data about the key officers and even their families. You can find out if a company is a family business whose prime purpose is to provide jobs. If the owners are getting up in age and have potential estate problems, you may be able to forecast that the company will be sold and that its aggressiveness may decline.

Public Sources

What the Competitor
Tells the Public

So far I have been reviewing sources where the competitor is promoting the firm to its current or potential investors as well as those responsible for guiding others in their investment decisions. Investor sources are a good starting place, since the firm must be honest in its dealings with these groups or suffer the consequences of declining stock values or increased costs of funding its growth and defense. But it is promotion and must always be taken with a grain of salt. Another important source is the data provided to the customers and the public in general. If people have a poor attitude about the institution, they may refuse to buy the company's products, and this will impact sales and earnings.

There are numerous sources of information about the competitor which relate to the public and are available to those interested in having it. These include advertisements, promotional materials, press releases, speeches, books, articles, personnel announcements, and even help-wanted advertisements. Let's review these and determine what you can deduce from them.

Promotions, Press Releases, and
Speeches

Many executives think that advertising of the competitor is just bragging, and they read it with skepticism or even hostility. This is a mistake. First, the advertising of the company enables you to see what the company thinks is important and the type of image it wishes to project. Some companies are using advertising merely to build reputation, while others use it exclusively to gain or enhance share and competitive position. This style or purpose relates to the company's priorities and vision. IBM has used advertising to create the image of a dignified, responsible industrial leader. It has sponsored cultural and nonprofit events and programs, and even though consumers hadn't bought IBM computers until the advent of personal computers, they had a significant awareness of the company. Mobil Oil has used its advertising dollars to educate the public about the economy and the risks of oil exploration and energy development. Warner-Swasey, a small machine tool company and now a division of Bendix, has been educating the public for over a decade on the need to restrain the growth of big government and big labor and to rely more on the private sector for growth. There are other companies that use advertising to contrast their products with those of the leaders. The Avis campaign emphasized that though it was number two, it was the quality and service leader, since its people "try harder." Motorola has been advertising to explain what its priorities are and why it decided to exit the television receiver market.

There are thousands of examples of good and bad advertising. An advertisement should be evaluated to understand the message that is being communicated and whether it is consistent with the rest of the strategy. Continuity of the message is also important. The relationship of this message with the one in the annual report may help to determine whether advertising is considered strategic or merely tactical. Inconsistency may mean that it isn't the reflection of the top management but merely the product of the lower-level operating managers. Determine whether it is consistent across product divisions, since this may indicate whether the marketing strategy is centralized or decentralized. It is helpful to know what media are used for advertisements and whether the approach is national or local. If the company uses only national media, this may indicate that it wishes to be projected in a nondifferentiated way. Note the mix of television, radio, newspapers, and magazines. How does the size of the company's expenditure compare with that of the industry leaders and averages? What is the focal point of the advertisements? Is it innovative products and services, ease of use, the low cost of operation, or low purchase price?

Advertising copy is expensive, and so the message is brief and somewhat incomplete. Therefore it is useful to supplement it with other promotional materials, which can be made available in stores through distributors or even directly from the company. These brochures or displays can describe the uniqueness of the product, the number of models and styles, or the operations of the product. In emerging growth markets, such as the "office of the future," the competitor may reveal its total concept and the assumptions it is making about the entire system and all of the key components. Further, there may be an elaboration of the evolution and the schedule that the company plans to follow.

Another source is the press release describing a unique event or introduction. Press releases may give information about new products or features, the appointment of a new manager or team, a reorganization, and the settlement of a strike or lawsuit. The importance of these releases may be not that they describe truly newsworthy facts or events but that the management feels the need to explain or brag. They may give the company a feeling of tranquillity, or even overconfidence. If a company is continually discussing one topic, it may indicate a preoccupation or even a distraction. This may enable you to take advantage of the distraction. In many companies today, concern with liquidity, the problems of deregulation, or the need to hire a new management are all symptoms of unrest and the seeds of future problems. Press releases are common when a company is acquiring, disposing, or being targeted for takeover. Under these unusual circumstances, you can find out a lot about the individuals and their personalities. The television talk or interview show can be of particular interest. The choice of topics and the degree of firmness shown are other characteristics to look at. In the past few years, I have seen videotapes of executives designed for use in business schools. These have all been insightful and educational, and I've learned about the culture, leadership, and concerns of the executives' companies.

There are some companies that have a policy of not talking to the press or issuing press releases and not taking part in public debates. The number of companies with this attitude is declining, since it is becoming increasingly difficult to hide and not become involved. The fact that a company has this policy can also provide insights about the management's objectives and goals.

The CEO isn't the only spokesperson for the firm. The manufacturing, marketing, engineering, and financial staffs will also be on the podium from time to time, and you and your associates can be in the audience or read the results of their presentations. These events can be invaluable if you are willing to be an attentive listener and not be so defensive that you fail to understand what is being said and what is omitted.

The manufacturing professionals may explain how their organization attacks productivity, quality control, inventory, and the use of new equipment like robots, CAD/CAM, and even "the factory of the future." They may include their objectives and goals, the timing of changes, and the trade-offs between labor, materials, automation, sourcing, and use of offshore facilities. Are they trying to be the leaders or are they merely following? Do they encourage or discourage the use of fads, like quality circles? What do they omit, and is this consistent with other sources that have been uncovered? What is the talent of the organization as reflected by the spokesperson?

Marketing professionals are also apt to brag about their moves and how they are coping with their problems. Listen carefully to what they say. Are they explaining their company's approach to segmentation? If so what is their logic? Do they clearly articulate their reasoning for the segmentation? How does it compare with yours and that of the rest of the industry? What are their assumptions about the segments' growth and even current size? What about the drivers and concerns? Do they perceive your company as a major threat? Look at their forecasts very carefully, and compare with those you have made—the message is to learn and not to judge. Marketing professionals will also provide insights into what they think about the market. This may include the value of advertising, the need to expand, the key distribution networks now and in the future, and the sensitivity of market and share to service, price, and distribution. Being salespeople, they are likely to be optimistic and to exaggerate, but that is fine as long as you discount what is said and make sure that it doesn't distort your judgment.

Most financial executives have been shy and not very communicative. This is changing, and they provide other insights about the health and well-being of the corporation. Listening to this group may take the most effort, since financial executives may lull you to sleep with their concentration on numbers, ratios, and variances. But the effort may be very rewarding, since they will explain how the controls and measurement systems of the firm really work and whether there are any major current or potential problems. They will also explain how the rewards system works and the ratios or numbers that really matter to the top management. The top financial officer is often the confidant of the CEO, since he or she is so important in the banking and investment community. In recent years there has been a closer coupling of the financial and strategic management organizations, and so the financial officer may also indicate what the strategic plan and its financial objectives really are. Study what the financial officer perceives as threats to the company's funds and what he or she says about the problems of inflation and the need to adjust returns to reflect inflation. Determine whether these ratios and adjustments are vital to the decisions of the corporation. What about the exchange and foreign currency situations? These individuals can also explain the real resource allocation system and may differentiate those businesses and segments that are considered winners from those on the loser side of the ledger.

The final group of staff professionals to examine are those in the research and development and technological fields. They are most likely to give papers to their peers at the professional societies. In their papers, they will provide candid descriptions about their successes and failures. What are they predicting about the state of the art? What are their major concerns and the problems that they describe? Are these similiar or different from the assessments of your own professionals and those considered to be the industrial leaders? How do they foresee the technological trends, and do they vary from one part of the world to another? In the 1960s the technological winners were in the United States, while in the 1980s the balance of power in certain fields moved to other nations. This points out the need to attend technical meetings and trade shows in Europe and Japan as well as the United States to keep current and to know what is likely to happen in the future. Examine very carefully the concerns about the workforce and how a specific company is trying to cope with the scarcity of people they anticipate.

Books and Articles

During the past decade, the number of books and articles about companies has increased dramatically. This increase is due to an increase in the circulation of existing magazines and the initiation of new ones in all fields. The *Harvard Business Review* has become a major publication, and the large corporations are delighted to have their employees and executives write for it. In addition the alumni of the prestigious schools go out of their way to publish for recognition and career development. In the past five years, publications such as *Journal of Business Strategy, Strategic Management Journal,* and *Planning Review* have become successful. There are similar publications in finance, marketing, and technology.

Another source of material written about and by companies are the case studies used by the business schools. These may be written by academic professionals or others with or without the permission of the companies involved and may be used to illustrate both good and bad practices and performance. Regardless of the reason that the articles or case studies are written and the role of the authors, they can be valuable sources of intelligence.

The content may include the history of the company and its accomplishments or problems. There are books available on IBM, GM, Ford, GE, ITT, A T & T, and various Japanese companies as well as smaller-growth companies with a unique image or reputation. there are thousands of cases on companies of all sizes that describe the companies' histories, opportunities, and problems. If read correctly, they provide information on the culture, objectives, strategies, and even functional programs. At times these are disguised, and so a little interpretation and even filling in of facts is required. These documents also describe the planning and financial systems and will contain documentation directly from the company itself. The same is true of the articles, since they will be shorter and highlight only the key facts. There will be highly critical articles and cases that will describe all the things that went wrong and why. The questions to ask are whether these problems will be repeated, and if not, what has changed to prevent the repetition.

There will be other articles written by the marketing, manufacturing, and technical professionals. These will provide more details and explanations than the papers and speeches that I discussed earlier. Some articles will be written by other professionals with a different perspective. The contrasting views may be very informative. These different opinions may cause a change in strategy or priorities or may denote conflict in the organization that may result in poor implementation. It is useful to probe the reasoning for the differences and determine the strategic impact. There may be conflicts between the functional organizations. The engineering management may be stressing the value of computerized design and manufacturing, while the production management may be resisting the implementation. The manager of one division may be a supporter of the strategic priorities, since they favor his or her division, while the manager of a negatively impacted division may be fighting them.

Some publications may be for the company itself and not for the outside world. They may be available for the asking if you are a customer or supplier or if the company wants to build an image. If this is the case, then try and obtain what you can and evaluate its content and value. It is not worthwhile to obtain the documents in a devious or undercover manner, since it may get you into needless trouble. These publications can cover a variety of subjects, ranging from technical projects and patents to new methods in the plant. There are also special publications for the customer or the public in general. These sleek professional publications will provide pictures and diagrams to elaborate on the concepts or processes that are described in other papers. Regardless of the type of publication, these are a few questions to consider:

- What are the technological, production, or marketing accomplishments or projects that are highlighted?
- Is the company claiming something unique, and is this truly different?
- Is there continuity in the projects? Or do they change often?
- When projects are stopped or discontinued, is there a rationalization?
- Is the company visionary and ahead of its time, or is it conservative and adverse to taking risks?

Help-Wanted Advertisements and Personnel Announcements

The publications you read carry advertising for positions as well as announcements of key changes in the management and professional ranks. In local newspapers, there will be advertisements for hourly, salaried, and lower-level personnel. A careful analysis of these publications will provide insight into what is happening in the company and the direction that it may be taking. For instance, what type of technical positions are advertised, and what numbers are in demand? Are the skills required consistent with the past products and services, or are they different? What do these differences tell you about diversification and change? Is there a high turnover in the executive ranks? Are the new appointments made from within the company, or are new people brought in from other industries or companies? Do changes in the hiring of people who work on an hourly basis indicate changes in process or production method? What are the salary levels that are publicized? This may help in estimating the salary rates and the cost of producing the products. If the professionals are being offered salaries considerably above the rest of the industry or if the firm has moved from being the lowest payer to being the highest, this may indicate a change. All intelligence is important, and it will come from simple and complex sources.

What the Public Says About the Competitor

There are other groups of individuals who may be highly knowledgeable about the industry and your competitor. I mentioned those who make a living advising others about investments. In addition, there are consultants, reporters, and advocacy groups.

Consultants

In today's world there is an increasing number of small, medium-sized, and large consulting firms dedicated to the tracking and monitoring of businesses. Consultants are a valuable source of intelligence and should be used, but in a planned and selective manner. These individuals have a first-hand and current understanding of the critical success factors in an industry, and they know how various companies stack up against them. They may have already studied a company and may be willing to supply the data at a moderate price with the hope that they will obtain future and more extensive assignments. Often they will have generalized reports of this nature. They may have even done some consulting for the firm in question. This sounds as though I am saying that they are unethical and will act as double agents. This isn't the point I am making. I have had only positive relations with consultants, and most of them have been very ethical and have worked at protecting the proprietary and confidential nature of past assignments. Like all professionals, they must protect their reputation and will not sacrifice it in any manner. If they did, you would not be willing to hire them, since they would only turn around and sell you out to the next bidder. If a firm works for other competitors, they will assign different teams and they will forbid the teams to talk to each other or exchange data. However, even in such cases they will be able to gain total industry data, and this will permit them to have the head start. Consultants can be of significant help in the study of new competitors and especially those in other countries. In such cases they will have knowledge of the national scene and the unique relationships that exist between the government and the private or quasi-public firms. In addition they may be able to get first-hand interviews with key people in the government, the industry, or even in the firm, none of whom may be accessible to you. There are times when a competitor will exchange information with a consultant even if it knows the consultant is working for you, because the competitor believes that it too will learn. I believe that the consultant should be open and let the competitor know that he or she is working for you rather than let there be any possibility that the competitor can claim you hire spies. The consultant provides know-how on obtaining and analyzing the data.

Reporters

Behind every article, whether it is a few lines or a feature article, there is extensive data and usually a well-informed reporter. These reporters are most often bright and very conscientious, and if they work for the prestigious journals, they wish to write in a reliable manner. They use a combination of confidential and public sources of information. You can't expect or even try to get them to divulge confidential information, but I have found them willing to sit down and discuss the business in an informal and useful way. They are interested in learning, and the discussions can be "off the record." Let me make a few suggestions on how to progress and what type of information or intelligence to try to obtain. First of all, the questions reporters ask may give you knowledge of the key critical factors or the problems in the marketplace. The answers to these questions from different individuals can be helpful. For example, how are the various companies attacking productivity or inflation problems? Some, the reporters might tell you, aren't concerned at all, while others are very concerned. If the winners are in one category while the losers are in another, this may give you some indication of the impact of the problem. Probe which companies are being interviewed and why the companies were selected. Look for the surprises. If there is a company that you wouldn't have selected, then determine the reason it was included. This may surface a new threat. I've stressed how personal style can influence the success or failure of a business. Reporters can talk face to face with the leaders. What is their feeling about the competency, the leadership ability, the planning skills, the realism of the leaders? This is a unique source of this type of insight. If the leaders are manipulators or wishful thinkers who are not respected, then the probability of their success is low. If the leaders are shy and underestimated, then you may have a more difficult time than you expect to be successful. The top officers are not the most critical ingredient to success, and the reporters may have an opinion about the depth of skills throughout the organization. The real innovators may be hidden, but they may be known by the reporters. All strengths are relative. This is a concept worth remembering. The reporters may see this relativity and be willing to share their perceptions. Since the interview is a two-way learning device, don't hesitate to ask your own questions and probe what you wish to learn. This may enhance your reputation and increase your knowledge base.

Advocacy Groups

In today's world there are dozens of self-appointed advocacy groups that are promoting the protection of the employees, the environment, and the total society. These groups include the traditional unions, the consumer advocacy groups, the environmental protection organizations, the civil liberties groups, and the minority-rights groups. These organizations will track and monitor the institution at the local, state, and national levels. The union leaders and their negotiators will have opinions and do special research on the labor climate, the wage levels, and the people orientation of the company. How does the company compare in wages, benefits, turnover, movement of plants to countries with lower labor costs? Advocacy groups will know about the conditions of business and have inklings about harvests, exits, and divestitures. When there are problems or changes, the management will increase its communications effort. Be particularly observant when the union is trying to organize a new plant, or there is a new professional organization.

The consumer groups will spend time tracking a company's accuracy in advertising and the quality or safety of its products. Though there is always a controversy about the validity and objectivity of tests, they are useful to compare the ranking of various products and even the extent of the offering. There are also concerns about the truth of advertising. This can give you some indication of the credibility and long-term commitment of the management.

In the 1960s and 1970s, environmental and ecological groups became very strong and forced companies to change. They did this by picketing, boycotting, and taking legal action. The companies that were involved exhibited their character. Some resisted and took extreme actions. This is what happened in the General Motors incident with Ralph Nader, who is a consumer advocate but who also became involved in the environmental movement. General Motors hired private investigators to probe the private life of Nader in order to obtain incriminating data so that Nader would stop his effort to get GM to make the Corvair safer. Nader found out, and General Motors was embarrassed and forced to apologize publicly for invasion of Nader's privacy. This incident showed that the company managers had a belief in their power that wasn't in tune with the reality of society. Other companies ignored the situation and hoped that it would go away. Still others negotiated and tried to be constructively responsive. I am proud to include my company in this latter category and believe that the other winners were also in this group. Reactions to such incidents are highly revealing about the perception that a company has of its role and how it considers the stakeholders in its strategic decision and objective setting. Stop and think about your industry and how the various firms have reacted or responded to such situations. Did some of the firms actually benefit, and what can you learn from their example?

Have you taken time to talk to the leaders of advocacy groups and determine how they see the changes influencing the industry, the availability and cost of resources, the scarcity of water, land, and skills? Have you thought about what firms they are targeting and how this can help or hurt you? If you are going to be forced to clean the rivers and the air and pay for past pollution, it is better to include it in your economic evaluation and not pretend that the problem will go away.

"Who's Who"

Finally, I would like to mention the value of the various publications that provide biographical information about the leaders in business. I believe that the background of the executives can give you some indication of what they are likely to believe is important and thus enable you to predict their actions. Of course, graduates of one school will cover the complete spectrum and not be the same. But the pattern of experiences, the time spent on jobs, and the number of opportunistic moves may help you predict future actions. Further, educational and regional backgrounds and religious beliefs do set the tone and the values of a company. For example, it may be useful to know if the management is primarily from a single religious group. Whether the managers are all newcomers or long-time employees may be indicative of their stability. This isn't the whole story, but it may fit the puzzle and confirm or cause you to question other sources or hypotheses.

Trade and Professional Sources

Professional Associations

Another source of intelligence is information given by and for the trade and professional associations. Participation in these associations ranges from merely filling out the questionnaires and providing statistical data to attending and addressing meetings, courses, and seminars. Information about the company and its industry will be documented in transcripts or publications. In these publications, you can find out the sales and shares of the major participants, the segmentation practices, the cost of production and distribution, the type and cost of research and development, the capital expenditures, the labor costs, and the advertising and sales expenditures. There are also special reports on manufacturing techniques, process improvements, and quality control as well as reports on the changes in channels of distribution, sales approaches, and incentives programs. In addition there are conferences and seminars that focus on areas of concern and opportunities. If you attend these seminars, you are most likely to hear the competitors first-hand, and as I pointed out, it is important to listen and not be smug or critical.

Suppliers and Vendors

You can also learn a great deal about the competitor from the suppliers and vendors in the industry. This may be more indirect than direct. Vendors cannot and must not do anything that will be considered a violation of trust or a disclosure of confidential information. But they are interested in selling, and so they will give you some indication of what company is using the material or process or the new component. They may indicate whether the process or the new automated system is in use, and, of course, it won't take a great deal of wisdom to figure out which company is using it. The fact that they are selling a new innovation will mean that it will be used by someone in the industry, and it will most likely be the traditional innovator. For instance, suppose that you are in the automobile business. Which company is likely to take advantage of the new sonic devices for preventing one car from backing into another? Or which company will use the new electronics system for instrumentation?

The real insights can be gained from those who sell production equipment, since they can help you to anticipate which company is going to add capacity or try and obtain a cost advantage. However, don't overlook the suppliers of workforce or capital. These recruiters can enable you to know which companies are recruiting for specific skills, and knowing this can enable you to anticipate what is likely to happen in the future (remember that the analysis of help-wanted advertisements and personnel announcements also helps). But universities and trade schools may also be workforce vendors. They have knowledge of overall demand and know which companies are recruiting in their schools. Some firms restrict their recruiting to certain types of schools—the Ivy League, the Big 10. Others only go for the smaller, less well-known schools, and still others will recruit anywhere.

The suppliers of funds are another source of knowledge. Like vendors of materials, people, or components, bankers and credit agencies can also offer a perspective of what is happening in the long and short range. They can help you see which companies are financially innovative in exiting, acquiring, joint venturing, and so on. For instance, which companies are using leveraged buy-outs, spin-offs, or royalty trusts? This source of intelligence can be of particular help in foreign markets. Which companies are connected with which banks? How supportive are they, and are they interested in your particular industry?

Trade Press

Regardless of the industry, the trade press is a must, and it should not just be read but studied and contemplated. In any typical trade publication, you will find several different types of material. First, articles will cover the leading indicators of sales, earnings, and productivity moves. Second, there will be information about new products and their features. This will include descriptions of the newest innovations and their producers, explanations of what makes them innovations, and prices. Third, there will be features about the changes in the distribution, technologies, and so forth.

There will be special features about companies and their management. Personnel changes will also be included. Finally, the advertisements themselves are worth studying, since they are aimed at those who should know the most and are the toughest ones to impress.

Customers and Subcontractors

The customer may be the most obvious and best source of information about what is happening in the industry and what the competitor is trying to do. This source is the most obvious but the most ignored or underestimated. Customers' needs and wants are the crux of the game, which all companies must ultimately address. What customers think is the key to the winners and losers. If their needs are being satisfied by one company more than another, that company will be the real and lasting winner. So ask what the customers or ultimate users think and whether they think your product is better, equal, or worse than the others. Try and be objective. Don't be so confident that you ignore what they think. This data will include the quality and performance of the product as well as the service that is provided and the total economics. The total economics will include the cost of use and repair as well as the cost of not having the products available or in use when needed. How does the competitor achieve its results? Is it through a superior design or through a better response to the customers' needs or problems? Most of the computer competitors missed the point that IBM didn't have a superior product but rather a better-serviced product and that its real strength was in presales and postsales services. If auto companies had asked their customers about Japanese cars, they would have found out earlier that the superiority was in exterior finish and "rideability" and not in design or speed or even in fuel economy.

The interesting point to remember about customers is that they can quite often afford to be honest and aren't constrained by confidentiality, which is a limitation of the other sources. The words "quite often" are worth noting. Customers do have some constraints, since they also have vested interests and may be playing one competitor against another in order to obtain preferred terms and costs or even to have capacity added to serve them, if and when they need it. Have you asked the key questions: How do customers rank the competitors and you, and why? What would they like to see improved overall, and who is best equipped to do the job? Are there any needs that none of the competitors satisfy?

A related group is the dealer or distributor of the product or service that you provide—or, if you go directly, the salesforce itself. These intermediaries also have a direct connection to the users, and they may have the answers that you seek. The only caution is that they may interject their own opinions and miss some of the real answers that may lead to change.

Government Sources

In the United States, governments at local, state, and federal levels require many reports that give data about the company and its strategy. Because of the "right to know" legislation, these reports are available to anyone just for the asking. These reports are only part of the story, but they must be accurate, and the company will be punished if it lies. I'll outline a few of these documents and the type of information that they will contain.

The Securities and Exchange Commission requires quarterly and annual reports for any company that is listed on the major exchanges. Fortunately, most companies are listed on these exchanges, and so this type of information is readily available. These quarterly and annual reports provide information similar to that found in the corporate annual reports, but in some cases it is more thorough. I have seen reports that describe the entire product lines and the competitive position of the company in each. There will also be listings of the plant locations and the products made in each. The law requires a disclosure of the compensation and tenure of the top management. When a company is engaged in an acquisition or merger, the reports are of particular value, since they contain the rational behind the move and also an explanation of how the companies complement each other.

There are also reports required by the Federal Trade Commission, which will cover other aspects of the company's operations. The more regulated the industries, the more the requirements and the more detailed the information. This may seem useless to many, since these companies are in noncompetitive markets, but as the world changes and these traditionally regulated companies move into new markets, it may be more useful. Thus it is worth studying them and considering the assets and liabilities that the regulative environment provides. If a company participates in government-funded projects, there will be additional data about them that is worth studying. Such projects include military projects, exports receiving federal funding, or minority-training programs. The list is extensive, since the number of regulatory agencies is also extensive. If the companies are properly assessed, you may derive data that isn't available from any other data base.

In addition there is information filing that is related to a company's problems with the law. For instance, antitrust or restraint-of-trade suits can be very helpful. These are normally voluminous and will require discretion and selectivity. The ten-year file related to the IBM and A T & T trials would fill many warehouses. Some of these files are not available to the general public, but some of them are, and they may be useful. There are also individual and class-action suits, both by and against the company. Look to see how many suits have been filed by the firm. Some companies have large legal staffs and will sue extensively to neutralize the competition and make it expensive to participate in the industry. At one time, these suits were used to prevent smaller companies from entering or even using their own patents. This isn't the case today, but some still work at the technique. A systematic evaluation of the patent portfolio and the patent filing can help you determine the direction the firm is going and the next innovations that may appear on the horizon. Some companies have extensive portfolios and yet aren't able to capitalize on them. This may denote a weakness in implementation or even a lack of integration between its laboratory and its operating managers. It is also worth noting that patent filing will take place in some countries before others. For instance some patents will be filed in Europe before they are filed in the United States. Take a look at the individuals involved and their locations. Some individuals are prolific filers, and they may be wooed away by others or even retire or die. The locations may indicate the business obtaining the largest share of the resources, making it the highest priority business.

State and local governments also require reports and documents. The state documents may help you determine the products made on the local scene, the labor costs, and the benefits paid by the company. You can determine what the cost of exit will be and even whether the exit can take place at all. If a government imposes large unemployment costs on firms, they may find that it is cheaper to stay in business than to get out. The taxes imposed at all levels will also tell you how expensive it is to participate in the business. At the local level, you can find out about the size and capacity of the plant from the safety and fire plans on file.

Information about companies isn't available in the United States alone. It is also available in other countries. There are national plans that describe the nation's priorities and the key companies that make up its planned attack. If you are in an industry where such plans are available, it is worth studying them to determine how the attack will be implemented. If there are extensive research dollars allocated for the industry, you may determine that success will be sought through innovation. If there are export incentives, price may be the key factor. If there are productivity supports, then a combination of price and availability is the key. These documents are normally in the native language, and so it is important to have competent translations.

In summary, there are dozens of sources of information about the competitors, prepared both by those who are in the firms and those who follow the firms' actions and anticipate what they will do next. Each source has its

EXHIBIT 9-1   Sources of Competitor Information

	Investors	Public	Trade/professionals	Government
What competitors say about themselves	Annual meetings Annual reports Prospectuses Stock/bond issues	Advertising Promotional materials Press releases Speeches Books Articles Personnel changes Want ads	Manuals Technical papers Licenses Patents Courses Seminars	SEC reports FTC reports Testimony Lawsuits Antitrust suits
What others say about them	Security analyst reports Industry studies Credit reports	Books Articles Case studies Consultants Newspaper reporters Environmental groups Consumer groups Unions "Who's Who" Recruiting firms	Suppliers/vendors Trade press Customers Subcontractors	Lawsuits Antitrust suits State/federal agencies National plans Government programs

SOURCE: William E. Rothschild, "The Missing Link in Strategy," *Management Review*, AMACOM, 1979.

advantages and disadvantages, and none is perfectly accurate. Exhibit 9-1 provides a handy summary of all sources. You must be willing to be objective and understand before you judge. Further, you must be willing to test and validate and use the pieces to fill out the full puzzle. The key is to be a practical and thorough student, not a know-it-all.

In the next chapter I will discuss the various methods of using this data and obtaining the best judgments.

10 Making It Work— Documentation and Teams

I have experimented with a number of approaches designed to make competitive intelligence a way of life and not just another routine and meaningless exercise. I would like to share my experience with you and describe what I believe works and doesn't work. I would also like to share my ideal with you, even though, as with any ideal, it may not work for everyone.

What to Avoid

1. *The overkill.* The first thing to avoid is the publication of a voluminous report or book on a specific competitor or even on multiple competitors. Most managers and those making the strategic decisions are very busy and don't have the time or aren't willing to take the time to read a large book. This is like providing an encyclopedia or other reference book and expecting someone to read it. If the publication isn't used, it is worthless, regardless of how much time was spent preparing it. Thus the report must be simple and concise. It must emphasize only that which is strategic and not get bogged down in details. It is very helpful

if the report is written by people who can write with interest and even suspense. Remember that a good spy story is read with more interest and attention than an encyclopedia.

2. *The single competitor.* Another problem is the emphasis on only one competitor and not on the interaction of several competitors. One competitor is rarely important enough to warrant the exclusive attention of the top management. Thus, you must evaluate a number of competitors and be able to compare their relative strengths and how they impact each other. You can't do the job in isolation.

3. *The clipping or data-dump problem.* I have subscribed to clipping services, and these have been overwhelming and have provided scraps of information that haven't been very useful or even discriminatory. Those doing the clipping are often just mechanics, and they don't know what you are looking for and don't separate the strategic from the tactical information. Often you get the same data from a number of sources, and since you pay by the piece, this is uneconomical. Sometimes you even wonder whether the collectors read what they clipped. Since the data comes in bundles and you rarely have the time to do the evaluation and analysis in a timely manner, you often put it in stacks or files, and then it is lost in a pile of irrelevant data.

4. *Too low in the organization.* The prior point ties into who you assign to do the reading and the evaluation. You can't assign the task of competitive evaluation to a novice or to someone very low in the organization who may not know what you are looking for or even how to determine the critical data. This isn't a clerical job. It requires a combination of insight, knowledge of the business and strategy, intelligence, and a sense of purpose. In addition, it will require continuity and commitment. It is most helpful if those responsible for the decisions and their implementation can also do the intelligence job.

5. *Form-filling exercises.* Forms are easily filled out without a single thought. I have seen forms sent to salespeople or manufacturing people, only to be completed in a rush, without the thought and dedication necessary to make them useful. If those doing the task don't want to do it or are not sure of the purpose, you will not get good results.

6. *Too much precision and quantification.* We are dealing with an art (as well as some science) that can be improved with some thought and discipline. Often intelligence work reverts to a number exercise, and the total focus is on getting the "facts." This isn't sufficient, and it can prevent the activity from becoming strategic and actionable.

7. *Too much past and present and not enough future.* Finally, the activity quite often provides merely a description of the past not a forecast of

future changes in the competitor's strategy and results. It must be recognized that the real benefit is to anticipate and make some assumptions that can be used and monitored.

How to Do the Job

Step 1—Clarify the Issue

The first step is to clarify the competitive issue. This means that you must understand the purpose of the competitive analysis. Is the purpose to defend or make a gain against existing competitors? Is it to defend against a new enemy or potential enemy that may be moving from a different region, backward or horizontal integrating, or even using a new technology? Are you planning to diversify or expand in some associated market? The answers to these questions along with the sense of urgency may have an impact on the makeup of the team, but the approach I will recommend is fairly consistent.

For instance, suppose you want to anticipate the moves of existing competitors. The first step is to appoint a team for the specific competitors. This team should be comprised of individuals from various aspects of the business—marketing, manufacturing, finance, engineering, and probably the planning staff. The planner may be the integrator. Have the team members describe each competitor's strategy as they see it for their given area of expertise and also describe the resources they have. Be sure to appoint one individual to be responsible for the management of the team. Have the planner or an outside consultant summarize the results of this activity. You may have each team member be responsible to describe and document his or her area of responsibility, but insist that descriptions be concise and clear. This will provide a reference point and a statement of the case and hypotheses. Next have the team or an outsider do a search of the written sources and attend appropriate meetings or programs.

Step 2—Examine the Differences in the Data

The emphasis should be aimed at determining the differences found in outside and inside sources. The need for objectivity is vital. Differences and similarities should be noted and not rationalized too soon.

Let's examine some of the typical differences in the data and the reasons for them. First of all, there may be a difference in the size and growth of the market given in different sources. This was noted in the previous chapter, and it is a result of the differences between the total market and that which is considered the served market. Most managers use the numbers that they think will best defend their position. This is an excellent example of differences that are explainable but that can lead to different decisions and priorities. If you define the market very narrowly, you will most likely miss the real growth and even become convinced that you are the leader. There isn't just one way to define the market, and it shouldn't be rationalized before all the data is in and the total situation can be judged.

Another common difference is the share in the market. There are always a number of ways to define share. Some companies use yearly sales data in dollars (or any other currency); others use orders, which are different from sales in long-cycle businesses. For instance, in a dying business, the sales can be high and the orders zero. The sales are the result of the past performance, and orders tell you about the future. You may not use currency at all but rather use units sold as your measure. This is physical volume, and it is important in higher-volume markets. But you can also measure the share of brands or manufacturers in the market. For example, should you compare Sears against the manufacturers of appliances or lawn mowers or even computers? Or does it make more sense to look only at those that make the products for Sears? This is important, since in one case you are measuring marketing and distribution strength, while in the other, you are measuring manufacturing strength. Another aspect that can lead to different share analysis and perceptions is the time frame. Some companies use a longer period of time and look at change, while others, as I said, only measure the current year. Thus, you must evaluate why there is a difference and whether one way of measurement distorts the decisions. Some companies lull themselves into complacency because they use a self-serving measure and the others use a more realistic measure. It is valuable to have both insiders and outsiders to evaluate the relative position of the company in its critical segments.

Another critical difference of perception is in the technological comparison. This is important because the company may be comparing itself against the current technology and ignoring the substitute. This has been mentioned several times, but it is worth remembering, and so I have included it in this last chapter. The team you select to do the evaluation should have someone familiar with the other technologies, and his or her opinion should be recorded, even if it is discounted or ultimately not included.

The listing of the differences and their causes should then be the focus of further evaluation and validation. The need for selectivity must be kept in mind, since not all the differences really matter and you can get lost in the details before the strategies are really understood.

Step 3—Convene the Team

You now have a document that describes the individual judgments of the team members. But individual judgments aren't enough, and the judgment of the entire team must be obtained. Distribute the document that you have prepared to the team members and ask them to assess it from their perspectives and note the similarities and differences in the same manner that we recommended with the outsiders. Where there are differences that are strategic, the individual team member should record why he or she thinks his or her perspective is correct and if possible the backup material that may prove the case. This step will force all to think.

Given sufficient time to do the job, the team members should meet to discuss their perceptions and concerns. Start with the similarities and get them out of the way. I believe that the similarities should be discussed first, since it is likely that there will be more of these than differences. Thus, you can spend the most time on the problems or areas where further evaluations need to be made. But of more importance is that the team will start off constructively, feeling that the job can be done and that it can make a contribution. If you start with the negatives, or the differences of perception, the group may wind up in conflict and it may be impossible to work constructively.

Let's take an example of a typical session. The team members all agree that the competitor is aggressive in a specific segment and that it is focusing on innovation. The marketing staff considers that the competitor has a strong ability to differentiate the product and add features in a consistent and effective manner. It concludes that the company has strong product-planning and market-research capabilities. The engineering staff, however, doesn't see any evidence that the company is truly a technical leader. It has examined the products and even the literature on the product and concluded that the company is standard and isn't in the forefront. The production organization, however, concurs with marketing that the company's facilities are capable of making changes and that they are highly automated. Thus a case is being made that the competitor's strength isn't product innovation but differentiation based on an ability to anticipate the users' needs and then to meet them rapidly. This raises the issue as to how this was achieved and whether it is worth replicating. But it may also deserve further in-depth evaluation of the competitor's technical staff and its ability to respond. The engineering staff may be missing something. Differentiation may be the key to meeting the competitive challenge.

The output of the first meeting is clearly a listing of areas of strength and limitation and issues that need additional clarification. This is where the additional research needs to be focused. It may require the assistance of outsiders or additional staff. If it conforms to my experience, there will only be a few of these issues and resolution should not be very expensive or time-consuming.

Step 4—Move from the Past to the Future

Once the past strategy and actions of the competitor have been resolved, even if not perfectly, the team's attention should be directed to the future. What is the competitor likely to do differently in the future, and what is likely to cause the change? These are key questions. The need to answer them is the reason that the analysis is being done in the first place. One of the first questions that should be thought through is whether or not the same team should be used. There are two factors that influence this decision. The first is whether or not the first team can be objective and think like the competitor, and the second is whether the change in the competitor's strategy is likely to be dramatic. Let's explore both of these factors.

Some individuals are so imbued with their own situation that they can't think about the decision that others might make that might be different than their own. If this is the case, you need to select other team members. Even if the group is objective, there may be situations that require a new team. Suppose the competitor has been acquired or taken over by another company whose background and skills are different than those of the competitor. This may be a conglomerate that is only interested in getting the asset base of the company to invest it elsewhere or that is interested in combining the company with another subsidiary to move it into a new arena or market. Or it may be a multinational that is using the company to gain access to the domestic market. In this case the future strategy may be very different from the past, and the team must be capable of seeing the world differently and using the competitor to serve their new objectives. The team members' job isn't to determine what they would do but rather what the management of the competitor will do with the assets. To achieve this objective may take several meetings and much discussion, even argument. Several options may exist. These should be properly evaluated, and then it should be determined which are most likely. It isn't a simple task. Preserve all the work, and don't throw away any of the alternatives, since they may turn out to be the contingency plans that ultimately are selected. Document the findings of the group, and make them as clear and concise as you possibly can.

Step 5—The So-What Step!

If you have followed my advice, the team has worked over weeks, possibly months, to develop what it thinks are the most likely strategies of the competitor. You may even have used multiple teams, each looking at the same competitor and then reconciling their differences. Or you may have had them looking at several competitors and then trying to understand the interactions of the competitors and how they may have an impact on you and each other. But as I stressed before, the key questions are "So what?" and "What do we need to do differently?" The concept has been covered before, but I would like to make some recommendations on how to do the logistical implementation. The same team or teams we have used should have a crack at comparing your strategy with that of the competitor or competitors. They should point out differences and also make suggestions on changes. I would start with them because they may not be attached to the current strategy. Further, they have tried to put themselves in the place of the competitor and may have a new perception of the world and your company. The team should set up a special meeting with the management to review its results and to point out the differences in the companies' strategies and why they vary. It may also make recommendations for changes. Another use of the team is to have it react to the recommended changes in your strategy and what the competitor might do if you change.

Thus far I have described the establishment of teams to evaluate the existing competition, but there are also nontraditional competitors, which may not even be in the same industry. This may be a result of companies moving from one region to another or from one segment to another. Or it may be a result of new technologies that can do the job equally well or even better. It is useless to have teams consisting of your own employees, who may know nothing about the competitor. Therefore it will be necessary to hire outsiders to do the job and accomplish the first and the second steps. These individuals or firms should be knowledgeable about the company or at least about the industry or technology. This will expedite the process and give you a running start. For instance, it may be necessary to have them write the preliminary report or offer a briefing session. This may then be given to the employee group that is already functioning or to one that is new. After the briefing and description of the past, the insiders and outsiders may then combine to determine the future strategy of the company. One of the critical issues to be resolved is whether the new company will change the success factors. What will this mean to your past strength or limitations? There are many such situations. The watch industry provides an example. In this case, the traditional watchmakers witnessed a change that came from a combination of digital electronics technology and the technology of the Japanese companies, which are among the best in this applications area. The success factors of the past changed and will never be the same again. Today the winners are those that mastered both of these technologies and were able to combine the best of both for different segments. Another example is found in the field of personal computers. This market has been created by Apple Computer and Tandy (Radio Shack), but they are being attacked by the traditional electronics and mainframe-computer giants, including IBM and the Japanese companies. In both of these situations, the incumbents should have evaluated the new competitors well in advance of their entry into the markets.

Keeping Current

The use of teams comprised of people from many disciplines within and without the firm is my preferred method. This approach forces an in-depth view of the competitor in a practical mode by those who have a stake in the outcome. But this can't merely be a periodic exercise. It must be ongoing, and it requires a continuing surveillance. Each team member should feel responsible for tracking the company and noting anything that may indicate a change in direction. This can be casual, and the changes can be noted without much ado. If there is a major change, then the observing member should call a special meeting to report the change and get the team to make a decision about the need to change the strategy. Even if there isn't a major change, there should be occasional meetings of the team to update the evaluation and make sure that changes haven't been overlooked or that several minor changes don't add up to something significant. The "what if" questions should be asked and the need to modify the existing strategy should be emphasized. There may be a need to provide some written documentation of the findings of the teams about the competitors. If this is the case, then I'd recommend that you use some of the mapping techniques discussed in Chapter 2. You will recall that these included total arena and industry perspectives and reviews. Several competitors can be plotted on the same map to display overlaps and areas where there are conflicts. The use of colors permits you to show the future as well as the present and the past. When a team member determines that things are changing, either by addition or subtraction, he or she can make the changes on the map and circulate it to other team members and even the management responsible for strategy development. The use of segmentation matrices is also an effective way of demonstrating changes in strategy and even noting changes in the segment strengths and limitations. Again the use of color coding can also provide insights about the changes that have taken place and that will most likely occur in the future. You will be able to note how companies are expanding their horizons and whether they will overcrowd or change the profitability of the various segments. You will be able to spot segments that are unoccupied. Changes in segments can be noted on matrices, which should be circulated among the team members.

Diagrams should appear on the opening pages of reports, and they should be supported with statements about each of the segments or lines of business and with summaries of the competitor's investment and management strategies as well as its major programs and resource allocations. I don't need to review all of the data that I would put into the summaries. I have provided the tools needed for a competitive analysis. They should be adapted to suit your specific needs. The need for brevity and conciseness should be kept in mind, and if changes occur, the summaries should be modified and sent to the team members and strategists to keep the information current and to provide the *competitive advantage*.

INDEX

215

International Business Machines (IBM)
  (*Cont.*):
  product strategy of, 22, 108
  development of, 109, 110
  salesforce of, 118
  service strategy of, 99, 123, 201
  specialization by, 60, 68
  success of, 30, 40
International Paper, 61
International Telephone and Telegraph
  (IT&T), 64, 82, 83, 86
  management changes in, 92
Inventory status, 126
  accounting methods, 134
Investment strategy, 5
  case histories in, 150, 151, 160, 162,
    165, 170, 172, 176
  definition of, 79
  and strategic driver, 104–105, 137
  tax law changes and, 147
Investors as information source:
  information from, 186–189
  information to, 180–186, 190
Italy, state-owned industry in, 85

Japan, national priorities in, 80–81, 84
Japanese companies:
  automobile industry, 2, 60
    pricing in, 123
  as competition, 146
  computer industry, 72
  diversification by, 60
  electronics industry, 30, 33, 80
  financial strategy of, 110, 133
  geographic expansion of, 98
  innovation by, 40
  office equipment industry, 61
  product strategy of, 114
    licensing as, 111
  service strategy of, 125
  steel industry, 65, 80
  television industry, 5
  zaibatsu, 151–152, 161
Jefferson, Edward, 51, 91
Johns-Manville, bankruptcy of, 40
Joint ventures, 104, 110–111
Journal of Business Strategy, 194
JVC, 110

K-Mart, 48, 52
Kirby, R., 51
Kodak, 61
  innovation by, 107
    following, 108
  standardization by, 96, 114, 115

Lag demand strategy, 131
Land, Edwin Herbert, 37, 89
Law suits as information source, 202–
  203
Lawn mowers, analysis of industry, 43–
  45
Leadership:
  analysis of, 56
  product position and, 106–107, 109,
    114
  specialists versus generalists, 62
  (*See also* Management)
Learning-curve pricing, 121–122
Leisure and entertainment industry,
  competitive mapping of, 18–19
Licensing, 111–112, 114
LIFO (last in first out) accounting sys-
  tem, 134
Lincoln, 21
Little, Arthur D., Inc., 188
Location, luck as factor of, 38
Losers (*see* Success factors)
Luck:
  as a factor of location, 38
  as a success factor, 37

McDonald's, 36, 40, 47, 65, 98
McDonnell Douglas, 39
McIntosh, 61
Macroenvironment:
  assumptions about, 34
  changes in, effect of, 40
  response to, 66
Magazines and books as information
  source, 27, 193–195
Magnavox, 9
Management:
  background evaluation of, 88–89
    past performance in, 89–92
  changes in, 52, 89
    anticipating effect of, 91–92
  of domestic companies, 65, 66
  of multinational companies, 66, 69
  as a resource, 37
  of specialized versus diversified indus-
    tries, 62–63
  vision in, 30–31
Management strategy, 30–31
  case histories in, 151, 152, 161, 162,
    166, 171, 173, 177
  (*See also* Strategic drivers)
Manufacturing strategy, 129–132, 138–
  139
  capacity utilization, 130–131
  facilities, location and type, 130
  flexibility, 131

ABOUT THE AUTHOR

William E. Rothschild is a staff executive of corporate business development and strategy at the General Electric Company. His background combines staff and operating experience, which includes practicing and consulting on all aspects of strategy development and implementation, as well as marketing, finance, manufacturing, and human relations. His work covers a wide spectrum of industries, including consumer, industrial, aerospace, power systems, forest products, and automobile components (both domestic and international). He is the author of two international best-sellers on strategic thinking and implementation: *Putting It All Together* (1976) and *Strategic Alternatives* (1979). He has lectured at Harvard, Columbia, and also in Japan, China, and Europe. His books have been translated into Japanese, Chinese, and Spanish.

The next decade promises a new competitive environment in American business...with many new entries in existing markets...new multinationals in U.S. markets...slower overall growth...and numerous substitutes for existing goods and services. Intensive competitive analyses will be required in all kinds of business organizations. And the company that fails to make the right moves in this area will quickly find itself losing market share and position.

This practical book helps anticipate the coming changes and offers timely guidance for developing strategic plans to profit from them. It provides several unique but well-tested approaches to competition and competitor evaluation, and shows how to convert these insights into the **competitive advantage**—that all-important competitive edge that allows the leader to protect its leadership position or permits the new entry to gain on the incumbent. For example, the book demonstrates:

★ How to plot and anticipate *competitive moves*

★ How to identify the *winners* and *losers* in an industry and, by determining why they differ, highlight the current and future *success factors*

★ How to evaluate total industry structure and its potential for change

★ How to spot allies (such as suppliers and customers) who could become *adversaries,* and take proper countermeasures

★ How to plot the *competitive demographics* —to be ready for broad-scale changes that could permit new opportunities or threats

★ How to track the investment, product, marketing, manufacturing, financial, and employment strategies of *key competitors,* so you are prepared for—and can take advantage of—their future moves

★ How to *modify your own strategy* to meet changing conditions

★ How to set up a viable *competitive intelligence system* to deliver the information and input you need

Spanning a broad area, the book is logically organized, with each successive chapter building on its predecessors. All the various elements of strategic planning are gathered and woven into a pattern that spotlights competitive factors and brings them into sharp focus for analysis.

Each individual chapter is carefully organized as well. First, concepts and approaches are discussed. Then the author provides pointers, examples, illustrations, and checklists—plus application worksheets to help you adapt and apply the material to your own specific needs.

It's all based on real-world experience and is fully authoritative. And it's designed to be useful to organizations of all kinds and sizes—small as well as large.